STRANGE PEOPLE ON THE HILL

STRANGE PEOPLE ON THE HILL

HOW EXTREMISM TORE APART A SMALL AMERICAN TOWN

MICHAEL EDISON HAYDEN

New York

Cover design by Ann Kirchner

Cover images: Michael Ventura / Alamy.com; Library of Congress, Prints & Photographs Division, photographs by Carol M. Highsmith [LC-DIG-highsm-31389, LC-DIG-highsm-31390]; © Africa Studio / Shutterstock.com

Bold Type Books
Hachette Book Group
1290 Avenue of the Americas, New York, NY 10104
www.boldtypebooks.org
@BoldTypeBooks

First Edition: April 2026

Published by Bold Type Books, an imprint of Hachette Book Group, Inc. Bold Type Books is a co-publishing venture of the Type Media Center and Perseus Books.

Library of Congress Control Number: 2025046500

ISBNs: 9781645030607 (hardcover), 9781645030621 (e-book)

Printed in Canada

MRQ-T

CONTENTS

PREFACE

For the Living

I didn't write *Strange People on the Hill* to dramatize the psychological and emotional environment that birthed the second Trump presidency, but when I read it back, that's what I see.

I wrote the book throughout 2024, while looking back over the previous four years of my life and the country's. I didn't post on social media or follow daily election chatter because I was healing from a mental health crisis that had landed me in a psychiatric hospital. Logging into social media felt like a particularly dangerous choice after surviving that. I tried to tune everything out and write.

I rejoined social media and started to participate in the discourse again a little before Trump's inauguration in January 2025. I saw the same things you did: the Roman salutes, the abuse of ICE detainees without due process, the alliance with Russia, and the silencing of constitutionally protected speech by way of arrest. As I write this in the spring of 2025, our government is doling out new obscenities.

I spent years warning people that this would happen. From 2018 to 2023, I worked at the Southern Poverty Law Center (SPLC), the civil rights nonprofit based in Alabama. I wrote investigative pieces for the SPLC's Hatewatch about the activists who were helping to force these changes on us—white nationalist grifters, terroristic neo-Nazis, misogynist social media influencers—and I worked as a spokesperson, appearing on TV and radio to persuade people to take MAGA's push to undermine democracy seriously.

I liked my job—until it fell apart. My separation from the SPLC was traumatic, as you will read, but it has been equally hard watching the org crawl into a defensive crouch at this crucial moment. Known as a premier civil rights group, the SPLC raised millions from people concerned about MAGA, but then laid off scores of workers in a union-busting purge in 2024. Those let go included immigration lawyers who could have pushed back against White House Deputy Chief of Staff Stephen Miller's agenda. They eliminated the entire investigative unit behind Hatewatch and launched a vertical called "Hopewatch" as a nonconfrontational, public-relations-driven alternative.

It hasn't just been the SPLC retreating. The world I describe in *Strange People on the Hill* no longer exists. An entire beat of investigative reporters who wrote about right-wing extremism with the ambition of defanging it has vanished. When the action started in *Strange People on the Hill*, February 2020, I could have named for you about two dozen reporters, like me, with jobs focused primarily on investigating that topic. Today, I can't think of more than a few who still have those gigs. It feels like the "resistance" people talked about in 2017, when Trump first took power, failed, and the liberal institutions that supported the concept quit.

It was through my work at the SPLC that I discovered Berkeley Springs, West Virginia. That's where the action of *Strange People on the Hill* takes place. Like the book itself, I can no longer untangle my memories of the town from the symbolism of our current moment. Here, a somewhat queer-friendly town relative to the West Virginia county around it descends into acrimony after an SPLC-designated white nationalist hate group buys a historic castle there. That pro-Trump group quite literally stares down on the people below from a hill, their very existence triggering the discord. The parallels to the United States itself today are hard to miss.

I made a dozen trips to Berkeley Springs between 2020 and the end of 2024, some of them lasting a few days and some lasting nearly a month, but I haven't been back since November 6, 2024, the day after Trump's win. That's where the book ends, and where the town lies frozen in my memory. Although my memories of Berkeley Springs become more dreamlike with each passing day, preserved by the pages that follow this preface, the town will always live in my heart.

The last face I saw in Berkeley Springs before I left that Wednesday morning in November belonged to a woman in her sixties named Lisa Swanson. And I can still see her on that morning after the election, with her short black hair and pale, intelligent face, right before I pulled away from her house in my rental car. I connect our goodbye that day to what I now understand to be a profound shift in American culture.

Lisa Swanson is a retired nonprofit worker who did whatever she could to prevent Trump from taking power again. She traveled out of state to knock on doors and wrote postcards urging strangers to participate in our dying democracy. We talked over lunch that Wednesday about whether the Trump administration might use the law to harm low-level political activists like her. I worried at the time that we were indulging in crazy talk.

On Lisa Swanson's red-painted front door, next to a neighboring house covered in MAGA signs, she put up her response to the collapse of American liberalism. It was a white sign cut from stencil, quoting the labor organizer Mary "Mother" Jones:

Mourn the Dead, Fight for the Living

Trump has talked about serving the "forgotten men and women" of America, his supporters, and, like Lisa Swanson, they appear in *Strange People on the Hill*. But are Trump's "forgotten" people truly forgotten, after two election wins and an authoritarian government pandering to their biases? Every newspaper and television station has scoured the country recording the perspective of the angry white Trump supporters who form the base within Trump's base. I'd argue that Lisa Swanson, Trey

Johanson, Judy Gubinski, and other red-state progressives you will meet in this book represent a more neglected feature of American life.

Outnumbered in their towns, people like the women I mentioned are spiritual optimists who dig deep to donate to nonprofit groups and Democrats, and then feel let down when the money gets squandered. They live among reactionaries and fight quixotic battles to make their neighborhoods more inclusive. My impression is that our media finds them hokey and ignorable, because their nineties bumper-sticker political views cut awkwardly against a post-Twitter culture that centers cruel people with selfish ambitions.

The Berkeley Springs residents I mentioned also saw me at the darkest point of my life—when I truly didn't want to live another second—and responded with an empathy that matched the views they espoused around town. They saved my life, and for that, I can't regard them with cynicism. Their ideology has lost, but they don't stop imagining a more compassionate country.

When I feel down about what has happened to America, I try to remember that there are people like them in every town. You will find them waving hand-painted signs on the side of the road and meeting in coffee shops just like the one at the center of this book. They keep fighting, even after wealthy institutions surrender. They are my "forgotten men and women," and "the living" for whom I wrote this book.

Names and Dialogue

The majority of the names that appear in this book are authentic. I gave pseudonyms to some people who told me they feared retaliation. Dialogue has been built verbatim from a recording, reassembled based on my notes, or pieced together through multiple sources to produce a substantive approximation of what people said.

The Use of the Word "Movement"

When I worked for the SPLC's Intelligence Project, we categorized activists such as Peter Brimelow—whose purchase of a castle in Berkeley Springs, West Virginia, is the precipitating event in this book—based upon their ideology. The SPLC described Peter as a "white nationalist." He has condemned the SPLC and called labels like "white nationalist" and "white supremacist" "devil words."

I've chosen to use a broad term, "the movement," to refer to the group of people who coalesced around Peter and fought for the same things he did at the same time he did. The "great replacement," or concerns that elites are replacing whites in their homelands with nonwhite immigrants, animated these activists above all else.

Peter might have called this a "dissident right" movement, or simply a "nationalist" movement. Many others, including me, have called it the "white supremacist" movement. We all would likely agree that a political movement centered around the purported dangers of demographic change in America does exist. That is the movement to which I refer in *Strange People on the Hill.*

Berkeley Springs

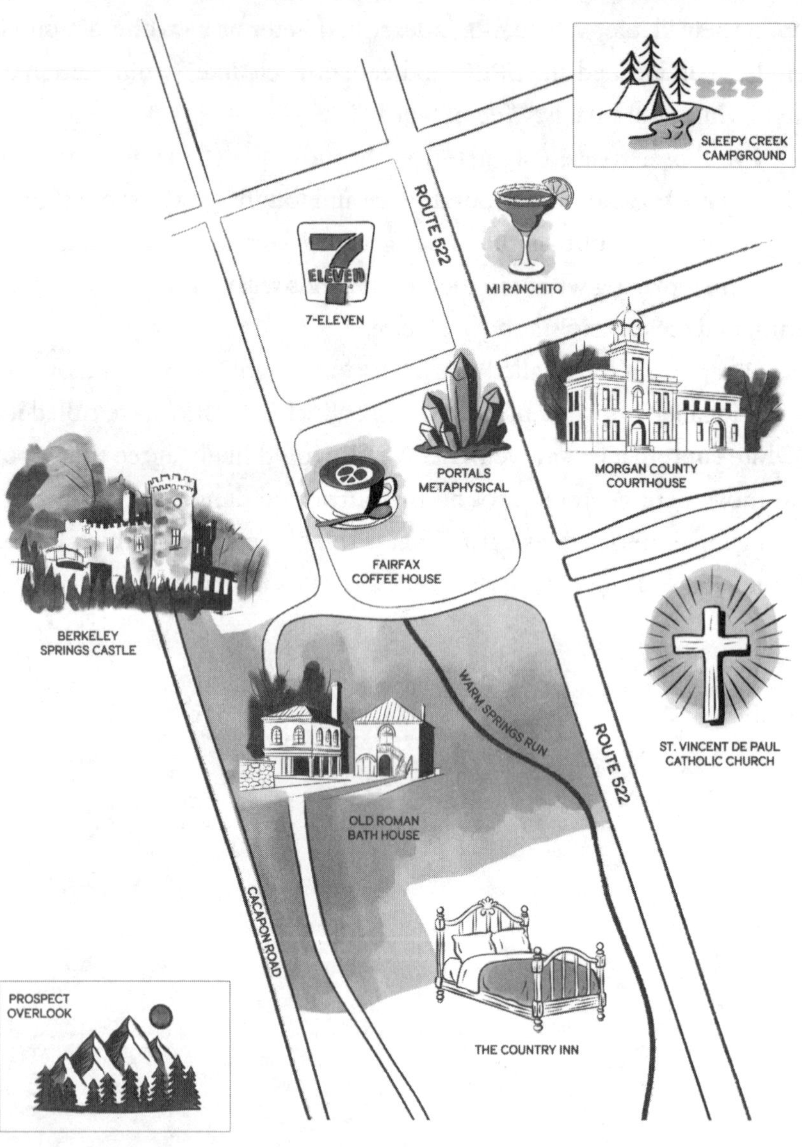

PART I

IT WILL COME TO BLOOD

1

The Great Replacement

When Trey Johanson drove down the roller-coaster hill that led into town on February 26, 2020, she saw the Berkeley Springs Castle and wondered if the new owners had already arrived.

Tourists and passersby found something haunting about the nineteenth-century sandstone building. Needly trees shot up all around it. Red-eyed gargoyles and a sinewy lion statue guarded it. No walking path existed near its perimeter, underlining the fact that the castle looked down on Berkeley Springs from a position of inaccessible dominance.

Trey, a petite woman in her fifties with wavy silver hair and pale blue eyes, prided herself on making strangers feel welcome when they walked into Fairfax Coffee House. That's where she was driving that morning. At the recommendation of her daughter, Trey had bought the red and yellow brick shop from a dentist named Magic Miller in 2017. She had married her third husband, Paul Johanson, two years later.

A worker for *The Morgan Messenger* hung a bundle of newspapers on the door of Fairfax Coffee House that morning, as they did every Wednesday, and Trey moved the bundle to the counter, preparing to sell the papers for one dollar each. When she pulled the yarn to free the stack, the face of Lydia Brimelow popped out at her on the front page.

The physically towering Brimelow family matriarch was holding up keys to the castle. Her husband, Peter Brimelow, who was nearly forty years older than Lydia, stood with her. Three young Brimelow daughters surrounded the couple.[1]

"Berkeley Castle Has New Owners," said the headline. Trey then read the photo caption: "Lydia and Peter Brimelow stand at the door of the Berkeley Castle, which they purchased on Valentine's Day. They are pictured with their three daughters. Photo courtesy of Peter Brimelow."

Trey's friend and neighbor—let's call her "Alicia"—had first told her who the Brimelows were. Lots of people from the town talked about them on Facebook after that. Trey's husband, Paul, started talking about them too.

Alicia, a middle-aged brunette mom with ruddy cheeks and a warm laugh, had moved to Berkeley Springs from Philly because she wanted a change from city life. She owned a shop adjacent to Fairfax Coffee House that sold multicolored pottery, candles, and lightly perfumed soaps. Alicia had first read about the castle purchase in a blog post authored by a reporter named Russell Mokhiber on Sunday, February 23. She told Trey about it soon after.

"These people are white *nationalists*," Alicia had said.

Trey tried to process the news as Alicia explained it. Everything seemed so surreal.

"White nationalists have over a million dollars to just throw down on a castle?" Trey asked.

"Apparently!"

Untethered to a weekly publication schedule, Russell had posted about the Brimelows three days before the *Messenger* published its own story. And he didn't embed cute, happy photos of the Brimelows in it. Russell focused on the nonprofit advocacy group they ran. The group was called VDARE.

Russell noted that Peter Brimelow had named VDARE after Virginia Dare.[2] On August 18, 1587, on Roanoke Island, Virginia Dare was the first white child born into an English colony on the land that would become America.[3] VDARE's founders modeled their organization's existence around her existence. Peter and his collaborators behaved as if, without their intervention, the memory of that white child was going to be wiped out of history.

Russell had quoted Peter as saying, "You know, I personally like living in a white society."[4]

Peter spoke in a thick English accent. Not infrequently, he muttered in it. Trey wondered if this alien Peter Brimelow character had blown in from Connecticut by way of England, with no clear connections to West Virginia, simply because it was a "white society." Maybe he thought everyone in Morgan County, West Virginia, looked at the world as cynically as he did.

Months earlier, in the fall of 2019, the Ku Klux Klan had dropped off flyers at both Trey's and Alicia's shops. The headline at the top of the page read, "The Cost of the Jews' Open Border Policy." Underneath it, the authors of the flyer listed a few dubious talking points maligning immigrants. At the bottom of the page there was a Klan logo tagged with the words, "Wake Up White America!!!" Alicia now wondered aloud if those Klan flyers could be connected to the sale of the castle.

"What if they sent the flyers to test us? And since we never did anything in response, VDARE felt it was safe to move here?" Alicia asked Trey.

Trey was skeptical. "Do you really believe that?"

"I'm not ruling anything out," Alicia said. "All I know is that it happened and then this happened."

"The Klan wears masks," Trey said. "These Brimelow people pose in photos with their *adorable* children."

When Alicia and Trey first received the Klan flyers, they had discussed launching a public-facing response to them. But Trey stopped short. She claimed that she didn't have the appetite to engage with whatever was left of the Klan in West Virginia. Then a new, second Klan flyer had arrived at their doors. This one decried the purported evils of queer people.

"I don't want to give this oxygen," Trey had told Alicia on the street between their shops, while autumn began a steady roll into winter. "I just don't think that's the right play. It might encourage them to do more."

Trey wanted to speak up for queer people in other ways. She put up a Pride flag at Fairfax Coffee House in June 2019 to celebrate Pride month. Trey then chose to keep the Pride flag flying, making the symbol a big part of Fairfax Coffee House's branding. In a deep red county in a deep red state, no one could miss the Pride flag she hung up at the front of her shop. Everyone could see it every time they walked through the adjacent Berkeley Springs State Park.

At the time Trey and Alicia discussed what to do about those Klan flyers, I was working as an investigative reporter and spokesperson for the Southern Poverty Law Center (SPLC), a nonprofit civil rights group that built "intelligence" on extremists. I didn't know who these women were, and I'd never heard of Berkeley Springs, but I knew about VDARE, because the SPLC listed them as a white nationalist hate group. They were one of the most prominent hate groups we listed. When VDARE purchased the castle, Trey's and Alicia's lives intersected with mine.

As I told these women weeks later, when I traveled to Berkeley Springs for the first time, Peter Brimelow had played a critical role in turning the country into what it became under Donald Trump. Not a Klansman from the era of lynching, but far from a typical conservative of the nineties and aughts, Peter effectively shifted Republicans away from neoconservatism and toward nativism. Eventually, that nativist turn would take America into a series of constitutional crises and to the edge of some American version of fascism. Peter established VDARE as a nonprofit foundation, but reactionaries primarily knew it as a website that published influential propaganda.

While Stephen Miller is often "credited" with shaping Trump's anti-immigrant, authoritarian persona, VDARE may have influenced Miller's mind first. I published a series of stories about Miller's private emails back in November 2019 for the SPLC. The emails showed that Miller read VDARE to reinforce his beliefs.

In his emails, Miller also referenced Jean Raspail's dystopian novel *The Camp of the Saints*, a VDARE favorite. In Raspail's tale, hordes of impoverished and dark-skinned brutes from India descend onto French shores by way of rafts, the first wave of an invasion of the civilized West by the brown-skinned developing world. A beast-man described as the "turd eater" devours feces as food, and a pack of dark men rape a white woman to death.[5] VDARE sold *Camp of the Saints* online, sometimes as a Christmas gift.

Another French author, Renaud Camus, coined the term "great replacement" in 2010, but it was VDARE that helped launch it into domestic prominence. The theory of the great replacement is that elites, or, depending on who told the story, Jews (not commonly a direct target of VDARE), have invited nonwhite immigrants with inferior bloodlines into white-dominated Western countries to weaken them and absorb more power for themselves. Long before Tucker Carlson brought great replacement talk into prime time on Fox News, VDARE treated the concept as the defining issue of our time.[6] Peter and his collaborators hammered on this idea that whites faced a genocide through immigration with persuasive repetition.

Violent extremists feasted on this great replacement propaganda, using it to justify terror attacks across the West. VDARE, in turn, published apologia about the writings produced by terrorists who killed innocent people, simply because they echoed the great replacement narrative.[7] VDARE did this in August 2019 after twenty-one-year-old Patrick Crusius slaughtered twenty-four people at a Walmart in El Paso, Texas. Crusius had referred to an "invasion" on the southern border in a bigoted screed he authored.[8]

VDARE also linked in their publication to a manifesto authored by Brenton Tarrant, the man who, in March 2019, gunned down fifty-one people in Christchurch, New Zealand, leaving bodies scattered throughout a mosque. The killer titled that manifesto "The Great Replacement." Peter Brimelow had said that to end such massacres, the West should stop "mass Third World immigration." It was never the movement—that group of people, including nativists, neo-Nazis, and white nationalists who performed activism in response to the great replacement—that was to blame. It was always others.

"We absolutely will not be having rallies, marches or demonstrations, if that is the concern," Peter told *The Morgan Messenger* in response to people expressing disgust about him and his movement on Facebook. "We've never been involved with anything like that, and we never will be." Peter denied that he was a white nationalist to the paper.

As Trey's anxiety about the new keeper of the castle grew, she started to research VDARE by reading its website and hated what she found. The bylines on articles posted there featured names that seemed fake or made up, as if the people associated with the group wanted to hide who they were. Why did they need to do that?

Some of the VDARE posts stressed purported differences between races. More than one post highlighted crimes committed by Black people against whites. Everything the authors posted to VDARE seemed to imply that the country was collapsing.

Trey saw two posts focused on a news story unfolding in China, something called "the Corona virus." She had heard about this phenomenon only in passing. VDARE's authors suggested that white people might be blessed with immunity to the new virus:

> The racial dimension to the Corona virus has fascinated me since the outbreak began. Despite some ethnic Europeans having caught it, including white Americans trapped on a quarantined cruise ship off Japan which has turned into a floating Corona epidemic... it's still true although as of today... no white people have died of the virus as far as we know. Two people in Iran have just died of Corona... but this doesn't necessarily undermine the argument that Corona is primarily—but, of course, not necessarily exclusively—an East Asian disease.

The author of the post went by the name Lance Welton. In it, he turned his thoughts to the "mongoloid" percentage in certain people's genetic composition. At the bottom of the post, VDARE announced that

"Lance Welton" was a pen name, although the real Lance Welton wrote for them out of New York.

Trey found the pseudoscientific posts on race repulsive beyond words. They had implications for Berkeley Springs that did not comport with the dreams she'd had for its future. She'd never considered Berkeley Springs a finished product. Trey imagined it would grow into a bigger tourist hub and that she would be a part of that change.

Trey wanted a Berkeley Springs that more consistently pulled in a multicultural crowd of visitors from cities like Philadelphia, Pittsburgh, Baltimore, New York, and Washington, DC. Liberals from these cities visited Berkeley Springs for its spas, hiking trails, and vistas—but not enough of them. Trey wanted the town to become a true outlier in red-state West Virginia. She was not the only person who felt that way.

"The first thing you see when you look up from my shop is the castle," Alicia said to Trey. "It's every worst stereotype of West Virginia."

That weighed more heavily on Trey than anything else. The town was so tiny. It was a micro-town, really—just a few blocks with a handful of tourist-targeted shops and a few eateries. It took someone in good health one minute to hike up the hill from Fairfax Coffee House to the Berkeley Springs Castle. The buildings were neighbors: one up, one down. The castle, with its rising battlements, overshadowed everything.

"This will obliterate our reputation," Trey told Paul. "The whole town. Everyone is gonna associate us with—"

"I think it's pronounced V-Dare," Paul said.

"Whatever it is," Trey said.

Trey had grown up in the Deep South, mostly in and around Atlanta. Neighbors had treated her father, a blue-eyed man of Swedish heritage, differently than they treated her mother. Trey's mother was a Jewish woman of Eastern European heritage, and that had made her and her sister two of only three Jews at their public school.

On March 7, 1965, when Trey's mother was seven months' pregnant with her, she'd carried Trey in her womb across the Edmund Pettus Bridge in Selma, Alabama, behind the Reverend Martin Luther King Jr.

Trey's father, a US Air Force captain, snapped photographs of the violence that day. Knowing that she'd been there, on Bloody Sunday, was one of the reasons Trey felt compelled to act against VDARE. Before she even realized that she was doing it, Trey started to set up a meeting of business owners to oppose VDARE's purchase of the castle. She did it without thinking about the repercussions she might face for putting herself at the center of such an action.

"We need to focus on the business owners," Trey said. "Our businesses are in jeopardy."

"Okay, so what should we tell people?" Alicia asked.

"That we'll see them on Friday," she said.

2

A White Man with Money

Lydia Brimelow discovered the Berkeley Springs Castle through Zillow.[1] There were a lot of real estate listings on Zillow, but nineteenth-century castles were rare. She thought that if VDARE could find the money to buy the place, it would be a fairy tale come true for the movement.

Lydia found her Zillow castle somewhere around the middle of Trump's first term. A tall brunette in her late thirties with an oval face and mournful eyes, Lydia worked hard fundraising for the nonprofit VDARE Foundation. Peter, significantly older and physically diminutive by comparison, with a big poof of white hair, had wanted to move VDARE's headquarters out of Connecticut and plant the group and his family somewhere new.

Because VDARE's activities tended to provoke protests, including phone-calling campaigns staged by people who wanted the world to hear about Peter Brimelow's views on immigrants, private venues slammed their doors whenever the group and its supporters tried to meet in person. VDARE bragged that this shunning produced impressive refunds from the hotels where they had booked their conferences, but it left them without a safe space to talk about their ideas.[2] The frustration peaked in 2017 when VDARE failed to find respectable venues willing to hold its conference.

Peter wanted to hold the 2018 VDARE conference at the Cheyenne Mountain Resort in Cheyenne Mountain Springs, Colorado. But on August

15, 2017, after months of planning, those at the helm of the wedding-centric establishment decided they didn't want to host it and canceled the event. Peter issued a statement through VDARE in response and partially blamed my future colleagues at the SPLC for what happened.

"I would like to pay tribute to the professionalism and courtesy of the individual staff members at Cheyenne Mountain Lodge over the several months we worked together. I regret that their innocent belief they live in a free country has proved unfounded," he wrote. "Cheyenne Mountain Resort's cancellation is a further example of what President Trump has correctly called the Alt-Left: a conspiracy against the civil liberties of Americans by internet vigilantes (such as Media Matters, Southern Poverty Law Center), and their allied troll army, and the violent Communist gang (the so-called AntiFa), plus complicit elected officials."[3]

When I first read the statement, I was working as a reporter for ABC News. I knew nothing about Peter Brimelow, but I felt the rage animating his words. We discussed Peter briefly during an editorial meeting, pondering whether the Cheyenne Mountain Resort story would be valuable to a national audience. The answer was "not enough."

VDARE ultimately sued the city of Colorado Springs, alleging that a statement from its mayor had caused the cancellation. At the time the group purchased the castle, the case was very much alive, and the Brimelows believed they had a chance to win it. Peter had also quietly sued *The New York Times* in January 2020 for labeling him a white nationalist.[4] He had high hopes about that case too.

Cheyenne Mountain Resort dumped VDARE three days after a twenty-year-old admirer of Adolf Hitler, named James Alex Fields Jr., murdered the thirty-two-year-old Heather Heyer, a counterprotester, in a car-ramming attack at the now-infamous Unite the Right event in Charlottesville, Virginia. Hundreds of young white men had assembled to defend a statue celebrating the Confederate general Robert E. Lee. The only thing anyone seemed to remember about the event afterward was the violence.

Jason Kessler, a VDARE blogger known in the movement for his tendency to be self-aggrandizing, had helped lead Unite the Right. Peter had repeatedly attempted to distance VDARE from the "white supremacist" label, but now his associate, Jason, had secured the permit for the most infamous event publicly associated with American white supremacy since Timothy McVeigh's 1995 bombing of the Alfred P. Murrah Federal Building in Oklahoma City. Peter had to admit, though, that the August 11, 2017, torchlight procession around Robert E. Lee's statue was "remarkable."

Jared Taylor, another old head of the movement, cross-posted on VDARE from his website, American Renaissance.[5] The Yale grad and former editor for *PC Magazine*, known for his stilted manner of speech—he has long pronounced the word "white" as *hu-whyte*—said the white activists of Charlottesville faced anti-white racism.

"There is a clear pattern to these events that not one mainstream outlet has noted," Taylor wrote on August 13, 2017, as backlash against the movement grew across the country. "There is confrontation *only* when anti-whites harass and try to stop pro-white events. The reverse never happens. Lefties and non-whites can mount the most brazenly anti-white events, unmolested and with full media approval. It would be hard to imagine a clearer example of this contrast—and of the entrenched bigotry we face—than yesterday's events."[6]

After Unite the Right, people scrutinized and ostracized everyone in the movement. When Lydia found the castle on Zillow, she thought that it could counter that problem. The castle offered status to the movement, for one thing. It carried an air of historical mystique, recalling a whiter time in America. It offered opulent rooms that would dazzle other "patriots" at conferences. The castle also had built-in security. The infiltrators who tracked them would get nothing.

To secure the Zillow castle, VDARE faced the obstacle of cost. Several townspeople told me that the Gosline family, the castle's previous owners, would not have allowed anyone to even tour the castle without ascertaining that they had the money to buy it. And the expected cost, well north of a million dollars, didn't include the future expenses of upkeep, which could be large given the size and age of the place.

To get their money, the Brimelows tapped wealthy supporters. VDARE pulled in $4.5 million in 2019. It was a surge of millions of dollars in donations, more than they'd collected in any previous year. According to Peter Brimelow, two big-money donors stepped up.

The secretive people who funded the castle purchase appeared to have used DonorsTrust to do it, because one-third of the amount collected came from there. DonorsTrust bundled billionaire money together from figures like the libertarian business titans Charles and David Koch and the even more reactionary Mercer family.[7] I don't know which rich people facilitated the purchase of the castle, but I do know that Peter and some of his collaborators were connected to wealthy people.

Kevin DeAnna, an early-middle-aged blogger who wrote thousands of posts on VDARE and on social media under the name "James Kirkpatrick," met privately with Peter Thiel before the 2016 election—although he has since denied being part of the so-called Thiel network of propagandists alleged to be on the billionaire's payroll.[8]

DeAnna, a lanky blond man who has always looked a decade older than his age, moved to pseudonymous writing after years of butting up against the mainstream conservative movement under his own name. On a podcast, he explained what kind of wealthy men funded the movement in secrecy. He described them as flirting with the movement, rather than joining hands with it in a way that fully satisfied him.

"I know of a few donors to some right-wing organizations," he said, "and I'm not gonna give the names to that, but I would say they don't give a lot. They give very, very little. But the reason I think they're doing it is they're sort of putting their finger in the wind. They're trying to see what's going on. Occasionally you read stories about elites, real elites... talking about a lot of interesting ideas that really don't vibe with multicultural democracy."[9]

A woman named Teresa White-Curtis of Perry Realty brokered the sale of the Berkeley Springs Castle. Nothing about Teresa seemed ideological to anyone. Her father ran a junk shop in town with an impressive collection of cast iron skillets inside. People in town gossiped about how she had hit a substantial payday on the deal.

VDARE officially purchased the castle on Friday, February 14, 2020. The parties signed the paperwork at the offices of Trump and Trump.[10] The Berkeley Springs firm served as the law office of Charles Trump, a local politician who has no connection to the populist, authoritarian president. The date marked VDARE's most significant moment since Brimelow had founded his group in 1999.

Despite being born in Lancashire, England, Peter Brimelow romanticized the lost cause of America's Southern Confederacy. That made VDARE's move south intriguing to me. Peter published, and republished, a post on VDARE titled "Time to Rethink Martin Luther King Day." He started it with the exclamation, "Happy Robert E. Lee Day!" and noted that the Confederate general's birthday fell on January 19. He then bemoaned the celebration of Martin Luther King Jr.'s name.

"Diversity is not strength: it is weakness," Peter wrote. "The celebration of a deeply flawed figure like Martin Luther King was a confession of weakness, and the attempt to turn him into a national role model has required unsustainable myth-making. Perhaps in the future, Americans will be allowed to celebrate their own races' heroes separately, just as Italian villages have different patron saints. Right now, however, the cost of the King cult to white America is too high."[11]

Peter's road to authoring commentary like that started when he worked as a financial journalist contributing to *Forbes* and *The Wall Street Journal*. He made his name on the right by contributing to a mainstream conservative publication, *The National Review*. He made it as far as a conservative writer could go, and then, over time, slowly pushed his commentary into edgier territory.

The United States granted Peter citizenship in 1992, and in the same year, he published a scathing statement about nonwhite immigration in *The National Review* highlighting his desire for a whiter America:

> Perhaps because the 1965 Immigration Act was slipped through in such a deceptive way, many Americans, and many conservatives, just do not realize that it is directly responsible for this transformation of their country. They tend to assume that a kind of natural phenomenon is at work—that Hispanics, for example, increased from 4.5 per cent of the U.S. population in 1970 to 9 per cent in 1990 because they somehow started sprouting out of the earth like spring corn.
>
> But no natural process is at work. The current wave of immigration, and America's shifting ethnic balance, is simply the result of public policy. A change in public policy opened the Third World floodgates after 1965. A further change in public policy could shut them. Public policy could even restore the *status quo ante* 1965, which would slowly shift the ethnic balance back.[12]

In 1995, Peter's mentor, John Tanton, urged him to write a book on immigration, and he provided him with funding to do it too. Peter obliged with the book *Alien Nation*, in which he treated the idea of a multiracial American society with utter contempt.[13]

"There's a plain fact to be considered," Brimelow wrote: "the evidence that multiracial societies work is—what shall we say?—*not very encouraging*."[14]

Some publications typically associated with liberalism praised Peter and *Alien Nation* then. *The New York Times* did. So did *The Economist*. David Frum, who later wrote speeches for George W. Bush before rebranding as an anti-Trump commentator at *The Atlantic*, praised *Alien Nation* and offered Peter up as an intellectual force.

"Don't be misled by verbal pyrotechnics: Brimelow presents his case with a prosecutor's thoroughness," Frum wrote. "No reformer can avoid grappling with the formidable work of Peter Brimelow."[15]

As more people grew aware of *Alien Nation*, and of Peter's writing at *The National Review*, the risk of writing about race from such a reactionary perspective became more apparent. People labeled Peter racist. He became the kind of thinker that other reactionaries read but pretended not to read. Peter founded VDARE in that atmosphere.

"I'm an immigrant doing a dirty job," Peter told the Black journalist Bryant Gumbel on NBC's *Today* in 1995. "Nobody else is prepared to talk about this."

Lydia Brimelow's identity had been tied up with Peter's for as long as anyone else in the movement had known her. She'd first linked up with him only a few years north of the end of her childhood. Lydia started contributing to VDARE under the pseudonym "Athena Kerry" back in 2005, when she was only twenty years old, according to personal details described by the person writing under that byline.[16]

Peter claimed that he started dating Lydia that same year, when she served as an intern at the conservative nonprofit Heritage Foundation.[17] His first wife, Maggy, a conservative journalist, died of cancer in 2004.[18] So, the couple forged a romance roughly one year after Peter lost his wife and while Lydia was studying at Loyola University in Chicago, a Catholic school.

Katie McHugh, a former Breitbart writer who participated in the movement and socialized in it before eventually leaving, leaked Stephen Miller's emails to me in 2019 and later became my friend. Katie knew the Brimelows before they moved to West Virginia, because she dated Kevin DeAnna. She told me that Kevin made sexual remarks about Lydia behind the boss's back, and that people around the Brimelows privately snickered about them because of their age difference. Katie said that she viewed Lydia as a humiliated figure because of the mean-spirited gossip. She also described her as being smug and haughty.

"She told me I 'was just a waitress, and Peter picked me,'" Katie said, recalling conversations they'd had as friends.

Katie visited Peter and Lydia in their Litchfield, Connecticut, home twice. She babysat their daughters and liked them. Peter kept a large hand-painted portrait of his first wife on the wall of one room, Katie said.

Katie also remembered that the couple pinned photos of Lydia's sister on the refrigerator, and that Peter quipped, when Katie and Kevin were there, "Your sister could be a Victoria's Secret model." Katie thought that Lydia felt wounded by the remark, based on her reaction. She remembered the event as being typical of the way people in the movement treat women.

"That was just the way it was. You had to be happy that a white man with money picked you," Katie told me. "And then you had to shut up about everything else."

Katie told me that a man in the movement raped her in December 2017. One month later, Katie called Lydia and told her what happened, seeking support. She was startled when Lydia registered the accusation of rape without expressing sympathy.

After she hung up the phone with Lydia, Katie was overcome with feelings of paranoia. She snapped, she told me, and called Lydia back to tell her that she was, in fact, completely wrong in claiming that she was raped, and that the rapist friend had never *really* raped her. Lydia was equally unmoved by the second call, Katie recalled.

"I was just so frightened of what people would do to me, of how I would be treated if everyone found out," she said.

Richard Spencer, who in 2016 and 2017 emerged as a figurehead of the movement, once stayed at the Brimelows' Litchfield, Connecticut, residence as a guest. He told me that Lydia changed around 2017—that she had always been a warm person, but abruptly turned colder. Spencer said he didn't know whether this change reflected Lydia's response to him specifically or a switch in her personality.

The Brimelows flew a VDARE flag from a battlement atop their new headquarters after they secured the keys for it. They memorialized the sight in GIFs and used the imagery in a VDARE post announcing their acquisition of the castle. They published the announcement on February 26, 2020, the same day that Trey first decided to organize against the couple.

In the post, Lydia thanked the anonymous people who had paid for the castle and expressed optimism about the future of the movement.

"Having a space where we can meet and share ideas without fear of deplatforming will make a difference so material it is hard to overstate," she wrote. "And for that we will be forever grateful. Thank you, donors large and small, for making such a huge impact. We are enormously grateful to you—and everyone who is helping to keep America *American*."[19]

3

What Matters to Us

Paul Johanson, tall and slim with a slight whitish beard and a neatly kept blond ponytail, read the post on Russell Mokhiber's blog on Sunday, February 23, 2020. Paul was the opposite of Peter Brimelow as far as mature white men went, and not just because he worked with his hands. When Americans rallied Barack Obama to his presidential victory in 2008, Paul felt so moved by the historical magnitude of the occasion that he created a time capsule out of campaign artifacts. He embedded the sentimental material in a sliding drawer in his kitchen table and kept it there.

Paul moved from reading Russell's blog to the SPLC's website. The SPLC described Peter's ideology in prosecutorial terms: White nationalist. Anti-immigrant. The SPLC made Peter sound really, really bad, highlighting his own words to support its conclusion.[1]

"We're facing what was called in the case of the Civil War an irrepressible conflict. But this is America. People have guns. It will come to blood," Peter said in one quote.

The submission form the SPLC posted for website visitors to send in tips asked for a report of a "hate-related incident." Paul knew of none but chose to proceed anyway.

"No incident just yet, but everyone in my town just learned that yesterday a group called V-DARE purchased a large, famous property in our small town's center known as The Berkeley Springs Castle," he wrote on February 24. "The castle overlooks our town and is a historic feature with its own unique history. People in the town are presently reacting with fear, anger and deep concern."

Paul also wrote about "rumors and confusion" infecting the town. He expressed concerns that VDARE would use the castle to host conferences.

"What advice do you have about how we as a community should progress? Can you send someone here to advise us if the town council asks for that? If local citizens ask? Thanks, Paul."

Paul hit send and his words dropped into a mountain of emails that sat in SPLC staff inboxes. When I worked there, emails marked "New Hate Incident" popped up every few minutes announcing obscure troll campaigns, intolerant neighbors, and swastika graffiti in high school bathroom stalls. The repeated pinging always left me with a faint paranoid feeling whenever I closed my laptop at the end of the day.

The next morning, before anyone had read Paul's words, a woman from the Berkeley Springs area named Mary called the SPLC's tip line and left a voicemail. Mary and her fiancé had moved from Charleston, South Carolina, to Morgan County in 2018 to be closer to her mom, who had become overburdened with her husband's diabetes-triggered health decline. Mary had hoped that Berkeley Springs might be a more open-minded community than the one she'd lived in farther south, but she was wrong.

"I'm a resident of Morgan County, West Virginia, and I'm calling because there's information starting to kind of percolate, through town, indicating that VDARE, a pretty well-known white nationalist organization, has purchased a piece of property here in our town, and a lot of us are not happy about it, and we are kind of looking for help, or information, or guidance, on how we can organize kind of a . . . protest against this," Mary said.

Mary's voice rose an octave as she spat out the word "protest." She said it like it was a thing that could kill her.

February 25, the day of the voicemail, was my forty-first birthday. I was walking to see a doctor in Manhattan when Rachel Janik, a fiery, fast-talking SPLC editor in her late twenties, called me up. Our team was small, and Rachel and I worked closely on almost every story I did there.

"Did you see this thing about VDARE buying a castle?" she said.

"What castle?"

"See what Howard posted," she said, referring to a colleague from the Deep South who monitored white nationalists. "So, apparently, VDARE bought a castle—"

"What do you mean by they *bought* a castle?"

I ducked into a bookstore to block out the street noise.

"A castle," Rachel said. "In West Virginia. There's a castle down there. And if you can get down there—I think you can get down there, can't you? It's probably pretty close?—you should do a piece on it. They're also looking to talk to someone in person... hold on. I'll send you a link."

This was not something we typically did. I spoke at conferences and colleges. Sometimes, I spoke on TV. I had never briefed a town.

My phone vibrated when her text arrived. "Read what I sent you," she said. "I also feel like these are the exact type of people we're supposed to be helping, so... it's a good thing to do."

"Help them how?"

"Go there, and you help them understand—Who are these people moving in? What kind of group is VDARE?"

Although Morris Dees, the SPLC's very white founder, used advertising to tether his org's image to the civil rights movement, he formed it in 1971, years after the major events of the period had already passed. Still, Dees worked to weaken the Klan through litigation, and the Klan once tried to repay him by burning down his office, so generations of liberals associated the SPLC with the fight for civil rights. They flooded the SPLC's coffers with money—to the tune of three-quarters of a billion dollars annually as of 2025.

The SPLC formed the Intelligence Project in 1981, and it was through that division's monitoring activities that it earned the polarizing reputation it held by the time I worked there. Workers at the Intelligence Project griped privately on Signal chats that the SPLC grifted off the civil rights movement in an undeserved manner. However, we overlooked that problem, because the well-funded organization provided us with resources to take on what those on the left colloquially called the "fascist threat"—a term that encompassed purveyors of a broad range of far-right ideologies, such as people who thought that immigrants poisoned the blood of the nation, preachers who wanted to criminalize gay sex, and misogynists who celebrated rape.

At the time that I had that phone conversation with Rachel Janik about Berkeley Springs, the SPLC was going through a particularly weird time. It had forced Dees out of his own organization in 2019 following allegations of sexual harassment, and other executives left soon after.[2] Heidi Beirich, the longtime director of the Intelligence Project, and a mentor of mine, left shortly before the Berkeley Springs call, citing exhaustion. It was in that atmosphere that the SPLC formed a sorely needed labor union.

A woman named Margaret Huang had taken over the SPLC as president around the same time that VDARE bought the castle. She had worked at Amnesty International, where we heard she'd had a contentious relationship with their union. Huang, whom the SPLC paid nearly half a million dollars per year, had the aura of someone who would smile to your face and then immediately spit venom about you after you had traveled out of earshot. My colleagues and I wanted as little to do with her as possible.

Rachel and I started making editorial decisions alone at that time because we had no leadership—no managing editor, no director. It sometimes felt like we were children parenting ourselves. Rather than simply writing a response to Paul Johanson, or returning Mary's call, we chose to show up to fight for them in person. This direct-action response was our vision of what the SPLC should be like. We saw something and did it. That quickly made decision sent me headlong into a little town's drama for years.

Paul Johanson, the man whose email first got us talking about West Virginia, was an only child who had been born in Madison, Wisconsin, in 1964. Years later, when I stayed at his place as a guest, he would tell me that his father worked as an astrophysicist focused on measuring the size of the universe. Paul's mother, an artist, sculpted abstract objects with smooth edges. He showed me one in his house, and it impressed me. He called his parents "neglectful, narcissistic, not very good hippies."

Paul said that as a kid he'd moved from Arizona to Brazil to Finland, then back to Brazil, and later to Milwaukee. He'd failed at engineering at the University of Wisconsin. Then he walked, hitchhiked, and hopped trains from Wisconsin to New Orleans. He married "the wrong person," an attorney living in Tucson, in 1991. Paul endured an ugly divorce. He lost connection to his kids.

Paul then took up what he described as a low-paying job at the Pentagon. He ended up staying in Washington, DC, where he transitioned to gardening. That's when he discovered Berkeley Springs. It was just a two-hour drive from the capital. He fell in love with it. In 2004, he started building an octagonal house on top of a hill on the edge of town.

Paul cleared the brush for the house himself. He embedded wine bottles into its walls that sprinkled colored light into every room, and he implanted oversized blue wine bottles into glass panels around the front door. He built two real trees into the core of the place like a wooden spinal column. The trees made the place feel almost dreamlike. It was as if you were walking outside in West Virginia while surrounded by the physical walls of a house.

On the morning of Friday, February 28, 2020, two weeks after the Brimelows finalized the castle purchase, Paul sent an email to plan the meeting focused on business owners that Trey had discussed with Alicia. He sent it to Trey and to Patti Miller, a local food security activist and lesbian in her sixties with short, buzzed hair and a firm but gentle demeanor. Patti had moved to Morgan County at the turn of the millennium and knew everybody in town. Paul issued his plan to facilitate what they hoped would be the first of many meetings focused on rejecting VDARE's message.

The fact that Paul would be facilitating the meeting would later become the subject of some gossip among his allies. His experience as a facilitator came from participating in a men's group called ManKind Project, which focused on men overcoming trauma together, sometimes in the woods. Some critics have called ManKind a cult. Devotees, however, swore by their experiences, claiming the group saved lives.

Paul's email read:

> Hello Patti and Trey,
>
> We've asked Russell (the blogger) to keep this meeting confidential (who and what said) until further notice. I have also asked Trey and Alicia to help keep the meeting focused on my facilitation so we can get through it with maximum engagement. I need you both to help remind people to stay contained in the space as it will be hard to hear one another if it's crowded.
>
> We need a sign-in sheet at door (name and contact info, email) that can be passed around.
>
> A—Determine length of meeting practicing feedback process (hand level to indicate investment, interest). 1.5 hrs suggested
>
> B—Agreements:
>
> — Confidentiality—what is said or who says it is not to be broadcast publicly.
>
> — Stop talking when I stop you, so more will have a chance to speak and be heard.

— All respond to "temperature" questions when asked so we can see what matters to the group. We'll capture some items.
— Raise hands to indicate you understand this.

C—Introductions: (I'll need someone to capture items on white board if/as needed) Name, Business, why you are here (30 seconds or less) [Raise hands if you have a shared interest or if someone speaks your concerns/experience].

— Please meet one another afterwards to talk at greater length. This is about mutual support and coming together right now.

Questions to consider:

1—Who are we as a business group and town?
2—What matters to us?
3—Actions to take on behalf of group?
4—Commitment level and availability?
5—Join in ways that fit for you (I'll share the SPLC list for examples).
X—Next meeting's place and time—we'll connect by email for now if you have given your contact information.

Through an automated signature, Paul ended his emails with a quote, from civil rights leader Martin Luther King Jr. about loyalties transcending race, tribe, class, and nation. He followed it with another quote from the Russian dissident Aleksandr Solzhenitsyn, who wrote of oppression in Soviet gulags: "But the line dividing good and evil cuts through the heart of every human being. And who is willing to destroy a piece of his own heart?"

As it happened, my email to Paul offering to meet would arrive just a few hours after he sent his to Trey and Patti. I told them that I planned to drive down sometime between March 9 and 13. A few hours later, Paul introduced me to Trey by email. Trey's response percolated with excitement. It seemed like the town was coming together to do something big.

"Thank you," she said of my agreeing to meet them. "Oh, thank you so much."

Between thirty and forty Morgan County business owners and a few of their friends walked from their houses and cars to gather at Fairfax Coffee House for the meeting that Friday night. They streamed in through the park and past the Old Roman Bath House, or across the street from the Morgan County Courthouse, their hands in their pockets to protect them from the cold.

Paul took notes on a whiteboard. Patti, the food security activist, was quieter than she had intended to be. She found herself losing patience with some of the other queer people there. Some of them had barely been in town for a year, and now they wanted to leave.

"I don't feel safe here anymore. That's it," one man said. "This town was supposed to be a safe space for us in this county."

Patti believed that seasoned neighbors dealt with one another in ways that transcended identity or politics. She had pro-Trump MAGA friends too. People handled conflicts among themselves with blunt conversations. Outside of horrific emergencies, calling the police on someone in Morgan County was a last resort. You worked things out.

"The reason I'm here is to give every person an opportunity to speak, one at a time," Paul said, trying to keep conversations from colliding and creating tension.

One of the people in attendance was Geoffrey Wendel, a man with long, thinning blond hair and an urgent manner of speaking. On Facebook, Geoffrey had once posted a photo of himself standing outside in a blizzard wearing a head-to-toe purple wizard outfit with a matching stovepipe hat. People considered him eccentric, and several of his neighbors impressed upon me that Geoffrey owned a truly exceptional pair of boots.

The idea of the Brimelows moving into the Berkeley Springs Castle disgusted Geoffrey. He toyed with the idea of publishing a letter to the editor of *The Morgan Messenger*, but that never materialized. Geoffrey ran

Portals Metaphysical, a shop that sold crystals and other artifacts. He also gave tarot card readings.

Geoffrey wanted to make clear that racists didn't deserve to tap into the metaphysical realm. Portals Metaphysical issued a statement on February 23, right after Russell's blog post about the Brimelows zipped through Berkeley Springs, declaring that "Portals absolutely repudiates white nationalism and bigotry. We are welcoming of many sorts, but if you are a supporter of this toxic lifestyle... you are most certainly not going to find a friend here."

The day the *Messenger* published its article about the Brimelows purchasing the castle, Geoffrey posted a comment to Facebook through his personal account, saying, of white Christians, that "their whiteness is the universe's immune system actually trying to take them out because they are a disease."[3]

Toby Moore also attended the meeting. He lived in Berkeley Springs only part time—it was his getaway home—making him more of an outsider than others there. Toby perceived the conflict differently than many other people in the room.

A social scientist focused on voting rights, Toby had no local business to protect, but he felt morally opposed to "Nazis," to use the colloquial term that people bandied about that night. Toby dug into VDARE's IRS filings. He found Peter and Lydia to be unimpressive people, floating into town on some rich person's life raft.

"I have been looking into this and so has Russell," Toby said. He had spoken to Russell Mokhiber after Mokhiber's blog post about the Brimelows' arrival had gone live. "This is a husband-and-wife team with very little real money," he told the room. "They're small potatoes, riding off of a few big donations."

Toby waited out a few comments before speaking again.

"I actually view this as a huge opportunity for the town," he said. "If people from DC and Baltimore and Philly find out that the businesses here are unified, standing up against these people, then you can get people to come out and support you. Get people to have a beer with the resisters. People will be honored to shop in your stores when they know you're standing up against this hate. It honestly could be a boon for your businesses."

Jeanne Mozier, who was sitting next to Trey, shook her head. A bespectacled Ivy League–educated woman in her mid-seventies, with gray and white hair, she had been recruited by the CIA straight out of grad school. But it was Jeanne's impact on Berkeley Springs, not her Washington, DC, credentials, that gave her disproportionate stature at the meeting.

Jeanne had relocated from DC over forty years before VDARE arrived, and she ran the Star Theater, a gorgeous redbrick movie house with an origin story going back to the early twentieth century. The theater's marquee lit up North Washington Street at night. People became accustomed to seeing Jeanne serving popcorn clad in a tie-dyed shirt. She had formed an arts council in Berkeley Springs, and she had helped establish its local museum too. She had also authored historical books about the town, an occupation she downplayed as being something she did for extra money.[4]

People treated her like an oracle. Many townspeople believed that it was Jeanne who'd made Berkeley Springs into a refuge for liberals and queer people. She'd enticed visitors from Washington, DC, by highlighting Berkeley Springs as a strip of living history. That was why Trey felt so shocked to hear her express passivity about the Brimelows.

"I met with the Brimelows and they're polite," Jeanne said during her turn to speak, a soft but noticeable edge in her voice. "They told me nothing would change and that they would preserve the castle and keep it open to the public. I just don't think this panic is warranted. Nothing has changed."

Trey felt a jolt of fear when she learned that not everyone in town was as outraged as she was. As people started to leave, Trey pulled Jeanne aside, trying to understand her.

"Now, Jeanne, I want to tell you, respectfully, that I disagree with what you said there," Trey said. "These Brimelows may have been nice to you, but—"

Jeanne interrupted, pushing through the conversation with a force she'd repressed during the meeting.

"Nothing has *changed*," Jeanne said. "We will continue to sell my book about the castle. Everyone will continue with their business."

Jeanne's book was a light read about the castle and the legends surrounding it that shop owners stocked as a souvenir. Titled *The Story of Berkeley Castle: What's True and What's Not*, its back cover declared, "If JEANNE says it, it must be true!"—with her name capitalized for emphasis.[5]

"Nothing has changed! Nothing has changed! Nothing has *changed!*" Jeanne shouted at Trey, pounding her hand into her own thigh each time she said it.

4

Ghosts

Peter and Lydia Brimelow walked into the Berkeley Springs Castle as new characters in an old story. When Berkeley Springs residents gossiped about the Brimelows to me, a few of them said things like, "You know about the history, right?" And they said it with a smile that held back an indelicate thought.

The "history" was that an older man had built the castle in the mid-1880s to impress a much younger wife. After that, everything spiraled for the castle's first owners. They went broke and allegedly committed murder. They became ghosts. For the Brimelows to find a happy ending in the castle, they would have to defy what people perceived to be a curse.

Morgan County residents have treated Berkeley Springs—sometimes still also called by its original name, "The Town of Bath"—as a mystical place controlled by vaguely understood, preordained currents. Trey Johanson described this to me as the town's "woo woo" energy.

Some have attributed a spiritual significance to the water—the springs that have poured out of the hills for centuries and for which Berkeley Springs is named. They believe these springs direct the flow of life in the town as well as in the hills and hollers around it. At minimum, the springs are the reason why the town has attracted travelers.

Doug, an employee of the state-owned Old Roman Bath House, proudly instructed me that the water in Berkeley Springs pumps out at a warm 74 degrees Fahrenheit at a rate of 1,250 gallons per minute. On weekend mornings, residents from around the county drive to the park next to Fairfax Coffee House carrying jugs to fill up with the water that flows from the spigots beside the bathhouse.

On a laminated sheet at the front desk of the historic spa, the state park laid out the composition of the town's water. I've stayed in multiple rented rooms around town where the hosts also kept laminated cards containing the information. They put it out there like it is a beautiful poem:

Mineral content: Grains/US Gallon
Sodium Chloride: 0.142
Sodium Sulphate: 0.598
Sodium Nitrate: 0.026
Potassium Sulphate: 0.116
Calcium Sulphate: 0.526
Ferrous Carbonate: 0.005
Magnesium Carbonate: 1.110
Strontium Carbonate: Trace
Alumina: 0.045
Silica: 0.496
Ammonium Chloride: Absent
Albuminoid Nitrogen: 0.0012
Organic Matter: 0.275
Calcium Carbonate: 6.749
Total: 16.8592
Gasses: Cubic Inches
Free Carbonic Acid: 2.2
Carbonic Acid in Bicarbonates: 7.14
Dissolved Oxygen: 0.41

Long before Berkeley Springs had an English name, Native Americans pursued the healing effects of the water. It made the region a place for tribes to converge and talk. Archeological artifacts have placed the existence of Native tribes in the area as far back as 8,500 years.[1] The Massawomeck people lived in the region. Later, The Susquehannock people did. Both tribes spoke the Iroquoian dialect.[2]

On July 4, 1876, David Hunter Strother, an author who wrote under the pen name Porte Crayon, issued a speech commemorating what was then the centennial for Berkeley Springs. He described "the Tuscaroras, the Delawares, The Six Nations from the banks of the Susquehanna and as far north as the Great Lakes and the Catawbas from the Carolinas" converging at the springs. Strother claimed that they "established a standing truce among these sacred fountains, that all might enjoy in peace and security the beneficent provision of the Great Spirit."[3]

White colonizers started joining Native Americans at the springs by around 1720. Strother noted that they first "mingled with" Natives and finally "superseded" them at the sacred waters. Two English-language maps flagged the springs as far back as 1737. One map called the place "Warm Springs," and the other called it "Medical Springs."

Lord Fairfax first controlled the area around Berkeley Springs as part of his inheritance. In 1747, he detailed a plan to build a town there.[4] A sixteen-year-old George Washington, while working for Lord Fairfax as a surveyor, bathed in its waters the next year. The future first president did so in what looks today like a ditch in the ground. "We called this day to see YE FARMED WARM SPRINGS. We camped out in the field this night," the teenage George Washington wrote in his diary on March 19, 1747.

George Washington repeatedly returned to the springs. He came as late as 1796, three years before he died of complications surrounding an infected throat. Washington liked what would become Berkeley Springs so much that he bought two plots of land there. Historians told me he never lived on them.

When colonizers founded the Town of Bath in 1776, they created "America's First Spa." What the local tourism website doesn't boast about is the culture of liquor, gambling, and sex work that white settlers brought to the spas then. People knew Berkeley Springs for this debauched culture more than anything else.

In 1775, when the Reverend Philip Vickers Fithian, a Presbyterian, traveled down from his native New Jersey to experience the healing waters, he discovered "amusement in all shapes." He witnessed men enjoying "promiscuous company." Fithian wrote about one man driven wild by "those vigor giving waters" engaging in what seems from his description like a rape. Fithian said this man overdosed on spring water and willfully broke into the room of a Maryland maid named "Buxom Kate."[5]

The newly formed US government established a local post office in the town in 1801. They called it Berkeley Springs because there was already another town called Bath. So Berkeley Springs became Berkeley Springs, but it was still Bath to many—and, to devout Christians, something akin to a wetter version of contemporary Las Vegas.

Zach Salman, a historian who grew up in the area and who has fought to preserve the town's buildings, told me that the Town of Bath emerged as "the adult playground of the mid-Atlantic" after its founding. The idea carried forward for over a century.

Berkeley Springs peaked in the mid-1800s. At that time, wealthy visitors arrived on the newly constructed Baltimore and Ohio Railroad, which ran adjacent to the Potomac behind the area where Berkeley Springs Castle would later rise. They partied in grand hotels, like the sprawling Berkeley Springs Hotel. Then, at the start of the American Civil War in 1861, the revelry paused. The same railroad that had brought revelers became a way to transport troops and resources.

Maryland and Virginia had among the highest populations of freed slaves by the nineteenth century. Still, a significant portion of the white population wanted to perpetuate white dominance.[6] Only three men from Morgan County, Virginia, voted for Abraham Lincoln in the election of 1860. The majority voted for Democrat John C. Breckinridge, who emerged as a high-ranking Confederate during the war, but disappeared to England in self-imposed exile after the fighting ended.[7]

On the first day of 1862, Stonewall Jackson, chasing proximity to Union-held Maryland, led 8,500 secessionist soldiers into town, supported by artillery. The pale-eyed Virginian seized the Berkeley Springs Hotel to house his soldiers and held it for two days. Jackson sought to destroy the Baltimore and Ohio Railroad, and in the ice and snow that collected alongside the rolling Potomac, Confederates from Virginia and Arkansas clashed with men from Indiana and Illinois.

Jackson tore up telegraph lines and railroad tracks, but the Confederates retreated.[8] During Jackson's broader, dead-of-winter campaign, the extreme cold being a relative rarity for Civil War action, nearly 2,000 of his men fell ill because of the inclement weather and died.[9]

Lincoln recognized West Virginia as the thirty-fifth state on June 20, 1863. It formally severed from Virginia and criminalized slavery. Unionist Virginians engaged in two years of legal maneuvering to complete the extraction, which eventually included Morgan County and Berkeley Springs. The 1871 Supreme Court decision in *Virginia v. West Virginia* made Berkeley and Jefferson Counties, now neighbors to Morgan County, a permanent part of the state.[10]

Following the end of the war, Samuel Taylor Suit saw opportunities in Richmond, Virginia, the conquered capital of the Confederacy, and opened the First National Bank of Richmond. Suit then returned to Maryland and invested his time in the distillery business. He also invested in the railroads, another booming business of the era. A widower at an early age, Suit, called "the Colonel," remarried and saw his wealth expand, but his appetite for his second marriage declined.

Suit met a seventeen-year-old girl named Rosa Pelham at a party in 1878. She was pretty and he became obsessed with her. His divorce hadn't even been finalized yet, but he wanted to marry Pelham. Literature promoting Berkeley Springs and the castle gives their story a romantic, storybook flair. But a description in the 2005 hobby magazine *Bottles and Extras* made reference to Suit's appreciation of youth more generally: "All his life the Colonel had a soft spot for young people. He raised a special breed of white ponies on his estate to be given as gifts to the children of his friends. Contemporaries portrayed him as very sentimental and loving. He particularly loved Rosa."

The age gap between Suit and Pelham was actually smaller than that between Peter and Lydia Brimelow. Still, it bothered Pelham enough that she refused to marry him because of it. To change her mind, Suit offered to build her a castle in Berkeley Springs, right above the fabled healing waters. Pelham acquiesced. They married in 1883, when she was twenty-two years old and he was fifty-one.

Suit started construction on the castle in 1885, with workers bringing in local silica sandstone for the project. Alfred Mullett, who designed other historic buildings, including the State, War, and Navy Building in Washington, DC, likely contributed to the look and feel of the castle, given his repeated visits during its construction. In total, this project to woo young Pelham cost Suit $100,000. Adjusting for inflation, Peter and Lydia bought it for about a third of that, relative to the era in which they lived.[11]

Builders completed the roof by May 1887. By May 1888, Suit was dead. He never quite got the chance to experience the castle he gifted to Pelham.[12] The twenty-seven-year-old then lived alone there with the couple's three children. She became a celebrity in town. People said she took lovers and went mad. Pelham blew her inherited fortune on parties within five years. At the same time, the financial solidity of the region deteriorated around her. Pelham went bankrupt. She lost the castle in 1903.

Pelham had one of her affairs with a colonel known only as "Jawbone." According to legend, she pushed Jawbone to his death from the battlements. Both of their ghosts were reported to have started haunting the castle in subsequent years.[13]

Another suitor of Pelham's allegedly fell down the stairs and impaled himself on an umbrella before he became a ghost. People have also reported seeing a young female ghost in the building who liked to "sing and giggle."[14]

The now-defunct Bank of Morgan County owned the Berkeley Springs Castle for two decades before a family called the Cunninghams purchased it. Around the time the Cunninghams bought the place, the Ku Klux Klan marched hooded through Berkeley Springs during Fourth of July events. They did it in 1924, 1925, and 1926.

In 1938, the Cunninghams sold the castle to the Kesecker family, which kept it until 1954. The Keseckers sold it to the Bird family. The Birds owned it from the 1980s to the turn of the century. That's when a man named Andrew Gosline took over the castle. Patti Miller told me that Gosline boasted of being a direct descendent of Stonewall Jackson. Otherwise, she said, he stayed out of controversial matters. People raved to me about Gosline's willingness to use the castle to bolster tourism.

Gosline died in December 2014, leaving the castle to his children. A Facebook account for the town's tourism board mourned his death:

> R.I.P. to Berkeley Castle's owner, Andrew Gosline. He loved the castle, returning it to its original purpose as a private residence. Gosline expanded and enhanced the castle grounds as well as the interior and exterior of the structure adding his pet gargoyles. He opened the castle for the use of several community groups including the Museum of the Berkeley Springs which held an annual holiday tea there for a decade. Future plans for the castle are not known but Gosline left it better than he found it. Thank you.

Drug overdose deaths spiked in Morgan County during this time. Overdose deaths related to the opioid fentanyl nearly quadrupled at the same moment that Donald J. Trump emerged as a national force in American politics.[15] Trump expanded his influence over the party, and West Virginia grew more openly reactionary, according to residents with whom I spoke.

The Berkeley Springs Castle emptied out. People in town told me that Gosline's heirs never really wanted to commit to the local community in the way Andrew had. Shop owners in town, including many of the men and women who ventured over to Fairfax Coffee House on that chilly night in February, prayed for someone interesting to swoop in and restore the castle to the role it had in the life of Berkeley Springs before Andrew Gosline died. They hoped new ownership would fire up tourism.

And that's when VDARE showed up.

To some residents, bad luck had become as much a part of the Berkeley Springs mystique as its water. But the decline had started long before VDARE's arrival. Rosa Pelham's financial fall coincided with three of Berkeley Springs' major hotels burning down, decimating the tourism industry that had sprung up before the Civil War and then roared back to life after it. More fires plagued the town's hotels in future years. Then heavy rains flooded Berkeley Springs on St. Patrick's Day in 1936, ravaging much of the town's property.

On August 25, 1974, the Washington House, the last of the old resort hotels, burned to ashes during the darkest hours of the morning. The death of the hotel marked one of many setbacks that advocates of historical restoration have faced in recent decades in the region.

"The sight is awesome, appalling—the central core of Washington House Hotel already a mass of flames and two fire companies—Berkeley Springs and Hancock—fighting bravely, but losing ground to the raging, spreading inferno," a witness told *The Morgan Messenger* about the overnight blaze.[16]

The yellow brick neoclassical-style Morgan County Courthouse, built in 1907, burned down too. More than one person I spoke to when I first visited Berkeley Springs on March 12 placed the arrival of Peter and Lydia Brimelow within this narrative of fires, floods, and tragedy.

People talked to me about these things the way fans of losing sports teams talk about the inevitability of heartbreak. Each new setback reinforced a vague, otherworldly feeling that everything in Berkeley Springs was cursed.

5

High Weirdness

On the night of March 7, Paul, Trey, and Mary, the South Carolina transplant who had left the voicemail for the SPLC, met with a small group at The Troubadour, a dive bar in Berkeley Springs. The Troubadour offered cheap pours of liquor, obscure country music acts, a place to dance, and "five piece Wing Ding and Fries" plates.

Mary was, at thirty-eight, a youngster relative to the median-age Berkeley Springs resident. She hated the unfocused, hippie-ish vibe of the conversation about taking on VDARE. Mary felt that Trey and Paul were unequipped to lead a confrontation against someone as imposing as Peter Brimelow.

She knew the power that big, wealthy people could wield in a small town, and it frightened her. She had agreed to meet me during my trip, but she also said she felt pessimistic about it mattering.

"It's just that I don't see any reason to believe the Brimelows won't just steamroll this place and make it their own," she said.

"I'd love to hear why you think that," I'd said.

"We can meet at the coffee shop when you get here."

Other people from town had reached out to me when they heard that I was a subject-matter expert coming down to analyze the castle dilemma. They wanted to pass along intelligence on VDARE and almost anything else that came to mind.

Some emails people sent me came fermented in a small-town broth I struggled to digest. Geoffrey Wendel emailed me on March 11 to warn me about Toby Moore, the part-time resident who spoke up at the meeting.

"From behavior and some poking around . . . Toby Moore . . . may very well be an agent provocateur with ulterior motives. I do not know if he is of the folk that bought the castle, or an opportunist who sees a power opportunity," Geoffrey wrote. "I do not feel comfortable being more active, or communicating with the growing groups around the Fairfax coffeehouse, as he is enmeshed in all of them."

Geoffrey went on, writing about the various things that made him feel nervous.

"And please do not tell these folk I have given you a heads up. There is high weirdness going on here," he concluded.

I wrote back to Geoffrey, saying, "Okay—message received."

In a literal sense, that was true. I'd received his message. I told him I would meet him alone at his Portals Metaphysical shop. This new coronavirus thing was spreading rapidly, but my conscience started telling me I couldn't cancel on this town. I decided I could simply drive down to West Virginia, where there were very few cases of infection, and keep myself away from any airport.

The gravity of the virus hit me coming back from a media training in Atlanta at the start of March, where the SPLC briefed me on how to discuss their latest round of hate group designations. I was leaving from Hartsfield-Jackson Airport that evening and I waited in no lines. One guy flew out of my gate wearing two layers of surgical masks. I emailed our team.

"Hey friends, I am at the Atlanta airport right now and there were no lines for Delta during rush hour on a Wednesday night. I am not an alarmist, but there is an undeniably eerie vibe and it prompted me to send this email," I wrote.

Then everyone started canceling everything.

My wife, Aadya, had two reasons to be concerned about a forthcoming trip to Berkeley Springs. The first one was the coronavirus. Our two sons were now trapped inside with us in a tiny apartment in Jackson Heights, Queens, where there was no room for social distance. The second one was other potential threats to my health, both physical and mental.

"What's this for again?" she asked me.

"I have to talk to some people in a town," I said. "One of the groups we cover bought a castle there."

"A castle," she said.

"Yeah."

We moved carefully, balancing different things, trying not to bang into each other in our little kitchen.

"What am I gonna do with the boys?"

"We'll work it out," I said.

"The timing is not great, Mike."

"The timing sucks."

I finished making my coffee.

"So, what kind of group is this?" she asked.

Peter Brimelow's activist war against the Immigration Act of 1965, also known as Hart-Cellar, which opened the United States to a new wave of immigrants from Africa, Asia, and the Middle East, meant that he would likely not think well of me, even without my associations with the SPLC. The fact that I was an Arab American journalist who also wrote inquisitive stories about him and was married to an Indian woman made me a script-perfect VDARE antagonist.

After I had published Stephen Miller's emails in 2019, VDARE had responded, burying an intriguing phrase, "which may explain something," between parentheses: "Michael Edison Hayden (he apparently has an Egyptian mother and an Indian wife, which may explain something) just published an article based on [an] email treacherously leaked by Katie McHugh, a disgruntled ex-Breitbart staffer and former Alt Right groupie, showing that Stephen Miller, Trump's much-hated immigration adviser, reads VDARE.com."[1]

I'm culturally white, and the only Arabic I learned growing up were the curse words. My mother, Magda Antoun, immigrated to the United

States from Cairo in 1968 as an eighteen-year-old, three years after Hart-Cellar passed the House in a vote count of 320 to 70. No way around it, I wouldn't exist if Lyndon Johnson hadn't signed Hart-Cellar into law.

Aadya, an immigrant from Mumbai, represented a far worse case than mine, from VDARE's perspective. She had obtained a green card through marriage in 2006 and then lived here for decades without bothering to apply for citizenship. She walked among white people, entertained herself in white spaces, but felt no pressure to assimilate or vanquish her Indian perspective. This was the exact type of person the movement believed shouldn't be allowed in America.

Aadya had very severe dark eyebrows and an elegance that felt otherworldly to me when we married in 2006. When doctors diagnosed her father with lymphoma, I traveled to India with her and lived there for five years. I started working as a journalist in India, writing stories for the digital versions of *The New York Times*, *The Wall Street Journal*, and others. We almost lived there for good but changed our minds after I came up just short on a position with Reuters as an enterprise reporter covering the subcontinent.

When we returned to America, I took a job as a contractor with ABC News during an expansion of the broadcaster around the 2016 election. I started reporting on the MAGA phenomenon, from Trump to the white activists who supported him. When I returned from India, America felt like a different place entirely from when I'd left. The mood around politics had gotten acrid. Trump's rhetoric around immigrants terrified me.

A colleague of mine at ABC News, Morgan, needed me to take her shift so she could attend a wedding in August 2017. It turned out to be the weekend when white supremacists marched on Charlottesville for the Unite the Right rally. On the Saturday night that James Alex Fields Jr. murdered Heather Heyer, I dropped to my knees and started sobbing into my couch, my work bag still slung over my sweaty shoulder and my ID badge still dangling over my shirt. It shattered something in me. I decided to start writing about the movement full time after that, hoping to destroy it.

Back then, I kept Gab open in my browser every hour I was awake. Gab was an obscure version of Twitter populated by people who hated women, Jews, Muslims, Latin American immigrants, Middle Eastern immigrants, Black people, queer people, liberals, socialists, anarchists, vegetarians, vegans, artists, pit bulls, and anything else you might find in New York City. When a mirthless middle-aged white man named Robert Bowers murdered eleven Jews at the Tree of Life Synagogue in Pittsburgh on October 27, 2018, he announced his intention to kill by posting on Gab. I didn't have to scramble to figure out what happened because I already knew Bowers. I knew all the obsessive maniacs on Gab, personally. They kept threatening to kill me, so they became hard to forget.

Lots of people threatened to kill me. Someone on a neo-Nazi forum promised to throw a Molotov cocktail through my childhood home to "celebrate" my dad's seventy-second birthday. They described the front window by the kitchen. That made everyone, including the police, worried that they'd scouted it. The police installed cameras at my parents' house and scheduled nightly loops around the property for multiple weeks. The racist street-marching group Patriot Front sent mail to my parents' house. They sent one card I remember with a very simple message on it: *PATRIOTISM WITH TEETH.*

A guy affiliated with Patriot Front, going by "Braxton Bragg," the name of the Southern Civil War general who led the South's ill-fated Chattanooga campaign, published my sister Katie's address in Los Angeles and publicly fantasized about someone raping her.

"I'm fine," Katie told me. "These losers are fucking hilarious!"

"I don't think it's a joke, Katie," I explained.

White supremacists also repeatedly messaged me photos of Alan Berg's gory, mutilated corpse. In 1984, neo-Nazis from the group The Order murdered Berg, the Jewish radio host upon whom the Oliver Stone film *Talk Radio* is based. His picture showed blood and brains splattered across his driveway. Every few days someone sent me the same photo of Berg, newly dead, his head no longer looking like a human head, gore splattered everywhere.

"What do you want me to do with this?" I asked one of the pseudonymous guys on Gab who sent it to me.

"Look at it to remind yourself of what you're doing," the person on the other side of the screen responded.

Berg had lit up a Pall Mall right before they shot him to death, and police found it still smoldering near the blood that poured from his body. Police struggled to determine how the bullets entered Berg's torso, because he had contorted in so much pain as they landed in him. Multiple bullets entered and exited his skull, which is why the photo looked the way it did.[2]

"Are these more violent people?" Aadya asked me.

"I don't think so. These racists are old racists," I said.

"Okay."

Aadya picked up our two-year-old son and he looked at me.

"Well," I said. "*She's* not old, the wife. She's younger than we are."

"They're a married couple?"

"Yeah."

"Are you going inside this castle?" she asked.

"I doubt it."

Early on the morning of March 12, carrying an overnight bag, I hiked forty-five minutes from my apartment in Jackson Heights to LaGuardia Airport to rent an SUV. I was too paranoid to get into a cab with someone who could have the virus. I picked out a black RAV4 from the lot, and a masked worker opened the doors to air it out while looking back at me for approval.

"That's fine," I said.

Living with the threats and darkness—hate, rage, scapegoating—was beating me up. I longed for consistent therapy but found it prohibitively expensive. What I needed was a doctor I could see every week. I visited a superb psychiatrist on the Upper West Side named Dr. K, who prescribed medications. But I could only afford to see him once a year. Insurance wouldn't cover it.

The SPLC's answer to our mental health challenges was a subscription to a meditation app on which everyone spoke in an English accent. They also gave us telehealth therapy subscriptions, where the staff seemed unequipped to handle trauma. I tried a guy on there once and the first thing he said to me when I explained my situation was, "That sounds terrible."

I put in the coordinates for Berkeley Springs in the RAV4's GPS system. It dawned on me that I had never actually stopped or spent time in West Virginia. My minimal understanding of the state came from an amalgamation of news programs I'd half watched on TV.

Driving down, I saw gray New York, gray New Jersey, gray Pennsylvania, and gray Maryland, all hushed by growing fears over the coronavirus. The sun didn't seem to come out the entire way. The hills rose to meet me as I crossed the Potomac, went past a roadside diner, and pulled into Berkeley Springs for the first time.

6

A Promise

I arrived on the afternoon of March 12 and did a loop around Route 522, also named North Washington Street, which cut through the middle of the little town. Berkeley Springs looked like a movie set of a small American town.

A hardware store. A standalone doctor's office sporting a Trump flag. A junk shop littered with what looked like dangling cast iron skillets. A mural of a druggy-looking cartoon cat. An ancient movie theater trimmed with red lettering. A white gazebo. Some indistinguishable tan buildings, maybe government. A church. An old-fashioned hotel, draped with flags, including an Irish flag.

Something very big and gray lurked in the trees to the right of my car and to the left when I reversed course. It was the castle.

I checked into the bed and breakfast and threw my bag on the floor. I found a Bible waiting for me in an open nightstand drawer. The B&B was one of those places where everything gave too much under human weight. The stairs talked. The bedsprings drooped to the point just above total deterioration. I peeled off my glasses, washed the day off my face, and went out.

The castle wasn't hard to find. I walked the path up the hill and within a minute stood in front of it. On foot and close up, it looked incredible. I saw no VDARE. I saw no Peter or Lydia. It was just this bonkers, haunted-looking castle in West Virginia, with tree limbs shooting up all around it into the overcast sky. I snapped pictures of the gargoyles. Whoever designed the eyes had made them look sentient.

The Brimelows had moved an hour-and-a-half car ride away from Washington, DC, and gotten themselves much closer to power. That's what I thought about as I headed down the hill to meet Trey. Proximity to power, and an ability to organize without being seen, were the keys to understanding how VDARE ended up in that building.

If the leaders of the movement wanted to turn their town into a home base, the neighbors in Berkeley Springs had a challenge ahead of them. I envisioned buses with tinted windows letting people on and off without detection. If Peter wanted to host a powerful sympathizer of the movement who needed to remain invisible, he could easily handle that in this location.

When I turned up 522 on foot, Trey waved. She was petite and had the ability to project earnest joy, something I could never do when meeting new people. She hugged me straight off, as if I were her favorite nephew.

"Did you get in okay, hon?" she asked.

"I think so," I said.

"So, you saw the castle?"

"I did. Wild. It's actually really beautiful," I said. "I was telling my editor that that area should be a public park or something. How old is it again?"

"Nineteenth century," she said.

"It's amazing."

"I mean, you can't miss it, it's right here," she said, pointing.

We turned the corner. I saw the castle again. It loomed over everything, particularly her shop. Trey's smile dropped into a straight line when she looked at it.

"Crazy," I said.

"Paul?" she called over a dividing wall, then, to me, "Paul's right there."

I had forgotten about Paul from that SPLC email. A blond man with a bandanna around his neck bounded up from a space next to the coffee shop. He looked like he had been performing manual labor. We shook hands.

"You made it," he said.

"I wish I were visiting for different reasons."

"People are really united here against the whole thing," he said. "They really are. Lots of energy behind the whole thing."

"Well, I love the town so far."

"Do you?" Trey asked.

She seemed genuinely pleased to hear me say it.

"I haven't seen much but yeah. I feel like I want to come back here and vacation. I bet it's beautiful in the summer."

"That makes me so glad to hear," Trey said. "And we have hiking, and all that good stuff. Do you have kids?"

"I do."

"Boys or girls?"

"Two boys," I said.

"You're going to have to bring them over in the summertime," Trey said.

"Maybe I will," I said.

"The coffee shop is right here, obviously," Paul said, pointing. "And this is the biergarten. We are building this up right now and hoping to get it ready soon."

He showed me a loosely arranged space next to Fairfax Coffee House. Paul also pointed out a mural of a multicolored sun with birds and dragons circling words for "love" in different languages.

"That's lovely," I said.

"Our friend Matt made it," Paul said.

"Isn't it something?" Trey said.

I admired the mural for a beat.

"So, how are you guys holding up with the whole coronavirus thing?" I asked.

"We haven't seen much of that," Trey said.

"But are you prepared for it? To be honest," I said, "it's kind of weird for me to be just interacting normally. We're not doing this in New York."

I made a hand gesture to demonstrate our physical closeness.

"It's spreading very fast?" Trey asked.

"I almost canceled this trip," I said.

"Well, I'm glad you didn't," Trey said.

"Our family has been isolating, so you should be fine," I said. "I mean, we haven't been making contact with anyone."

"Don't worry," Trey said.

From out on the street, the castle gave off a mean look, and I again imagined it with vans running in and out of it.

"I'll be back for the talk," I explained. "I just want to take a quick look around."

"We'll be ready for you," Trey said. "Also, Joe Bernstein from BuzzFeed is here too. Did I mention?"

"No," I said.

"Yeah, he's been here already," she said. "Just so much energy around what we're doing right now! It's incredible."

I had never met Joe, but we'd crossed paths online. I had no issues with him, but I hated the idea of becoming a detail in a BuzzFeed dispatch from Berkeley Springs.

I walked the little town. Less than a thousand people lived there. Only seventeen thousand people lived in Morgan County, which included and surrounded it. The few people I passed were white and none of them were young. I saw a Mexican restaurant called Mi Ranchito and decided I would eat lunch there before leaving on Friday. It looked like my best bet for talking to anyone of color.

I returned to Fairfax Coffee House. Trey had dimmed the lights to create a mood, and she had layered the shop window with obliquely antiracist slogans promoting love and tolerance—these appeared to be her everyday decorations. She also used a jellyfish as her logo and had plastered an illustration of the creature onto mugs and along the walls.

The shop had two connected rooms for customers. The first led to a white countertop where people could place their coffee and food orders. It was closed for the occasion. The second room acted as a parlor, and it expanded into a small wooden bar. Trey directed me into that room to speak.

I shook some hands and scanned the place. It looked like about twenty-five or thirty people were in attendance, all white, mostly middle aged and older. I saw Joe Bernstein, and we acknowledged each other. Then I sat down in the middle of all the faces and Trey introduced me. She expressed gratitude on behalf of the town. No one wore a mask.

"Hey everyone, thank you for coming," I said. "Particularly in the middle of this coronavirus stuff. I try not to give out my exact location publicly, but I live in the New York area. And it's getting very scary over there now with the virus. So, it means a lot to me to see you prioritizing this. The first thing I want to say is that I'm sorry about what you're going through. You didn't invite Peter Brimelow here, obviously. We don't get to choose our neighbors."

I explained the great replacement conspiracy theory, and I talked as much as I could about Peter and Lydia and what they did. I told them I didn't know who had funded the castle. I told them to stay strong.

"I've heard that they're litigious," someone interjected.

"A lot of people in the movement are," I said.

"What if they try to sue us?" the person said.

"I think if you stick to the truth, you should be fine. They're not going to run around and sue people for showing up at meetings. They might want to, but they can't."

"What can the SPLC do to help us get rid of them? Beyond this," someone said.

I knew that the SPLC wouldn't offer legal help, because we were too dysfunctional, but I couldn't say that. Everything would have to break perfectly right for the SPLC to take it on. I had only come there because my friend Rachel thought we should do it.

"I'm obviously not a lawyer but I'm going to write about this situation, and I'm going to stay on it, and use whatever platform they give me to help. I really believe in this town," I said. "You'll outlast Peter Brimelow."

When the meeting ended, I shook hands. Toby Moore greeted me, and I found him to be not at all like the person Geoffrey Wendel had described in his email. I met Matthew Hahn, a local doctor with a big smile, who kept his remaining hair buzzed close to his head. He was running for Congress in West Virginia's Second Congressional District as an anti-Trump voice but immediately came across as far too gentle to win a race.

"It's good to have a Republican here," I said.

"Well, I can't stand this VDARE stuff."

Hahn's pro-Trump opponent would later obliterate him in their primary, beating him by over 50 percent of the vote.

Trey approached to thank me.

"You meant what you said about staying on it?" she said.

"I'm going to come back one day," I said. "You're stuck with me."

"You mean it?"

"Absolutely."

"Who else would you know in the mainstream press? Would you know anyone?"

"I'll give that a thought for you. But I'm going to keep the pressure on."

Everything closed early. The number of people I saw on the street diminished from few to zero after nightfall. I ate dinner at a place called the Ravenwood Pub, where I was the only customer. It appeared to be carved out of the back of someone's house.

A gray-haired woman, Regina Amacha, served me an off-menu vegetarian dinner with a cold bottle of stout. When I asked her about the VDARE castle, she told me wistfully about how her mom had brought her and her brother up from Birmingham, Alabama, to see Martin Luther King Jr. speak in 1963.

I retired to my room and turned on CNN. Anderson Cooper and Sanjay Gupta were interviewing a guy who had contracted the coronavirus on a cruise ship. Then a doctor from the University of Nebraska promised the audience that the virus wasn't like the Black Death of the Middle Ages.

"Having said that, this is a very serious event, and one we need to take seriously, and prepare for, and do everything we can to blunt the spread during this pandemic," the doctor said.

The trazodone that Dr. K had prescribed for me took me under. Nightmares woke me up. I dreamt I was moving through an apartment complex in a city something like Amsterdam, looking for my youngest son, and he was somewhere in another room.

7

America Is Burning

On the afternoon of March 13, 2020, I interviewed Mary at Fairfax Coffee House and asked her why she had reached out for help. She told me how shocked she'd felt when she'd read Russell Mokhiber's blog. She didn't know what to do.

"Nobody got a heads-up about this group from *anyone*," she told me. "We had no idea that they were coming into town—from *anyone*."

I asked Mary what she would have done if she'd found out earlier. She didn't know, but she took VDARE's castle purchase personally. Mary now woke up in a place that she believed was defined by unvarnished white supremacy. And she had nowhere else to go, because of her stepfather's health problems. She was stuck there, and the local resistance leaders, like Trey and Paul, had no real plan.

Later, I ordered a veggie burrito with an iced tea at Mi Ranchito and invited the server to talk. She was Leslie Robles, the matriarch of the family that owned the place. In 1999, her husband, Oscar, had ventured out on a road trip from Virginia to Seattle and blown a flat tire in Berkeley Springs. The town's mayor, Susan Webster, helped him. Webster urged him to open a restaurant, and he agreed to do it.[1] I asked Leslie about being an immigrant in a town that had very few of them.

"When I came here twenty years ago, people didn't know what to think of us," she said, speaking slowly to choose her words carefully. "Now it has changed, in a good way."

"May I ask... have you heard about all this stuff at the castle? There's this group that is, um, *against* immigration that moved there. Have you heard about that?"

"I'm sorry," she said as she left the table. "I don't know."

Before I left, I drove to Prospect Overlook, a place someone from Fairfax Coffee House had recommended. To get there, I had to drive on Route 9—a road that stretched out deeper into more rural West Virginia towns—past the castle and then beyond it, crossing winding roads and a few homes embedded in a forest. I pulled my car onto the shoulder of the road and took in the vista.

The sun crept through the overcast sky. It illuminated one of the most incredible views I've ever seen. I might have been looking at the country before European settlement. Sporadic bursts of the rushing freight train sounds of the Baltimore and Ohio Railroad broke the silence of the hills. The wide Potomac River cut perfectly through the middle of the landscape, twisting through hills and clusters of trees. Those trees seemed to crawl on forever, stretching into the horizon before they hit the sky.

I read a charming black and white sign posted where the shoulder met a cluster of trees:

> This headland overlooks the Potomac and Great Cacapon valleys and the three states, West Virginia, Pennsylvania, and Maryland. The National Geographic Magazine rates this scene among America's outstanding beauty spots. WEST VIRGINIA DEPARTMENT OF CULTURE AND HISTORY, 1983.

I sat in my car for another ten minutes, thinking about life and death. I checked my fuel. Half of a tank. I pulled a sharp U-turn, drove past the castle on my way out, and headed for Queens.

A few times, Aadya and I had taken our older son to Elmhurst Hospital, less than a mile from our house. Suddenly, Elmhurst became the epicenter of the American coronavirus outbreak. We never left the apartment after that. The trip to Berkeley Springs was the last thing I did before the pandemic consumed everything.

The SPLC started canceling in-person gatherings. It canceled reporting trips too, making my jaunt to Berkeley Springs the last one of an era. Reporting trips followed on the other side of the pandemic, but that trend didn't last more than a year or so, and SPLC workers were never given the same kind of respect or autonomy again. Through tremendous distraction over the spreading virus, I worked up a story on the castle. As it got closer to publication on March 17, I emailed Peter and Lydia Brimelow.

"A group of residents from Berkeley Springs reached out to me with concerns about the castle you purchased, speaking critically of your organization. Many were concerned about the deleterious impact it will have on tourism, which is an important part of the local economy. This was hardly a small number, relative to the population of the town," I wrote.

My tone was pathetically snippy, and it would have been more to the point to have referred to the people as business owners rather than residents. In truth, I didn't know whether the residents I hadn't met sympathized with the Brimelows. I had convinced myself that the town I had seen in twenty-four hours was, in fact, the town.

Peter responded to me a day later. He conflated his beliefs with "patriotism," which is a rhetorical device used by the movement to imply that their critics stood in opposition to American values:

> That's funny, a LARGE group of residents (relative to the population of the town) spontaneously emailed to welcome us after local leftists started ululating. Of course, besides being beautiful, Morgan County voted 74% for Trump and what we've long advocated on immigration is basically what Trump outlined in his August 15, 2015, position paper. So patriotism may not be as shocking to them as it is to you. We look forward to being a

vital part of the local economy and the business community in Berkeley Springs for years to come.

The SPLC published my story, titled "West Virginia Tourist Hub Rejects VDARE's Negative Message," on March 19, along with the pictures I took of the castle's gargoyles.[2] When I posted it online, nobody cared. Everyone in the world had disappeared into the vortex of the coronavirus, which people increasingly called by its more sci-fi dystopian name, "COVID-19."

On the day the SPLC published the story, the Old Roman Bath House shut down operations in Berkeley Springs. People in the town started to withdraw into their homes. The minimal foot traffic around Route 522 ground to a stop.

"In response to COVID-19, for the safety of our guests and staff, the Main Bathhouse is closed until further notice. Updates will be posted as we receive them," an account associated with the Berkeley Springs bathhouses posted on Facebook.

Days earlier, West Virginia had shut down the fountains where people traveled to fill up jugs of water. Shutting down access to the water attractions in town was the equivalent of pulling the plug on a power grid.

Geoffrey Wendel's Portals Metaphysical told people to stop coming into the shop a few days after the article was published.

"We would like to underline something. Stay home. Seriously. We are at a point that the best thing you can do for the next 2 weeks (at least) is to isolate, and see if you have been exposed to Covid-19. We are a business focused on physical and spiritual health. It would be completely irresponsible of us to put our customers at risk. We serve a diverse set of communities . . . some of whom are very much going to do badly if they catch this and the healthcare system is overloaded," Geoffrey posted on Facebook on March 21.

As it did to every other business in town, COVID-19 bludgeoned Fairfax Coffee House. Trey watched her revenue dip 90 percent overnight. Filled with grief, she told her staff to apply for unemployment as soon as possible to avoid any crunch brought on by the inevitable cave in the economy. She started working seven days a week on her own. To get by, Trey stocked provisions from a restaurant distributor and sold them to people struggling to get food.

On March 26, VDARE responded to my story by publishing a post authored by VDARE's managing editor, James Fulford, titled "SPLC Thug Michael Hayden Demonizes VDARE.com's Castle Purchase. His Twitter Followers Plot Violence. WHERE IS FBI!?"[3]

I had to squint at the headline. Was it a joke? Then I read the thing. The post began, "Michael Edison Hayden, 'investigative reporter' a.k.a. Cultural Marxist Enforcer for the Southern Poverty Law Center... has been spying on VDARE.com's recent purchase of Berkeley Springs Castle in Berkeley Springs WVA. He's found and interviewed a few local Leftists (most of them, we're told, are Washington D.C. interlopers)... and his Twitter followers have responded with terroristic threats."

I had no idea what VDARE or Fulford were talking about regarding the "terroristic" threats. When I scrolled down on the page, I saw that some of my Twitter followers had indeed shared images referencing catapults, people storming the gates with torches, and other bits of castle humor under my tweet promoting the story. Another anonymous person wrote, "Aluminum powder mixed with iron oxide. Or Gallium if you're trying to be sneaky."

I agreed that maybe posting the recipe for thermite was in bad taste. But as the pandemic swelled in importance, the thermite recipe and VDARE's castle slipped from my mind. Trey slipped from my mind too. And Joe Bernstein never even wrote a story about Berkeley Springs.

Peter posted about his lawsuit against *The New York Times* for the first time that April, referring to "the sin of SULLIVAN," the 1964 US Supreme Court case *New York Times Company v. Sullivan*, which granted protections to the press against defamation lawsuits. Peter spawned part of his lawsuit off one of *The New York Times* articles focused on my investigation into Stephen Miller, making me a tangential part of it.

"Maybe suing won't work. Maybe we will indeed be driven entirely out of the public square. But we have to try. What alternative do we have?" Peter wrote on VDARE of the lawsuit. "And there are heartening signs that the flawed *SULLIVAN* decision is—after nearly sixty years—finally collapsing under the weight of its own contradictions."[4]

My colleague Hannah Gais, a close friend, repeatedly reached out to Facebook and YouTube with me about VDARE during those early COVID-19 months, because VDARE kept using the pandemic to lean into race-science material. Facebook suspended the organization's account on May 5, citing "inauthentic behavior."[5] We had no idea how much of a role we played in that because the company never answered our questions, but I suspected that we did play one.

On May 6, a lawyer serving the family of a twenty-five-year-old Black man named Ahmaud Arbery leaked footage of white men chasing him down with a truck and shooting him to death. Liberals and activists circulated the video across social media. A day later, the Georgia Bureau of Investigation arrested Gregory McMichael and his son, Travis McMichael, for murder. Mugshots of the men, featuring Travis looking somewhat doll-eyed and slack-jawed, played into every negative stereotype that liberals held about Trump supporters. They quickly linked MAGA to the violence.

A LeBron James tweet, boosted over 100,000 times, enraged people in the movement: "We're literally hunted EVERYDAY/EVERYTIME we step foot outside the comfort of our homes! Can't even go for a damn jog man! Like WTF man are you kidding me?!?!?!?!?!? No man fr ARE YOU KIDDING ME!!!!! I'm sorry Ahmaud (Rest In Paradise) and my prayers and blessings sent to the heavens above to your family!!"[6]

The movement snapped back at James with derision. VDARE highlighted it on Twitter and posted something by contributor John Derbyshire, or "Derb," an elderly Englishman *The National Review* had fired for his racism. Derb argued that Black-on-white crime had risen and urged people to dismiss the NBA star.[7] "News-wise, I'd been beginning to get desperate. It's been coronavirus, coronavirus, coronavirus, for weeks now. But this week we got relief, of a sort. We got an Emmett Till," Derb wrote in VDARE in a post published May 8, portraying that brutal murder of a Black teen in 1955 as a trope. He continued, "You know the script. Evil, gap-toothed, leering Badwhites, secure in their white privilege, most likely resident in some state of the old Confederacy, hunt down and murder an innocent young black guy. It's the core fantasy of Goodwhite Americans, and has to be acted out every so often for their moral satisfaction, like a medieval mumming play: a clear narrative restatement of the eternal conflict between good and evil."[8]

In 2022, when a judge sentenced the McMichaels to life in prison, Derb argued that the case demanded that America repeal the Civil Rights Act of 1964.[9]

Michael Thompson, a blogger writing under the pseudonym "Paul Kersey," published a little-noticed VDARE article on May 13, 2020, informing the site's readers that the great replacement had descended on the city of Minneapolis.[10] The once 99 percent white city had dropped to 60 percent white between 1910 and 2020, the article said.[11] Thompson's timing was awkward, because on the afternoon of Monday, May 25, a video circulated across social media showing a white Minneapolis cop kneeling on the neck of a Black man named George Floyd. I don't even remember where or when I saw it that day; I only remember that I wanted to shut it off.

In Minneapolis, rioters burned fires across the city, and protesters, including a far-right extremist who sought to contribute to the atmosphere of chaos to suit his own ends, burned the city's third precinct police station to the ground.[12]

The symbolism of the fires erupting everywhere electrified and obsessed VDARE. Its contributors switched from entertaining COVID-19 conspiracy theories to railing against the impending collapse of America. Kevin DeAnna, writing under his "James Kirkpatrick" pseudonym, published onto VDARE's site a photo of Black rioters with the phrase "WE WANT THE TRUMP WE VOTED FOR" tagged across the center.

In the accompanying post, DeAnna called for a harsh crackdown against the rioters and leftists. He begged his readers to see the horrors in our streets with clear eyes.

"Now, he has nationwide riots and videos of businesses being burned to the ground, all being essentially cheered on by his MSM/Dem opponents. America is begging for a crackdown," he wrote in his post. "Instead, President Trump is blaming Democratic state and local elected officials rather than taking action himself. President Trump simply can't afford any more mistakes. America is burning. The nationalist that voters thought they were electing in 2016 needs to act."[13]

The urgency that DeAnna and others conveyed rippled across the movement.

8

America's Twenty-First-Century Fort Sumter

Trey and a group of neighbors stood on the northeast corner of Berkeley Springs State Park on a late May afternoon, asserting through signs and voices that Black lives mattered. The group staged their pop-up event in the same place where local Jehovah's Witnesses usually handed out pamphlets.

No more than a dozen people protested the killing of George Floyd at the pop-up. A Black woman from Africa named Oduwa was staying with Trey, and she joined the protest too. The inclusion of a Black woman added gravity to the action in the predominantly white town.

Trey's engagement in civil rights issues felt good to her, but it turned certain people off. And that went beyond causing neighbors to whisper. For some, it cultivated profound feelings of resentment.

Critics of Trey with whom I spoke assumed she took political postures to serve herself. Those that disliked her justified their resentment by believing that the Johansons hated them and their Christian faith. A fog blanketed Berkeley Springs in the months after VDARE bought the castle, but it was a fog that kept people from seeing clearly who hated whom, or who was attacking whom.

Some people blamed Trey for summoning me into town to give Berkeley Springs bad press. By taking this position, they implied that reporting on VDARE was more offensive than Peter and Lydia Brimelow operating a website that argued for the repeal of the Civil Rights Act. Trey believed that the press would have found the story regardless, and grew frustrated with this line of criticism.

Then there was the matter of the flag. Everyone could see Trey's Pride flag while driving down Route 522. Confederate flags also flew along 522, of course. There was one flying high near Charlotte's Cafe, where the banner took a repetitive shellacking from the elements. Charlotte's Cafe, a diner on Berkeley Springs' southern side that served plates of Fruity Pebble French toast, had nothing to do with it. The flag belonged to the person who lived in the house behind the café. But unlike Trey's public embrace of the rainbow, people considered Confederate flags to be simply part of the landscape.

Longtime residents of Morgan County told me that, from the time they were children, they'd never seen as many Confederate flags as they had since Trump had won the 2016 presidential election. The proliferation of the stars and bars demonstrated to them that social progress wasn't inevitable and didn't move in a linear fashion. Maybe people who had always wanted to fly that flag suddenly felt safe to do so.

Beyond 522, Confederate flags appeared routinely on people's commutes. They flew from isolated country homes situated along that route's offshoots: Martinsburg Road, River Road, Route 9. No one I spoke to who took offense to the Confederate flags ever tried to tear one down.

Trey's Pride flag sparked a different response. Back in the summer of 2019, a local teenage boy and his friend had snatched the flag down off the coffeehouse. Trey's staff, which included young progressives and queer people, perceived this as a hate crime. Paul watched video footage from the camera positioned at the front of the shop. He caught a clear image of the boy's face, printed it out, and tacked it up inside the shop with a note asking if anyone recognized him.

Another young person from town recognized the boy. The information he relayed sent Paul to Hunter's Hardware, housed in a brick building a thirty-second walk away with an old-fashioned wooden sign out front pointing a finger toward the store. Paul spoke to someone who was a father figure to the boy, and soon enough the culprit marched into Fairfax Coffee House to speak to him about what he'd done. Paul told the thief that he just wanted to know why he did it.

"I don't know," the boy said.

"Try again," Paul said. "I want to believe what you're saying, so tell me the truth."

"I thought it would be fun," the boy said.

"Okay," Paul said. "*Now* I believe you."

The boy agreed to apologize to the staff of Fairfax Coffee House. He assured them that he was just having a laugh and harbored no intent of committing a hate crime. Paul thought he seemed genuine. Nobody called the cops.

On June 1, the Johansons arrived at the biergarten space next to Fairfax Coffee House for a business meeting about its development. At the time, they intended the biergarten to be named "The Source," a name that referenced the waters flowing adjacent to it. Trey devised a menu, and the Johansons felt momentum building around the project. The biergarten became a centerpiece of their future plans.

The Johansons got into business on The Source with a man named Charlie Curia. Charlie, a heavyset man with a whitish goatee, ran Mountain Laurel Artisans. His shop sold original craft projects and glassworks created by local artists a few doors down from Fairfax Coffee House, at the corner of 522 and Fairfax Street.

Like Trey and Paul, Charlie dreamed of the possibilities that might open up once they launched The Source. Court documents show that he invested the bulk of the money in The Source, doing so through a limited liability company called Humble, Laughing and Iridescent, or "HLI." Geoffrey Wendel of Portals Metaphysical also invested, but at a significantly lower stake. So did the Johansons.

Charlie had arrived in Berkeley Springs as a pharmacist. Multiple people told me that he'd boasted of having worked for the CIA. When I reached out to the CIA to confirm it, they refused to answer and referred me to the CIA's database of documents that had been released through the Freedom of Information Act (FOIA). Charlie's name produced no results there, and he declined the opportunity to talk to me about it.

Paul knew Charlie and trusted him. Before he ever agreed to engage with Charlie on business matters, the men had met in the self-help-oriented ManKind Project, Paul told me. Paul and Charlie confessed their trauma to one another. They learned stories that could be embarrassing if repeated in other contexts. They talked about their relationships with women.

Charlie had endured the death of his wife in 2018 and recovered from the pain around it while attending ManKind with Paul. Soon after she passed, he struck up a relationship with a stout gray-haired woman named Sue Evans. Sue became a steadfast partner with Charlie in his work at Mountain Laurel Artisans and on the biergarten project. Charlie also recruited a middle-aged man named Vince who claimed expertise in construction to help with the planning of The Source.

If you stood at the center of the park by the gazebo and faced the direction of the empty, developing biergarten space, Charlie's Mountain Laurel Artisans shop, decorated with glassworks, art, and knickknacks, sat on the right of it, next to Alicia's sweet-smelling periwinkle blue store. Trey's brick-based red and yellow coffee shop sat on the left. The elaborate "love mural," as Paul and Trey called it, overlooked the empty lot. To an outsider, the gaping biergarten space resembled a kind of fenced-in, unfurnished backyard overlapping Trey's property.

One of Berkeley Springs' many fires had created the empty space where the neighbors intended to build The Source. In the dark morning hours of April 27, 2015, a fire burned down the building that had housed the Awakening Holistic Center, a previous iteration of Geoffrey Wendel's Portals Metaphysical, and a store called Himalayan Handicrafts, which later relocated around the block.[1] Firefighters rescued three people from its top-floor apartments but couldn't save the structure.[2]

Trey, Paul, and other neighbors solicited feedback about what could be built in the empty lot. Residents had called the lot the "Field of Possibilities" back in 2017. Paul drew up plans for The Source in August 2018 and got to work on developing it. Then Charlie and Geoffrey signed on as partners, filing documents to that effect as Halloween approached in 2018.

Charlie stopped attending ManKind around the time the pandemic shut everything down, Paul told me. When reopening slowly started in town, Charlie didn't return to meetings. Paul assumed that Sue Evans had something to do with the change.

The Johansons' version of events is as follows. Just before Paul and Trey arrived that evening for the June 1, 2020, biergarten meeting, someone—likely Charlie, or, if not Charlie, then Sue, or possibly Vince—removed a Pride flag that Trey and Paul had mounted there and tossed it aside.

The Johansons had mounted the flag years earlier, so Charlie, Sue, and Vince would most likely have seen it long before this meeting. Paul felt that sour, percolating feeling that starts at a sign of an impending conflict. Their flag just lay there, crumpled on the ground.

Paul said something like, "What is that? What are you doing with that?" he told me.

He said that Charlie responded to his question with a monologue comparing the rainbow on the Pride flag to a swastika. He repeated this sentiment three times. Charlie then purportedly explained that, like the swastika, the Pride rainbow appealed to only a small portion of the human population. He said that the swastika meant something powerful to Nazis, but offended others. The Pride flag offended everyone other than queer people, he said.

Charlie also purportedly said that the rainbow meant different things at different times to different people. He noted that this was also true of the swastika. The symbol meant something different to Hindus than it meant to Nazis. Paul told me that he found Charlie's speech perplexing, but it also angered him.

News of Trey being bisexual broke late in Berkeley Springs, given that it wasn't the first thing locals thought about when they saw someone in a partnership with someone of the opposite sex. She had confided in Paul about that part of herself long before. An attack on the queer community was also an attack on Trey.

"You realize you're saying this in front of my Jewish and bisexual wife," Paul blurted, underscoring not only the criticism of Pride but Charlie's weaving of Nazism into the discussion.

"*Abomination,*" Sue hissed.

Trey identified as queer, therefore she was an *abomination*. This was a difficult thing to overcome in a working partnership.

Trey prepared to come out to more people in town, but she realized Sue already knew about her sexuality when she punched out the word "abomination." Maybe Sue had gleaned it from the Pride flags. Maybe Sue assumed that no straight person would ever display something so sinful. Whatever she was thinking, her remark created a fissure along Fairfax Street that deepened over time. It was like a small crack in a car's windshield that gradually expands.

One hundred miles to the southeast, these same cultural tensions erupted on a much bigger scale. On May 28, fueled by anger over the killing of George Floyd and relentless police violence against Black people, protesters in Washington, DC, slammed into barricades near the White House, sending the White House itself into lockdown. President Trump tweeted, "when the looting starts, the shooting starts," at a minute shy of one in the morning, hinting at a story playing out in his mind that had a violent end.[3]

On the following afternoon, my friend and colleague Hannah Gais and her boyfriend, Tom, walked through Washington, absorbing the city in its simmering state. Anti-Trump protesters packed the streets that afternoon chanting "No justice, no peace." Hannah snapped photos of "Fuck 12" graffiti on the walls of a commercial building. For the uninitiated, the phrase—originating from resentment specifically for drug enforcement units—means "fuck the police."

Hannah, a thirty-something-year-old researcher and journalist, had hated the idea of moving to DC. When circumstances forced her to consider it, she envisioned a gray world of chattering careerists slinging politics. But the SPLC wouldn't let her stay in New York, because of some arcane rule about researchers, so she'd moved there in the fall of 2019, along with Tom and their black-and-white cat, Siyah. Hannah was still very much in the process of making DC part of her identity that spring.

As the noise of the DC protests grew louder, I counted on Hannah to tell me what was happening there. On the TV in my apartment, it looked like mayhem. It whipped Trump's fans into a state of mania. They imagined that Trump might be dragged out of the White House by his feet and pummeled raw by an anarchist mob. Maybe Trump would die beaten up in the gutter like Gaddafi, at the grubby hands of "antifa." It drove them mad.

"Be careful out there," I said to her.

"I'm just going out for a run," she said.

A little after noon on May 31, a Sunday, Trump tweeted, "The United States of America will be designating ANTIFA as a Terrorist Organization." He wrote "ANTIFA," short for anti-fascist, to refer to the people disrupting life in the city, with all caps, as if the people opposing Trumpism were COBRA from *G.I. Joe*.[4] Trump's political opponents quickly pointed out that the language he used served as a small step toward throwing them in jail. I certainly didn't feel great about it, given how many people in the movement labeled me antifa and made a huge deal about that online.

DC Mayor Muriel Bowser called for a citywide curfew at 11 p.m., but the protests and riots continued to rage. Anti-Trump people set fires on the National Mall. They incinerated the American flag on live TV. They torched the parish of St. John's Episcopal Church, the most prominent Christian symbol in close proximity to the White House.

I glued myself to a sock account I ran on Twitter as the fires raged. Aerial footage circulated across social media. The movement looked at the same news cycle we did but saw race war. Civil war. For some, the moment was a signal to purchase guns.

"One of these pictures is from black insurrection/antifa insurgency in Washington D.C. on May 31, and the other is from the movie *Olympus Has Fallen*. Which is which?" VDARE posted to Twitter on the afternoon of June 1, showing Washington, DC, burning in two different images.[5]

On the morning of June 1, I visited my parents in Long Island. That same day, VDARE called the protests an "anti-white insurgency." Hannah, feeling cooped up by the dual pressures of COVID-19 restrictions and the looming citywide curfew, went for another run, moving past boarded-up storefronts.

Responding to pressure from his own supporters, Trump ordered a hodgepodge of law enforcement agencies to clear the protesters from Lafayette Park, an area on the perimeter of the White House. I watched on TV as cops fired tear gas and chased people down on horseback. I thought it was a scene straight out of a movement guy's fantasy of a fascist leader taking control.[6]

It ended with Trump walking through a line of officers carrying transparent shields, and then Trump waving that infamous black Bible outside of St. John's for a photo op.[7] Like many things Trump staged, the Bible stunt looked like bad television trying to imitate bad cinema.

Hannah monitored VDARE's live feed on YouTube.

"VDARE has a crew in D.C. and they're pretending to be VICE Canada," she wrote to me late that morning.

"Huh?"

"Hold on, I'll call you—"

So much of our work involved texting back and forth about an issue until we talked ourselves into doing something about it.

"—So, on the VDARE livestream—"

"Okay."

"They're stopping the protesters to interview them and asking for their names and hometowns and telling people they're from VICE Canada."

"Like VICE the website but the Canadian version," I said.

"Yes, Mike."

I watched. A young blonde woman put on a performative, peppy-sounding voice. She stopped protesters on the street who had been walking toward the White House. The protesters seemed like upbeat college kids, eager to tell the media why they opposed Trump. Some of them were Black.

VDARE's blonde host introduced herself as being from "VICE Canada" each time. She asked for names and hometowns. Each time, the kids looked at the camera. They recited who they were and where they were from. It gave VDARE's audience a clear look at their faces.

"These people have no idea that they're introducing themselves to VDARE."

"That's what I'm saying," Hannah said.

I looked on VDARE's website. It said they had "sent a couple of volunteers with cameras and real microphones to talk to demonstrators who were, unintentionally, displaying various agendas behind the latest rioting."[8]

"Anyway, I'm gonna post about it on Twitter," Hannah said.

"Don't go to Twitter. We can get them on this."

We published the "VICE Canada" story on June 4.[9] VICE Canada released a statement denouncing the use of its name. The more substantial outcome followed months later, when YouTube suspended VDARE's account.[10] First we reached out to Facebook about VDARE. Then we reached out to YouTube. Although it's unclear what role we played in it, both companies 86'd them.

The Brimelows lost prestige—and access to mainstream culture—without those sites. We understood alerting tech companies about movement activism to be one of the core parts of our mission. Plus, we did have to reach out for comment as journalists. If companies took down their accounts, it was out of our hands. The movement portrayed us as censors assaulting the First Amendment. It built up tremendous feelings of resentment in them that they have carried around ever since.

Peter and Lydia never addressed who sent the blonde woman into DC, and I never saw her again. The movement cycled through a universe of pseudonyms, people who thought for a moment that it would feel good to take their private feelings about race public and then changed course.

On VDARE's site and on Twitter, which now hosted the org's last remaining major social media account, the group obsessed over the "anti-white revolution" happening on American streets. They fixated on young people with masked faces bringing statues of old white men hurtling down. Everything was proof of the coming "great divorce," a term embraced by the movement to describe the imminence of a new civil war.

On June 10, 2020, VDARE wrote, of the creation of a left-wing autonomous zone in Seattle, that it was "amazing" to witness "America's 21st Century Fort Sumter moment" happening, referring to the 1861 start of the Civil War.[11]

"We warned you. It's about whites. It's about WHITE people," VDARE posted to Twitter on June 21.[12]

9

In a Town with All Whites

The cragged roads of Morgan County stayed silent as May turned to June and the capital burned. At some point, though it's unclear when, a dead tree slammed into the Berkeley Springs Castle. The collision apparently forced VDARE to restore the castle's roof. Lydia Brimelow told this story on a podcast without mentioning a date. She stated that it happened after they obtained the building but before they mounted a conference.[1]

Peter and Lydia Brimelow and their children had not actually moved into town yet, according to Peter's telling of events. They still lived in Connecticut, he said, even as the neighbors who reviled him assumed he was already there. Peter said he made visits to the town and full-time residence followed later.

After my meeting with concerned townspeople, a history teacher at Berkeley Springs High School warned his class about VDARE and what their moving in meant. He warned about the dangers associated with what they believed, a former student at the school told me a few years later. It's unclear how much Peter knew about moments like that. He seemed focused on the national story about Black Lives Matter at the time.

VDARE used the chaos of the riots to defend the violent radicals within their own movement. Unite the Right organizer Jason Kessler claimed in a June 1 VDARE post that the men who marched on

Charlottesville, chanting "Jews will not replace us," fell victim to the same threats that lurked in America that summer.

"I think there indeed is a parallel between Charlottesville in 2017 and these latest riots," Jason's post declared. "We are looking at the same groups and ideologies that, with the aid of black street criminals, wreaked havoc on a legally-approved demonstration in Charlottesville, now upscaling their Anarchist and Black nationalist tactics to a nationwide campaign of terror."[2]

Michelle Malkin, a VDARE contributor of Filipino descent, cautioned white VDARE readers that they mustn't apologize for their race. Some protests that followed George Floyd's murder involved white people kneeling, and the movement depicted this as a capitulation to the enemy.

Malkin also celebrated the street-fighting Proud Boys as "unapologetic Americans." "Two Proud Boys are in prison, railroaded by New York Democrats, after a Kafkaesque trial in which the cop-hating antifa 'victims' who lured the Proud Boys into an October 2018 street brawl refused to press charges or testify," she proclaimed. "Their crime? These unapologetic Americans stood on their feet, not on their knees."[3]

Lydia used the anger over kneeling as part of VDARE's fundraising push. "Why do we allow our cities to be turned into war zones? These are our communities. We have a say," she wrote. "VDARE.com is the voice of the Historic American Nation—a nation that will never kneel to the mob."[4]

With the rate of COVID-19 low in Berkeley Springs, people took tentative steps outside again, although the town did cancel many events throughout that summer and fall. Organizers for the first-ever Berkeley Springs Pride event had to cancel it because of the pandemic. Backed by Scott Collinash, the head chef at the Country Inn, the event promised to launch in 2021 instead.

Some businesses that had closed reopened to almost full capacity by early June. Customers of the Berkeley Springs Salt Cave once again sat in reclining chairs, toes deep in salt, breathing whirring gusts of salt dust against the backdrop of spacey ambient music and oscillating orange lights. Boxed inside the reopened room, about the size of your average man cave, the family-run facility made do by moving the chairs as far apart as they could get them.

The Roman Baths and other related state-park-sponsored spa facilities in town had not yet reopened by the start of June because they were renovating. But they planned on opening again by June 6. The reopening of these properties carried symbolic significance, particularly during the start of what should have been tourist season.

In the environment of tentative reanimation, a kid in his early twenties—let's give him the pseudonym "Bill"—decided to bring the Black Lives Matter protests to Berkeley Springs in a more substantive way than a few signs here or there.

Although he was legally an adult by a matter of years, townspeople often referred to Bill as a "kid." This was because the median age in West Virginia made it one of the oldest states in America—Morgan County possessed a median age nearing fifty. Bill labored as a self-described working stiff for a solar power company. The strange idea of staging a Black Lives Matter rally in Berkeley Springs, with its tiny percentage of Black people, emerged in part from conversations he'd held with coworkers as they drove back to the office together from their jobsites.

The solar power company that employed Bill had a progressive workforce compared to that of the county at large. Bill said this was partly because it was centered around a renewable energy source, and workers would have to really go out of their way to perpetuate climate change denialism. Some of Bill's coworkers shared his criticisms of police violence and the mistreatment of Black men. Bill told me that even his more reactionary colleagues encouraged him to speak his mind about it.

An athletic-looking guy with long brown hair, Bill was a compelling figure at a rally. He belied the conservative media stereotype of a Black Lives Matter activist, for one thing. Beyond being white and working class, he also expressed mostly positive feelings about the local police. He didn't think the Berkeley Springs police would ever engage in the kind of abusive or violent behavior that regularly trended on social media in the form of horrifying video clips.

From his youth, Bill had in fact carried with him a sunny perception of Berkeley Springs as it related to race. When the video of the Ahmaud Arbery murder surfaced, followed by the video of Derek Chauvin murdering George Floyd, Bill felt compelled to show people how different the town was from the bigger national story. He decided to engage the local police and the sheriff early on about his plans to hold a rally. And when it came to VDARE, he ignored them. That was just a weird situation he knew nothing about.

Bill lived right on the edge of town with a roommate. When his roommate heard his idea of bringing Black Lives Matter to Appalachia, he hated it so much that he bought one of those black, blue, and white "thin blue line" flags. Bill knew the flag supported police but also doubled as a declaration of animosity toward Black Lives Matter. His roommate hung the flag up as a silent comment on Bill's life choices.

Bill promoted his Black Lives Matter event on every Facebook page related to Berkeley Springs he could find. Keeping an eye on the fire and chaos that subsumed Washington, DC, he urged people not to follow that model, writing, "Don't burn the place to the ground," he told me. He labeled the event "Justice for Floyd."

On Wednesday, June 3, three days after Trump designated all-caps-ANTIFA a terrorist group, a remarkable thing happened. About one hundred people marched out onto the lawn of Berkeley Springs State Park in support of Black Lives Matter.[5] They poured in from the direction of the high school, past the cream-and-evergreen-colored "WELCOME" sign evoking mountains, trees, and a stream, and bragging that the park was home to "America's First Spa."

Young people dominated the crowd that gathered, including young women of color. The kids shouted their slogans and held their signs under the shadow of the castle. They created a sight that upended the image of Morgan County that Peter and Lydia were promoting.

An older couple held a sign at the entrance of the park that read, "AGE 83 AND 76; CAN'T BELIEVE WE'RE PROTESTING THE SAME SH*T," with the expletive censored. People lined up along Route 522 holding signs that said, "I CAN'T BREATHE."[6] A young Black girl held a handwritten sign that read, "MY LIFE MATTERS TOO."[7]

Trey came down to the protest carrying bushels of bright yellow black-eyed Susans—rudbeckias—that she'd plucked from her property. It was her favorite flower. Trey started handing them out to random people in the crowd. Ashley Briscoe, a local mother of two biracial daughters who attended school in the area, told *The Morgan Messenger* that Bill's event spoke to the challenges she faced.[8]

"Growing up in a town with all whites is hard," she told the paper.

Bill asked police for permission to shut down the street for nine minutes, intending to symbolize the minutes that Chauvin pinned Floyd down by his neck. The police declined. Then Bill hopped up onto the gazebo to smatterings of applause. He wore a black BLM shirt, camo cargo shorts, black socks, blue shoes, and a gray cap. His hair blew around as he unfurled the paper carrying his speech.

"People of Berkeley Springs, West Virginia, and the United States. Lend me your time, briefly," he said, reading from the paper. "Right now, Americans across the country are being challenged. Amid a pandemic, we are being forced to think. Forced to think about issues *we* may not be comfortable with. But the time is now and enough is enough."

Bill talked about Arbery, Floyd, and Breonna Taylor, the Louisville woman police shot to death during a no-knock search warrant on March 13, 2020. He condemned the legacy of slavery. He thanked the police.

A guy in a pickup truck "rolled coal" at Bill's protest, meaning that the driver modified his diesel engine in such a way that it blew big streams of harsh black exhaust into the air. Police pulled the driver over and that was it.

Give or take a middle finger, onlookers ingested the passion and anger of the high school girls holding signs along 522 without rejecting it. And Bill's rally made it onto a map curated by *The New York Times*, highlighting where Black Lives Matter events had taken place throughout the country.[9]

In the months that followed, though, Bill started to distance himself from Black Lives Matter. He never changed his beliefs, but the tone of how things were going across the country frightened him. When a local lawyer announced plans for a second Black Lives Matter event in town, Bill wanted no part in it.

"People became willing to draw blood over this matter," he told me a few years later.

Bill was right. After that first wave of Black Lives Matter rallies swept through America, an acidic backlash rose in response. The acidity filtered into Trump's campaign for reelection, which faced new obstacles as a result of the president's chaotic response to the pandemic. Some polls showed Trump down nearly double digits against seventy-eight-year-old career politician Joe Biden, although no one knew whether they were accurate or not.

Everywhere Trump's fans turned, they hit new walls to tear down. That meant attacking the energy around Black Lives Matter with energy of equal measure. In terms of recent history, the powerful backlash against Black Lives Matter had roots in the fury over COVID-19 restrictions. Wealthy American reactionaries fueled the anger.

VDARE capitalized on this explosion of white rage. Its proponents discouraged compromise with those who called for police reform. They depicted no space for common ground between their allies and those who called white Americans racist.

More and more reactionaries—not just movement people, but regular people who watched Fox News—started demanding a powerful defense of whiteness as June wore on. They also wanted to protect Trump. VDARE responded by giving them more than they were asking for, latching on to the argument that the people who had taken to the streets to scream "No justice, no peace" had aligned themselves with Satan.

"We must . . . consider what many of us have, deep in our hearts, known all along: that the anti-white, anti-Historical American Nation malice now menacing the world is, in fact, the work of the Devil himself," a self-identified Catholic author going by the name Matthew Richer wrote for VDARE on June 26.[10]

On June 28, Republicans and Democrats alike started sharing images and videos on social media of two middle-aged white lawyers from St. Louis. A few hundred of the Black Lives Matter activists had marched on the couple's private neighborhood and made a racket. This couple wanted to end it.

The online images made me laugh. Mark McCloskey held a giant rifle suitable for John Wick, but physically he looked like he could play Fred Flintstone. Patricia McCloskey, his taller, blonde wife, held her pistol in a sketchy way. It looked like if she sneezed she might accidentally blow her head off.

Trump supporters placed the awkward couple on a pedestal. They presented them to the world as a symbol of fighting back against what people started to call "the woke mob." VDARE boosted multiple photos of the McCloskeys on Twitter. Of one such image, VDARE wrote, "Where were you at the turning of the tide?"[11] Another VDARE post called an image of the McCloskeys pointing guns at Black Lives Matter demonstrators the most powerful thing the twenty-first century had seen:

> Monuments can be replaced. Cities can be rebuilt.
> But it requires the people to stand.
> The GOP has failed to do this.
> Now, with this image, we see where it's all headed.
> This might be the most powerful image of the 21st century thus far.[12]

When I read this, I wondered, What was this world, where the McCloskeys awkwardly pointing their guns amounted to the most resonant image of our time?

On July 1, hosts canceled the annual Apple Butter Festival because of the pandemic. Jeanne Mozier usually helped host Apple Butter, and Morgan County regarded the event as the centerpiece of the region's tourism season. People normally booked rooms at the Country Inn months in advance for it. Most people seemed to understand the reason the event was called off, but when every tourist dollar mattered, closures like this hurt. The move angered the people who saw COVID-19 restrictions as repressive.

"Can't we just riot that weekend since those gatherings are acceptable?" a woman named Holly Smith quipped on the festival's Facebook page.

A few days later, a personal injury lawyer named Larry Schultz learned of an ugly incident at Sleepy Creek Campground that had occurred during the July 4 holiday. It involved a Black family.

Sleepy Creek Campground was a sprawling family establishment that sat adjacent to River Road. River Road shot west from 522, near the town entrance. Embedded in a patch of lush greenery, Sleepy Creek Campground offered bingo, karaoke, and fishing tournaments. It had a stage for guests to perform on and one of the better playgrounds in the area. Not far from where the freight trains of the Baltimore and Ohio rumbled past, the campground greeted visitors with childlike hand-painted drawings of smiley faces and peace signs.

"Welcome! Peace, Love and Happiness this way!" proclaimed a sign hammered to a tree at the entrance.

Larry heard that an older white woman had shooed a Black family off the campground. The white woman was local—people said she lived right near the campground—and she'd used an inappropriate word to describe Black people when she did it. The dehumanizing word the woman used was exactly the word you would guess.

One of the Black family members who had had to hear the woman utter this word was a six-year-old boy. This detail obsessed Larry. He couldn't digest the image of this boy learning about the cruelty of the world from some miserable racist.

Larry wondered where the kid might feel like he could find a friend in Morgan County. Nobody around town looked like him. The situation was everything Larry resented about his home and none of what he loved. The high-flying Confederate flag at the closest neighbor's home overshadowed that peace sign at the entrance of the campground, making it feel meaningless.

Onlookers had watched this happen without taking any substantial actions in defense of the family, Larry learned. Someone called the sheriff. The sheriff's office allegedly did nothing. (When I spoke to employees at the office four years later, they couldn't recall the incident.)

Larry described the sheriff's response as being, "Well, too bad."

Burly, bearded, and looking like a contestant in an Ernest Hemingway lookalike contest, Larry worked out of Martinsburg but lived nearer to Berkeley Springs. He told me he had the heart of a civil rights lawyer, but the prospects for being that kind of lawyer in Morgan County, West Virginia, were about nil. It would starve him.

Larry knew about VDARE. He knew about the impression VDARE left on outsiders who had read about Berkeley Springs' plight. He felt that good people ought to speak up then, at that moment, because of the castle. The region's reputation for being too white and too tolerant of bigots like Peter Brimelow would only grow if compassionate West Virginians stayed silent.

Larry secured a permit to bring people into the park for a protest. The event would take place on the afternoon of Friday, August 21. He started promoting it through word of mouth. Larry knew other people who were ready to speak up too. He felt good about it at first.

Bill had targeted an audience of young people at his event, but Larry, who had graduated from college several decades earlier, courted a more mature audience. That wasn't a deliberate strategy—those were his peers.

Larry's event also followed Bill's by two and a half months. In the social media age, the gap felt like decades. It meant that any Trump fan who'd watched Bill's event, stunned and angry, now had a chance to respond to Black Lives Matter through a second event. They could ride the wave of that rising backlash embodied by VDARE's beloved McCloskeys.

By July, polls showed the popularity of Black Lives Matter sliding.[13] This, more than any other factor, represented a challenge Larry faced that Bill hadn't. VDARE and similar voices had succeeded in pushing their perspective—which had formed only moments after Derek Chauvin killed George Floyd—into the mainstream.

"The Black Lives Matter campaign is a blood libel against white America," VDARE's James Fulford wrote in a post published on July 11, 2020.[14]

Around this time, another story provided fuel for the outrage machine: the city of Portland, Oregon. Every day in June and July, Fox News hosts and other influencers circulated footage of protesters there going to war with their own home, causing property damages in the name of anti-fascism and anarchy that would eventually creep into the millions of dollars.

Some of the protesters were indeed anarchists. And these anarchist Portlanders made the perfect foil. They were comic book villains whose actions felt unthinkable to ordinary Morgan County Fox News watchers. They'd torn down a statue of Thomas Jefferson on June 14. They'd shut down a bridge on Juneteenth. They'd torn down a statue of George Washington on June 21, and they'd rioted on the Fourth of July.[15]

What if Berkeley Springs became another Portland? What about Martinsburg? Could it happen there? What about Hagerstown, Maryland? Winchester, Virginia? People really thought these things. People asked themselves whether they had the bravery to stand tall and fight back against these invasive, terroristic, radical left-wing mobs.

As Larry watched the discourse on local Facebook groups crumbling into wild outbursts of surreal storytelling, he started to sense the possibility of something going wrong at his event. Larry's daughter, who went to school in Pennsylvania, had a friend whose parents said they heard Larry was dispatching busloads of Philadelphians into Berkeley Springs.

Larry noted to himself that to the average Morgan County resident, Philadelphia scanned as "Black." He felt sickened by the lie and wondered who in town could possibly be stupid enough to believe it.

10

The Land of the Rednecks

David Floyd DeGraw told me he grew up in Baltimore and hated it. He told everyone that he was a "city redneck" who simply hailed from the wrong place. David, deep into middle age with a syrupy baritone drawl and curly wisps of gray hair pouring out from under his cap, said he'd moved to Montana to get away from that life. And for years, he told me, he made his living building custom homes. When his mom died, David returned to Baltimore only because his father didn't want to live alone. Then his dad died too.

David gained sole control of his childhood home in Baltimore and stayed there during the Obama years out of convenience. He was living in Baltimore on April 19, 2015, when a twenty-five-year-old Black man named Freddie Gray died. That was a significant day for the Charmed City. Within a few weeks, Freddie was a symbol of police brutality across the country.

Baltimore police officers had thrown Freddie into their van in handcuffs. They let him bounce around in the back as they drove. This pulverized Freddie's body. His flesh slammed repeatedly into galvanized steel. Critics of the police identified this as a "rough ride," a term that connotes a form of police brutality that stems from willful neglect. Freddie hung on to life for a week after his rough ride. When he died, medical examiners said that his spine was severed almost completely from his neck.[1]

A flood of anguish swept through Baltimore's largely segregated Black neighborhoods when they heard the news.[2] People took to the streets, as they would do after the murder of George Floyd five years later. Some chanted the phrase "Black Lives Matter," which was how David had first become familiar with it. Following Freddie's funeral, ferocious riots broke out. President Obama lectured the Black residents of Baltimore, saying they had "no excuses" to riot.

Rioters burned buildings. They ripped an ATM out of a wall. They burned police vehicles. They burned a CVS pharmacy. They fought with Orioles fans outside of Camden Yards. They threw rocks at the police.[3] Black people living in Black neighborhoods knew the police harmed people around them with brutal force.[4] Emotions triggered by living through these experiences exploded into the open air.

As expressions of Black anguish dominated the hot weather months of 2015, David linked everything back to Black Lives Matter. He remembered that a Black woman on TV had said people should not burn down the Black neighborhoods, but instead "take that shit out to the counties," where he and other white people lived. David took that personally.

David claimed that someone broke into his car in the aftermath of Freddie Gray's death. He said that Black people with Black Lives Matter signs accosted him at his home and demanded that he vacate it. David said they threatened to smoke him out with fire. I tried to verify David's recollection of events, but it was challenging. Things like this happened, but after speaking to David myself, I found his mind too clouded with paranoid fantasies about the people he reviled to trust his account. Maybe what he said happened, and maybe it didn't.

By 2018, David had retired, sold his family home, and moved to "a nice little podunk town" somewhere far away from Black Lives Matter, 110 miles northwest of Baltimore: Berkeley Springs.

"I couldn't care about anything city-wise. I wanted to hunt some *deers*. Do some fishing," he told me of why he settled on that town of all towns.

David got a place for himself on the edge of Berkeley Springs, where winding roads climbed until cellphone reception dropped out. He bought a brown and tan wooden house and parked his custom Chevy Silverado in the gravel driveway. He put up a sticker over the garage that said, "Old Fart's Garage." He put a sticker with the National Rifle Association's emblem on the glass panel on the front door. David's neighborhood consisted of only a handful of humans within walking distance and their pets. One of them put up a street sign that said, "3 Dale Earnhardt Drive," referring to the NASCAR legend who died of a basilar skull fracture in 2001.

David set up his collection of firearms in the house. He didn't think of himself as a gun enthusiast. He kept "the guns that he needed": A personal protection pistol, easily concealed, "a small little carry." A .44 mag, "a fun gun to shoot." A couple of different hunting rifles. A couple of different shotguns. He cherished his favorite shotgun, a "wall hanger." That was a 1911 Browning semiautomatic with nickel plating and hand engravings that David's grandfather had willed to him.

As when he'd lived in Montana, David now had a place where he wasn't bothered by urban living. He didn't want to be around liberals, in particular. Here, he could ride his Husqvarna mower around his big backyard and forget they existed.

David leaned in to his self-described redneck identity while living in Berkeley Springs. He became an active Facebook user, engaging in content that supported Trump and excoriated Trump's enemies. He uploaded as his avatar an image of the Confederate flag with the words "522 *SOUTH*" spread across it, referring to that highway that runs from the southern tip of Maryland, across the Potomac, and through the middle of Berkeley Springs. The word "SOUTH" was emphasized, implying that the town belonged to the Confederacy. In the actual Civil War, that wouldn't have been true.

On July 23, 2020, around midnight, David posted comments to Facebook with his 522 *SOUTH* Confederate flag avatar. He claimed to have no tolerance for "Facebook and the law."[5] Then he tore into a series of posts that readers understood to be focused on Larry's forthcoming Black Lives Matter rally.

David snapped off a string of words addressed to "BLM and ANTIFA." Echoing President Trump, he wrote "ANTIFA" in all caps.

"I see you I'm gonna kill you. Not fight not argue. Kill you," he wrote. "You want it you got it. I'm always armed so please try me. Nothing would make me happier then [*sic*] ending your pathetic life. YOU STARTED THIS PEOPLE LIKE ME WILL END IT."[6]

David lived the next few weeks without feeling much of an impact from having posted these and other threatening words. Meanwhile, the conversation on local pro-Trump Facebook pages continued to mutate. A rumor started to circulate that Trey planned to stash anarchist, antifa soldiers in the basement of Fairfax Coffee House.

The Fairfax Coffee House myth bore similarities to a false national story from 2017 about "antifa supersoldiers." Pro-Trump influencers said that black-clad characters would come out in force to behead white parents at the start of a new civil war against Trump.[7] It obviously never happened, and no one at places like Infowars ever faced accountability from their audiences for promoting the lie.

By Monday, August 17, more people who hated Black Lives Matter anticipated attending Larry's event to disrupt it than those who sympathized with the host's cause. David grew more specific about his thoughts in a reply to another Facebook user. "I'm always armed and ready. They are planning a BLM rally on August 21st. Bet your ass I'll be there locked and loaded to put a stop to this," he wrote.[8]

In a response to a different Facebook user, on Wednesday, August 19, he wrote, "It's coming this Friday in Berkeley Springs WV. BLM has decided to bring their bullshit to the wrong place. I'll bet you see it on the news. Just might be the shot heard round the world."[9]

Liberal-leaning Berkeley Springs residents started to notice a terrifying hum coming out of Facebook thanks to David and men like him. On August 20, Portals Metaphysical addressed the growing buzz about Larry's Black Lives Matter event in a Facebook post of its own.

"We have heard folk say they are afraid of vandalism and violence from this event," Portals Metaphysical wrote:

> We have no fear of it coming from the Black Lives Matter folk. We ARE concerned by the folk talking about coming down to harass them, though. If we ourselves get affected this way, we suggest you look at the violen[t] agitators and agent provocateurs who want things to go that way. We expect that some of these people will try to pretend they are part of the rally.
>
> Admittedly, these Voices are mostly keyboard warriors . . . but all you need is one of them to get the feeling they are supported enough to do something in the physical world. All you need is for one of them to think their behavior is justified.[10]

Someone apparently tipped the police off about David's Facebook posts. Maybe the drumbeat on Facebook became so savage that the police had no choice but to monitor discussions on it themselves. David told me that he "pissed off one wrong person." He added, "and that person was connected." He didn't name the person.

On the afternoon of the rally, at a quarter to three, Sheriff KC Bohrer told Deputy Scott Lemon that they had a lead on a guy who had made terroristic threats on Facebook. Bohrer emphasized that they had enough to charge him. He showed the evidence behind it, all from Facebook. David said that "six cops" showed up at his house, including Lemon, whose name appears on the charging documents. David said they handcuffed him before they hauled him to the courthouse.

The Morgan County Courthouse sits in the center of Berkeley Springs, adjacent to Route 522. It was essentially the same spot where Larry's rally was about to start. David watched people gather from a window inside the courthouse.

Hundreds of "patriots" stood unified, armed with rifles, carrying the weapons openly along 522, as West Virginia law dictated they could. David couldn't discern everything that was happening, but he could see this wall of patriots standing tall.

A friend came to bail David out that evening. The two men "walked right through it," this wall of armed patriots. They marveled at the scale of the response. The armed heroes had saved Berkeley Springs from the masked anarchists and busloads of protesters from Philadelphia who they incorrectly believed had shown up.

The self-appointed guardians of Morgan County carried AR-15 rifles. David saw a pistol holstered to nearly every hip. The rally "was full blown going on" as he walked through the mass of people. He couldn't see the Black Lives Matter side. The patriots had drowned Larry's side out. It was a total victory and patriots were in control.

"I knew there was nothing gonna happen in this town because these are country boys," he told me. "This is the land of the *rednecks*. You might have a lot of liberals moving out here because they love the scenery, or whatever the fuck this is, but this is their [the rednecks'] town."

That night, David got back to his place and "drank a bunch of beer and whiskey." He logged onto Facebook again. This time he recorded two videos through Facebook Live, the website's live-streaming service. He recorded both from his garage.

A mess of junk consumed his worktable, which he anointed with a recently opened can of Bud Light. In the first video, David showed the American flag pinned to the wall. Fewer than one hundred people watched him, according to Facebook's metrics. He spoke to Old Glory before attacking her. "All's I did was defend this fucking flag," he told his audience. "And do you know what my fucking government did? They arrested me and charged me with fucking domestic *terrorism*. And you know what? That's fucked up, dude. Well, as far as I'm concerned, from here on out? This flag right here? Can fucking sit there on the fucking ground."

David awkwardly ripped the flag off the wall and threw it in the vicinity of some office chairs. He aimed the camera to show it sitting crumpled on the stone floor. His voice rose to a shout.

"I defended this *motherfucker*! With everything I had! And that same son of a *bitch* is charging me with terrorism!" he bellowed.

David brought the camera closer to the fallen flag. He spoke to it like you would talk to a guy you just laid out in a bar fight.

"See that, bitch? You motherfuckers. How fucking *dare* you, man? I spent my entire life being a patriot. No more. Fuck you, man," he said.[11]

David then recorded a second video, one in which he spoke directly to the camera. The video attracted a few hundred viewers this time. He included a written description for it. It said, "I'm done." David slurred his words and cried, visibly. He looked like he had been crying for hours. "You don't understand how bad I'm hurting right now. You don't understand. I fuckin', I got arrested today," he said and snorted up his tears. "For telling Black Lives Matter and antifa that I will fucking kill them on sight. *If* they fuck with my country. And guess what my country fucking did, man? They fucking *arrested* me!"

David leaned over the camera with his sunglasses balanced delicately on his baseball cap. He wore a Harley Davidson shirt with the sleeves ripped off.

"I'm lookin' at three years in fuckin' prison because of a Facebook quote. I said I was gonna kill terrorists like them. Now I'm the one, the fucker, who's going to jail," he said.

David was crying so much by then that he felt obligated to address it. He wanted to lay everything bare. He didn't care if it got him in more trouble. The feelings of injustice were simply too much to contain.

"I'm crying my fucking eyes out because my country has fucking *failed* me. My country don't *care* about me. They don't care about *you*. This country is *done*," he said, choking back sobs. "Fuck America!"

11

The Hidden Prejudice That Causes Fear

The strangest thing for me about Larry Schultz's Black Lives Matter event wasn't the swarm of armed men that jumped up to challenge it. People expected that to happen, even if the numbers of guns shocked them. The strangest thing was the inability of local liberals present to determine whether Peter Brimelow attended it or played any role in sparking the show of aggression.

One person swore to me that they saw Peter sitting on a chair in a distant part of the park. Another person thought they saw him sitting up front by the gazebo, near where people spoke about equality. Others said they never saw him. And Peter insisted that he wasn't there.

Everyone said with certainty that they saw a VDARE cameraman working the crowd. And the people who stood up for racial justice also felt that VDARE was there in a phantomlike way, gloating over the humiliation that befell them. The event became pivotal in defining VDARE's relationship to Berkeley Springs and vice versa. Until that point, not many people had seen signs of VDARE in town, because there hadn't been any.

Peter and Lydia, wealthy flatlanders from the North, represented an extreme version of the reactionary sentiment that already flourished around Morgan County, mixed with something distinctly foreign. This alien quality imbued Peter and Lydia with a mythical aura that befitted a town already enveloped in superstition. They became antagonists in every local liberal's story.

Peter never posted anything about the Black Lives Matter event on social media during the run-up to that day. At five that afternoon, August 21, at the same time the rally was starting, he occupied himself instead with an article in *Vice* that said that Lydia had dropped $2,800 on the Florida congressional campaign of Laura Loomer.[1]

Notorious for her hatred of Muslims, her entrenchment in Trump's orbit, and her appetite for plastic surgery, Loomer ran a 2020 ticket focused on internet deplatforming. More specifically, the gimmick was that she wanted to get her Twitter account reinstated. Maybe VDARE's leaders wanted to get their Facebook account back too.

"OK, this is the life we've chosen—but no civilian should be hassled by media like this," Peter posted about the Loomer donation. "SMALL DONATION SECRECY a cause now as important as secret ballot."

Someone replying to Peter's post remarked that not many people considered gifting nearly three grand to a longshot campaign a "small" donation. It was true that Peter often appeared to lack an understanding of working people's lives, including those of the white working class he celebrated through VDARE as the "historic American nation."

West Virginia ranked in the bottom four states in poverty as of 2020.[2] Much of the poverty was that of white people. Beyond the hills and hollers, a living, singular culture with which Peter seemed completely at odds percolated: Roadside dive bars. Tattoo joints. A gentleman's club in Martinsburg called "Lust" that hosted a periodic event called "Dwarf Toss," where men threw smaller men with achondroplasia against a giant dart board, surrounded by cheering strippers. Not to mention gun shows and side-by-side UTV rides in dirty hills.

A former securities analyst with an English accent and an MBA from Stanford like Peter Brimelow wouldn't be expected to blend into a crowd of local pro-Trump men, should he step down from the castle. Still, the white working-class reactionaries who showed up waving Trump flags and Confederate flags while opposing Larry's Black Lives Matter event validated the propaganda Peter was peddling in the wake of George Floyd's murder.

With or without Peter's direct participation, August 21 was a big win for VDARE.

Hundreds of men showed up, along with a few women. They rode in on trucks and on motorcycles. Biker gangs rode in from Martinsburg.[3] Many of them came armed, just as David DeGraw said they would. They stood tall and let people know how seriously they took their self-deputized authority to protect Berkeley Springs.

The mild late-summer evening breeze carried an undercurrent of violence, although none broke out. On Larry's side, not more than a hundred people filed in for his event. They brought messages of peace and reconciliation.

Adonijah Gilmore, a thirty-year-old Black man from neighboring Berkeley County who had spoken at a handful of different events since the murder of George Floyd, was one of those who addressed the Berkeley Springs event. He attempted to build bridges with the counterprotesters, who chanted "*All* Lives Matter!"

"We are not here to say Black lives matter more than anyone else. Brothers and sisters, we have this movement not to continue the hate, but to stand with each other," Adonijah shouted from the gazebo into a wall of sound.[4]

Everyone who spoke of racial justice that evening immediately understood that they were there to play the foil to their opposition. A local TV crew that attempted to cover the event struggled to get a shot in, because two men carrying a giant Trump flag performed a pendulum swing with their bodies behind the newscaster, turning it into a makeshift political ad.[5]

The visible array of heavy weaponry disturbed Larry's guests and his co-organizers. West Virginia was an open carry state. There was nothing Larry could say.

The speakers were trapped in the park, surrounded by people who thought they were taking their country back from what was, on that night, an invisible threat. *The Morgan Messenger* reported on a member of the biker contingent boasting about his group's ability to "flank" these liberals.[6]

A different Larry, Larry Omps, an older businessman with soft blue eyes and whitish blond whiskers who owned the Country Inn, purportedly pulled Paul Johanson aside during the event and said he heard that Trey was storing protesters in the basement of Fairfax Coffee House.

Paul looked at him. He had not been aware of what had been happening in the local pro-Trump Facebook groups. The only thing Fairfax Coffee House had posted to Facebook that day was a note advertising a new vanilla pound cake at the shop.

"We don't have any protesters in the basement," Paul explained.

Then there was the heavy police presence. Officers from the Morgan County Sheriff's Department, the Berkeley Springs Police Department, the West Virginia State Police, the Berkeley County Sheriff's Department, and the Department of Natural Resources showed up.[7] People spotted police with rifles on top of buildings.

From the perspective of the police, both sides had the capacity to inflict violence. The people on the pro-Trump side, many of them carrying guns, might kill in self-defense. And, obviously, the out-of-state anarchists who people said would eventually arrive could kill people too. Antifa could commit terrorism. Presumably, they also had guns, or even bombs.

A couple of years after Larry's rally, I interviewed the chief deputy at the Morgan County Sheriff's Office, Johnnie Walter Jr., at the sheriff's station, which stood perched above a parking lot overlooking the Food Lion, the Goodwill, and the McDonald's drive-through. A big, jolly-seeming man with fat, coal-black eyebrows and thinning hair, Johnnie corrected me when I referred to the reactionary counterprotesters by that word.

"They were protesting *too*," he said.

"I understand that," I said. "But they were responding to the initial protest, which is why I'm referring to them as counterprotesters."

"Well, they weren't counterprotesters. They were protesting *too*," he said of the armed men.

"I think you're ascribing a negative connotation to a word that has a neutral one. There's nothing inherently wrong with being a counterprotester," I said.

"I'm just saying. They were protesting *too*," he repeated.

"Okay," I said. "Got it."

Kate Lehman saw the police with sniper rifles on top of the courthouse. It was the same courthouse where David DeGraw sat, waiting for his bail process to finalize so he could go home and wash down the pain he felt with liquor.

Rebuilt after that 2006 blaze that took out its historic century-old predecessor, the yellow courthouse was usually a calming sight for Kate, stabilizing the landscape of Berkeley Springs. It represented democracy, the functions of government. Now it was something menacing.

Larry invited Kate to give a call-and-response prayer at the rally. A prayer, Larry hoped, might be a hard thing for vocal Christians in the crowd to attack. A transplant from Long Island who had lived in Morgan County since 2006, Kate was a retired Unitarian Universalist minister. She staged her prayer from the gazebo.

Hecklers immediately drowned her out. Something called a "Black Out" tractor trailer blasted music, bursts of sound, and chants. Only a fraction of the people there actually heard the ending of Kate's prayer:

> KATE: We are responsible for what happens next.
>
> ALL: We must strengthen our commitment to bring about greater liberty and justice for all.
>
> KATE: We must strengthen our commitment to bringing about more love and compassion for all.
>
> ALL: We must strengthen our commitment to combat the hidden prejudice that causes fear.
>
> KATE: We come together so that righteousness will flow like a mighty river until peace fills the earth as waters fill the sea.

ALL: May we strengthen each other to work for a world redeemed, with promises fulfilled and ideals made ever more real for all.

As Kate battled to be heard, she looked out at the jeering faces. Men on the perimeter of the rally mocked Kate as if she were a total joke. She felt like the whole thing had an undercurrent of misogyny to it. In the crowd, she spotted a young man in his early twenties named Gavin.

Cold disappointment flooded her stomach. She looked as closely as she could at Gavin, given how enmeshed she was in the task of finishing her obligation as a speaker. He was laughing at her.

Gavin had lived next door to Kate for over a decade. When he was a boy, she had acted as almost an extra parental figure to him. Kate had driven him places in her car after school. She had taken him to the local McDonald's for lunch.

Kate had soft features, short hair, and a warm, honeyed voice that put people at ease. She seemed like exactly the type of person you might turn to if you needed a stranger to reassure you about something, or if you felt like you were on the edge of giving up. Gavin had come to Kate when he felt sad, or when he felt like he couldn't speak to his parents. He once told her he loved her.

Kate knew that Gavin's family watched Fox News and held reactionary beliefs. But Gavin's father had also voted for Obama in 2008. This was the type of nuance about Appalachia that national media often overlooked. Gavin had struggled to find himself. In second or third grade, apocalyptic thoughts had plagued his developing mind. He had articulated fantasies about the world ending.

One time while on a trip out of the county, they'd passed a Black neighborhood, and Gavin had thrown himself onto the floor of the car to hide. He said that he was worried Black people were going to kill him. But he didn't say "Black people." He used the very bad word for Black people instead, the same word that had inspired Larry to stage the Black Lives Matter event in the park.

Kate had emphasized to Gavin that racism came from fear, just as she did now during her prayer. She had invested a lot of time in Gavin to help him find the maturity to reject those thoughts. Kate knew he had taken interest in pro-police Blue Lives Matter as an older person, but she'd never imagined that he would allow that to rise above their relationship.

There was no nice way to put it. Gavin had betrayed her.

As the rally wound down, the summer sun was still illuminating the streets below. The shift in the atmosphere between Bill's first Black Lives Matter event and Larry's couldn't have been starker or more horrifying to the people who attended both.

Larry left angry. He had brought his daughter down for the rally. He never thought he would be putting her in danger. The guilt of doing so tore at him. He could "never imagine that these people would be so *butt-hurt*," as he later put it.

Larry poured himself a drink and logged on to Facebook to catch up with the local discourse. Then he made a few phone calls to friends in town to try to process what had happened. Lawyers from surrounding counties congratulated him for taking a stand, but he couldn't stop thinking about his daughter and those guns.

After the weekend, VDARE published a post titled "Patriots Rout Black Lives Matter in Berkeley Springs WV!" Someone going by the name Noah Arnold authored the August 24 entry, and it had a much more local feel than anything VDARE had published before. The post included Noah Arnold's narrated video footage, which referred to "our historic castle." He noted the flags that the counterprotesters carried, including the Confederate flag, and said that some carried "the Union flag." It left a viewer with the sense that the Civil War had never ended.[8]

Noah Arnold also wrote about a guy named Ted Stein. Ted, a liberal who lived part time in Berkeley Springs, had posted to Twitter about the event. He blamed VDARE for the scale of the backlash that he and others had faced. He tagged them in his post.

"This is a tiny artists community, population 700. A racist org VDARE bought a literal castle in my town. They organized this violent counter protest to locals having a BLM vigil in the park. Biker gang. A militia. And hundreds of armed racists," Ted wrote. "Never happened before VDARE."

Noah Arnold pushed back against Ted's accusation that they had organized the counterprotest, calling it a lie.

"What did we learn? BLM tactics rely on strength in numbers. In Berkeley Springs, local patriots refused to kneel," Noah Arnold wrote in a follow-up post.[9]

On the night of August 25, a seventeen-year-old boy with chubby cheeks named Kyle Rittenhouse, armed with an AR-15, killed two men and wounded another in Kenosha, Wisconsin. Kenosha had endured rioting after local police shot to death a Black man named Jacob Blake.

The boy killer had deputized himself to police the streets there, just as David DeGraw had wanted to do in Berkeley Springs. Groups like the Proud Boys hailed Kyle Rittenhouse as a hero. The story further polarized the country, instantaneously.

Larry had a conversation with Sheriff KC Bohrer around this time. The sheriff asked him, "Why did you do this?" Larry told him about what had happened at Sleepy Creek Campground. He asked him about why nothing was being done. Sheriff Bohrer dropped his head and said nothing, Larry told me.

In the days after the event, Gavin approached Kate to halfway apologize.

"I never meant to disrespect you," he told her.

Kate didn't believe him. She had been struck by feelings of pessimism following the debacle in the park. She thought about her grandchildren. Kate worried about their future. She saw the quality of American life declining everywhere she looked.

"Why were you yelling while I was speaking if you didn't disrespect me?" Kate asked him.

Gavin had no answer.

He later called on Kate for a favor. It was the type of little thing Gavin had done all the time with her, since he'd been a kid. This time, she turned away.

"Why don't you get one of your Blue Lives Matter friends to do it?" Kate said.

12

Ruling-Class Angry Apes

Jeanne Mozier, the town oracle, died on Thanksgiving. Her sister, Barb Wolfe, who owned a store called Berkeley Springs Memories that sold souvenirs and trinkets, announced Jeanne's death on Facebook.

"This is undoubtedly one of the hardest things I ever had to write. It is with a very heavy and broken heart that I tell all our family and friends that my sister, Jeanne Mozier unexpectedly passed away this morning," Barb wrote on November 26. "There will be no funeral or services but we will plan to have a 'Celebration of Life' as soon as we are able to congregate again."[1]

Barb had a birthday in a few days but postponed the party. Jeanne's family announced no cause of death. She was seventy-five years old.

Jeanne had always offered leadership to Berkeley Springs and a feeling of quiet balance, people told me. Some people in town admired Michelle Obama, and some admired Donald J. Trump, but Jeanne always sat at the center, emphasizing the appeal of Berkeley Springs to its visitors. Someone pinned a captioned photo of her onto the Christmas display at the gazebo.[2]

"Your gifts to Berkeley Springs will live forever," it read.

Some neighbors complained in private that Jeanne had built a reputation for herself that carried more weight than the mayor, or everyone else in Berkeley Springs combined, for that matter. Now that the town was without her for the first time in many decades, a significant part of its identity vanished. It was a hole that some residents feared would be filled by Peter and Lydia Brimelow.

Even if Jeanne had backed away from taking an activist line against the Brimelows, she still held distinctly different views from them. She had been posting criticisms of the Trump administration to Facebook right up until her death.

Toward the end, Jeanne wrote of Trump's election denial, writing about how "the idiot deniers in the GOP sat around making up conspiracies and lies."[3]

Trump indeed had lost the election and then acted like he won. I found this funny at first because it seemed so brazen and immature. MAGA acolytes had laid the groundwork for his election denial strategy through a #StoptheSteal campaign on social media—a voter suppression tactic dressed up as a genuine grievance by hatchetmen like Roger Stone—that had reinforced the president's narrative.

Trump's most vocal supporters staged events in swing states where vote tallies seemed close. At first, it stunned me to see these pop-up rallies attracting so many bodies, so many people waving giant flags and screaming. Armed men showed up at a vote-counting location in Maricopa County, Arizona. They stood alongside pro-Trump social media influencers there, including a men's rights activist named Mike Cernovich who sold a "cognitive supplement" called "Gorilla Mind Smooth" touted to improve focus.[4]

The VDARE contributor Noah Arnold, who had documented Larry's Black Lives Matter event, filmed a #StoptheSteal protest called the "Million MAGA March" in Washington, DC, on November 14.

In the video, VDARE highlighted the observations of a man named Shane Trejo, describing him as "a former Michigan poll watcher turned whistle-blower." Trejo had connections to the movement and had previously hosted a podcast called *Blood Soil and Liberty*, mirroring the Nazi slogan "Blut und Boden."[5]

"Three African American gentlemen show up with boxes of ballots at the dead of night, we have no chain of custody, have no clue where they were from and could have easily been fake," Trejo told VDARE's audience.

On December 8, a French computer programmer named Laurent Bachelier gave over $500,000 in cryptocurrency to American movement figures who supported Trump. Bachelier sent the bulk of his money to the young Hitlerite Nick Fuentes, but he also gave the Brimelows a full bitcoin, valued then at a little less than $40,000.

Bachelier killed himself in a room at the Hyatt Regency Étoile in Paris soon after. He had suffered from trigeminal neuralgia, a chronic nerve condition, and overdosed on the medications he used to treat his pain. In a note, he described himself as "a prisoner of his own body."[6]

Bad followed good for Peter. One week after he got his bitcoin, Katherine Polk Failla, a judge for the US District Court for the Southern District of New York, threw out his lawsuit against *The New York Times*.[7]

My entire family flew down to my uncle Raji's place in Fort Lauderdale over Christmas and New Year's that year. I spent most of the time jogging alongside the palm trees covered with multicolored Christmas lights on Galt Ocean Drive, rereading Mary Gaitskill stories, and ordering beach cocktails. I couldn't escape my work, which increasingly felt like it was destroying me. I deleted apps from my phone. I stopped consuming news. But my mind kept humming with the movement's chatter and rage.

On January 4, 2021, VDARE published a post authored by a pseudonymous someone going by the name "Charlottesville Survivor." "Why I'm Going to the Jan. 6 Stop the Steal Rally—While We're Still Allowed to Have Them," they titled it. The author argued that "everyone on the patriot Right, including conservatives, nationalists, and Identitarians, should stand with President Donald Trump on Wednesday January 6."

The VDARE author acknowledged that Trump had little chance of retaining power but argued that this was not the point of the endeavor. Republican elites had to learn that "nationalism" was the only way forward.[8]

"If there is to be any hope for the Historic American Nation, those Trump voters need to be a conscious political force that the Republicans can't take for granted," "Charlottesville Survivor" wrote. "They still believe in the national populism that Trump ran on in 2016 and still symbolizes today. A demonstration specifically in favor of Trump on Wednesday will show the needed strength and independence. It will show the GOP there is no going back."[9]

On January 5, the night before I was set to return to work, I picked up where I left off, monitoring hordes of mostly white, mostly male Trump fans calling his election loss fake. The #StoptheSteal people held a rally in the freezing cold in Washington, DC. Roger Stone cavorted with the Proud Boys and called Trump the greatest president since the Civil War.[10] Alex Jones barked with steam coming off his lips. "We have only begun to resist the globalists! We have only begun our fight against their tyranny! They have tried to steal this election in front of everyone," he said.[11]

When the hordes of Trump fans pressed their way into the Capitol on the afternoon of January 6, clawing and climbing on top of each other's backs to gain entry, I watched it from the living room of our new house. My family had recently moved from Queens to a New York City suburb.

It was a place where I could set up decent-enough security in response to the threats I was receiving. It had a backyard where my sons could play. I watched the TV and struggled to process this violent event that I subconsciously knew had to happen.

Some of the "patriots" who attended Trump's ill-fated rally rested at the Berkeley Springs Castle overnight. Peter and Lydia Brimelow played host to the travelers. Lydia posted about it on Gab.

"We just said goodbye to some friends who stayed at the VDARE Castle with Peter Brimelow and me after the rally last night. Our friends didn't storm the capitol, but they're not horrified by it," she wrote on January 7, 2021. "They had a great time. They met good people. They're energized. But mostly, they hate traitors."[12]

Peter published his own commentary on the violence on January 6, 2021, calling the insurrection attempt a response to what had happened over the summer. "Ruling Class Angry Apes Don't Like It, but They

Taught America That Violence Works," he titled it. Peter headed the post with an image from the melee—a behatted man waving a Confederate flag from a statue outside the Capitol. Peter called Black Lives Matter "blood libel on white America" and George Floyd's murder a "hoax." He also praised Trump for highlighting instances of fraud in "black areas."[13]

VDARE's Noah Arnold published a video on January 8 that showed the same event that Americans had watched on the news two days earlier, but from a different angle. The patriots starred as heroes in it. They were brave. They stood up to tyranny.

"We need men and women of courage and conviction who are willing to put their lives on the line for a cause, like our Founding Fathers did," an elderly man, with a hooded sweatshirt covering his head, explained to VDARE.[14]

John Derbyshire published an article in VDARE suggesting that January 6 "was a skirmish in the Cold Civil War," echoing one of his favorite catchphrases to describe the current state of America.[15]

One day later, Kevin DeAnna urged readers to brace themselves for short-term hell at the hands of elites. "In the end, no matter what we do, millions of Americans are about to feel the iron boot of repression—something we at VDARE.com have been dealing with for some time," he wrote.[16]

For me, Trump's failed attempt to flip an election made an already challenging work environment feel impossible. I got pulled into hundreds of January 6 press calls where the goal was to explain to reporters, from outlets ranging from *The New York Times* to a local Fox affiliate in Utah, what I thought had happened on January 6. I spoke to so many people that I lost my voice. Every time I spoke, I told the reporters some variation of the same thing.

I said that, for years, soft barriers had existed between the Republican Party and the movement, which was made up of white nationalists, neo-Nazis, anti-immigrant activists, and other people that Peter Brimelow called *patriots*.

After Trump announced his run, those soft barriers between the movement and the mainstream Republican Party started to erode. The barriers wore out a little more every time Trump validated the concerns of his activists, as he did when he told the Proud Boys to "stand back and stand by" in his first presidential debate with Joe Biden, on September 19, 2020.[17]

The barriers finally collapsed altogether on January 6. There were no longer any walls between the movement and the mainstream Republican Party.

13

The Motive, the Means, and the Proximity

My marriage to Aadya ruptured in the aftermath of January 6. Although there was no exact correlation between the two events, the stress caused by my SPLC job certainly contributed to the tension. I moved out of our new house and into my parents' place in accordance with the separation.

I worked in the same room where, in high school, I would sneak out of the window. I snuck out on Tuesday nights back then, close to midnight. I would take the train to the city and go to a goth-industrial night called "Communion." They hosted it at Limelight, a repurposed church. Then I'd head back to school on Wednesdays without sleeping. I felt nostalgia for my high school years as I sorted through the aftermath of January 6 and the separation.

While I was going through that, Peter Brimelow was busy infusing VDARE with paranoia about left-wing plots. He raised a more fearful tone about the future as the reality of a Biden presidency settled in. VDARE published the race-science champion Jared Taylor on March 10 in a post titled "Ruling Class Weaponizing 'White Supremacist Armed Insurrection' Hoax."

Taylor complained about the overuse of the descriptor "white supremacist" in the coverage of January 6. He told his allies to brace for the ascendancy of a totalitarian left.

"Blaming the Capitol takeover on 'white supremacy' will no doubt be a justification for surveillance and harassment of any racially dissident organization or person. It could even lead to laws that ban 'white supremacist' speech. Private companies are already actively suppressing speech with which they disagree. A climate is building in which our government could join them," he wrote.[1]

Peter Brimelow published content that seemed to use words and phrases like "deplatforming" and "cancel culture" more frequently, painting the cultural climate as akin to George Orwell's *1984*. Adding to this feeling of paranoia, VDARE's domain registry, Network Solutions, dropped VDARE as a client.

Peter and Lydia scrambled to find a replacement. On January 23, they invited Andrew Torba to the castle, along with his wife and child. Torba ran Gab, the social media site where many people had threatened to kill me, and where the Tree of Life terrorist had announced his intent to murder Jews. Torba himself had accused Jews of deliberately harming Christians around the time the Brimelows had him over.[2]

Peter interviewed Torba about how he had circumvented tech companies that had dropped Gab in the aftermath of the Tree of Life terror attack. But he really seemed to be searching for ideas, anything, to lower the pressure and keep VDARE online. Torba asked him how he was doing, and he spat out a cluster of misery.

"Terrible, awful! We could do with a revolution. Or more accurately, a counter-revolution," Peter grumbled.[3]

Peter and Lydia started attending Mass at St. Vincent de Paul Catholic Church in Berkeley Springs and formed relationships there with people who identified as conservative. Pro-Trump people who met with the Brimelows and their daughters face to face left with an impression that was incompatible with the SPLC's spooky-sounding "white nationalist" label.

Meanwhile, Ann Coulter repeatedly pushed a narrative about Derek Chauvin's innocence through VDARE, portraying the man who murdered George Floyd as a "human sacrifice." She said he'd faced worse treatment than any Black man had during the era of Jim Crow.[4]

White conservatives had learned to loathe the phenomenon they called "cancel culture," where people attempted to ostracize someone over their words and deeds. The backlash against cancel culture made some locals more inclined to like Peter and Lydia, who, in their opinion, faced cancellation by the very communists who had just colluded to steal an election from Trump. Through my work, I had certainly been one of the most visible people to try to cancel Peter, and I understood that I was seen as a villain in their world.

With Trey and other critics preoccupied by a pandemic that reactionaries now considered fraudulent, the Brimelows built alliances in Berkeley Springs without facing much in the way of protest. People were excited to access this mysterious couple who owned the town's premier piece of real estate.

In addition to forging friendships, Peter also struck back hard against one local detractor, Ted Stein. Peter threatened Ted with a lawsuit, and when other critics of the Brimelows from Berkeley Springs learned about it, they viewed it as a message from VDARE that it would use its financial resources to crush them if they spoke up.

Ted was the man who had tweeted that VDARE had "organized this violent counter protest" to Larry's Black Lives Matter event. On March 19, he responded to a tweet from Peter by reiterating that claim.

"BTW, the whole town knows it was you who brought the racists with guns in," Ted wrote. "You might end up getting sued out of existence even without those standards of truth (lol) you long for."

On Thursday, May 20, Ted opened his email to find a letter from Peter's legal team. The letter demanded that he retract his statements about VDARE or face consequences. Adrenaline swept through him. He wrote back.

"I am still sorting out my legal team. I have never been threatened with a lawsuit before," Ted wrote. "Once it is determined who will represent me, they will reach out. My father is a law professor. Do you mind if he gives you a call to sort out some clarifying questions?"

Ted sent me an email after the weekend passed, on the afternoon of Tuesday, May 25. He wrote that Trey had sent him my contact information and that Peter Brimelow had been waging "a bizarre intimidation campaign" against him. Ted noted that he had an office not far from the castle and that he didn't know what to do. He said that he thought the SPLC was his best chance to get help. I wasn't so sure.

I took a walk and called Ted. I had to stop several times to listen closely enough to hear him. His voice shook.

"I'm not a lawyer," I said, firmly. "But I can bring it to people here and see what they say."

"Would you do that for me?" he asked.

"Of course," I said. "Please be patient. I'll get back to you."

"Thank you," he said. "Thank you so much."

I tried to think of some words of reassurance.

"You did nothing *wrong*," I told him. "Peter Brimelow is bullying you. He wants to make an example of you!"

I sent the email to the SPLC's legal department.

As May bled into June, my phone pinged with cryptic messages. Someone was cycling through disposable cellphone numbers to send texts containing homophobic and racist slurs—shadowy comments that felt threatening without being specific—and evade detection. It was familiar territory. I forwarded some of the texts to the SPLC's security team.

My newly turned eight-year-old son approached the end of second grade, and on the afternoon of Friday, June 4, I knocked off work early and took him to a batting cage. Afterward, we drove to an adjacent 7-Eleven for a Slurpee. We were piling into the car when my phone rang.

It was someone from a North Carolina area code. When I answered, a man spoke in a tense-sounding voice. He said he was a special agent who worked for the FBI's Joint Terrorism Task Force—an "assistant WMD coordinator" out of their office in Charlotte.

"I just wanted to call you as a courtesy. We are looking at an individual who wants to kill you—I realize that is unpleasant to hear—and has been talking about ways to achieve that end," he said. "But we have eyes on this individual and we're hoping to take him out of circulation."

I froze. "Out of circulation" sounded like cop talk from TV. I wondered if they took on a performative tone like that to entertain themselves. I looked up at my son's green eyes in the rearview and he looked back at mine.

"Mr. Hayden?" the agent said.

"Yeah. I have company here."

"This is all out of an abundance of caution. You can stay put. We have it under control," he said. "And if you do experience any suspicious activity, please notify us."

A billion words rushed through my head, and I uttered the least expressive one.

"Okay," I said.

"Do you have any questions?"

"I can be home in less than an hour. Would it be okay to contact you back? I should probably also loop in my work."

"Yes, that's fine."

I hung up and stared blankly at the people coming out of 7-Eleven with their corn nuts, Red Bulls, and cigarettes.

"Something with work," I told my son.

I threw on sports talk radio and drove back to our house, not saying much. I got Aadya alone when I got there.

"Should I stay? I don't know how serious this is but if this guy has this address and something happens without me here, I won't be able to live with myself. I understand we have this—you know. Separation."

"Okay," she said. "I mean, obviously."

"Stay?"

"Yes. Obviously stay."

"I know this sucks. There's nothing else to say."

"Okay," she said.

"I can go back to my parents' place after, or—"

"We'll deal with it."

Night fell. I spent the hours in between pacing around the backyard, pulling up grass with my bare toes. Huey from the SPLC's security team called me. He spoke to me with a bassy southern drawl. His voice was firm and authoritative.

"The agent is a real person and the call was legitimate," he said.

"Okay," I said. "Do I need to move my family?"

"No," he said. "There are three things always in play for a threat of this nature. We look at the motive, the means, and the proximity. If they have all three, that's a problem."

"The motive, the means, and the proximity," I repeated.

"Correct."

"How many of the three does this guy have?"

"This man has a motive. He also has the means. But what he lacks is the proximity."

"So, he must be in North Carolina."

"You can go back to living your life," Huey said. "If you see anything suspicious, give me a call."

I walked onto the front lawn in my bare feet and stood there for a moment still thinking about who in North Carolina it could be. I had identified one guy in the movement based in North Carolina as a possible suspect. He was an Irish American neo-Nazi who went by the name "Potato Smasher." The guy was an ex-army mechanic who used to repair helicopters.

Potato Smasher had taken a selfie in which he was pointing his gun at a bathroom mirror, and a colleague of mine and I had used that image as part of a matching game while nailing down his real name. I had also identified his wife in the story, because she, too, was part of the movement. I'm sure he hated that. He seemed to particularly hate Arabs and Indians.

But the anonymous texter could just as easily be someone completely unknown to me, some person with whom I'd clashed online. I must have had thousands of acidic back-and-forth internet fights with different faceless, nameless bigots.

Aadya refused to let me get a gun, and I understood her logic, given the statistics. But deep down, I wanted a gun. I could imagine the gun in my hand and how reassuring it would feel. Instead, I slept on the floor near the front door of the house that night next to my son's old tee-ball bat.

The bat had a lightness to it that made it feel like a shillelagh. It occurred to me that if this person chose to bring significant enough firepower, there was not much I could do to stop him from killing us all. I guessed I would swing it at him and hope for the best.

Without any real progress made in repairing our relationship, Aadya and I suspended our separation in response to the threat. It worked, for a time.

14

Let His Way Be Dark and Slippery

In the warm weather seasons of 2021, Berkeley Springs rode what one resident described to me as a "mild sugar high" brought on by the pandemic. People who lived in cities sought refuge in places where social distancing was built into the fabric of daily life. City people coming from Baltimore and Washington, DC, escaped to more rural destinations in West Virginia for hiking trips. Morgan County not only eked its way out of the pandemic, but benefited from a small tourism bounce.

The Berkeley Springs Farmers Market thrived in this environment. The market opened on Sundays from ten in the morning to two in the afternoon. The growers and crafters set up their booths in the space between the parking lot of St. Vincent de Paul Catholic Church and the courthouse, below and with a clear view of the Berkeley Springs Castle, adjacent to a plaque commemorating a home previously owned by George Washington.

Under tents, people sold bread, meat, fruits and vegetables, and soaps and candles. And with visitors now bathing in the spring water across the street again, Sundays always pumped the market full of life. Regular visitors inevitably crossed paths with a trans woman named Lisa Marie. Lisa Marie, her last name withheld here in response to a request to protect her from threats, and her wife, Sharon, sold mushrooms they raised on their farm. Shiitake. Lion's mane. Oyster mushrooms.

Lisa Marie and Sharon had the best local selection of mushrooms you could hope to find in West Virginia. And visitors could get a handle on what type of folks they were by looking at the water bottle they placed on their display table. It was labeled with the words "Billionaire Tears."

West Virginia ranked in the bottom fifth of all states in terms of trans residents relative to the general population. And despite trans women emerging as consistent targets for reactionaries, portrayed online as sexual predators or disturbed maniacs, Lisa Marie rarely faced prejudice while selling.[1] With her large, round frame glasses and librarian-esque demeanor, few people would even pick up that she was trans, much less dislike her for it.

Lisa Marie said that the most negative things she heard around the market came from people belittling the farmers market itself. Some local supporters of MAGA portrayed it as a liberal, Democratic Party institution, despite some of the vendors being Trump voters themselves.

Lisa Marie commuted into Berkeley Springs every week from her mushroom farm. The farm was buried in an obscure holler several winding roads behind the castle. She and Sharon had converted a barn into a grow room. Shiitake mushrooms are grown on hardwood logs, and they had built up a cluster of them on their property for that purpose, securing them with metal fencing.

Inside their home, Lisa Marie cultivated a more intense relationship to the internet than most of the people I'd met in Berkeley Springs. She had dalliances with the hacker community, she said, and "used technology to uplift" herself and other trans people. She had worked for four years at Free Software Foundation, a group that advocates for the free use of software under "copyleft" terms. That essentially meant that she fought for software to be open sourced.

On Lisa Marie's very active Twitter account, she posted pictures from her foraging finds in the woods, along with the possums and raccoons that rudely sought to infiltrate their operation.

When an account operated by someone calling herself "the Trans Mom" asked her followers, "Heeyyyy what have you been obsessed with lately???," Lisa Marie responded, "Fun-guys" with two mushroom emojis.

Days later, on June 26, Lisa Marie brought up something different on Twitter. It was something that had been bothering her for a while.

"Going to the town next overs first ever pride today," she wrote across a thread. "Am both excited and nervous.... I also hope the nazis in the castle stay in their stupid castle.... I'm in no mood to deal with incel garbage today. Yes we have nazis in a castle, it's a long story... and yes they suck at life."[2]

Berkeley Springs finally held its first-ever Pride celebration, and Lisa Marie attended. Scott Collinash of the Country Inn helped to plan it. People considered the event a success, and the Brimelows never surfaced. Participants decorated the park with Pride flags. People set up booths on the park lawn and sold gifts and food.

Lisa Marie had familiarized herself with the Brimelows early after they arrived in town, but she never participated in any of the actions Trey had led. One thing she learned was that right next to the farmer's market, the Brimelows attended Mass at St. Vincent's.

That put Lisa Marie in proximity to them every Sunday when she traveled down there to sell her mushrooms. And she heard new gossip all the time. The Brimelows had started to dig their way into the fabric of Berkeley Springs. Lisa Marie grew angry with how openly some people seemed to welcome them.

On June 17, I published a story alongside the reporter Alex Kotch detailing how shadowy donors had infused VDARE with $4.3 million in the run-up to the castle purchase. At that time, we didn't know that the bulk of the donations had come from two unnamed individuals. Lisa Marie found the article a month later, on July 17.[3]

"Thank you @splcenter for your great work reporting on hate groups like VDARE.... Who have invaded our local communities in places such as Berkeley Springs, WV," she wrote.[4]

Peter Brimelow responded to the story through VDARE. He gave his article the headline "SPLC Thug Michael Edison Hayden Fears VDARE

.com's Prowess!" on June 18.[5] He also called me a "communist." VDARE had already written four posts about me by then.

Most of the posts on VDARE went through the org's standard material, proclaiming Biden's proverbial honeymoon was over and praising a moon-faced, Peter Thiel–linked Ohio Senate candidate named JD Vance.[6] But Peter then directed his publication into some more personal territory, focused on grievances.

VDARE made a miniseries called *Doxing the Doxers* that highlighted a blatant misnomer embraced by pro-Trump reactionaries. The idea was that they would "dox" the reporters who were "doxing" people from the movement, giving us a taste of our own medicine.

The word "doxing" meant publishing a person's private information online as a means of stirring up harassment against them. Doing it might even serve as an attempt to get someone physically harmed. Neo-Nazis swatted a ProPublica reporter's home, nearly killing him, after someone doxed him.

People attempted to dox me on Gab, the imageboard site 4chan, the messaging app Telegram, and the defunct forum 8chan, where the Christchurch killer had announced his plans to slaughter Muslims in New Zealand in 2019. Nobody ever got my information right, so they settled for my parents' address. Many of my reporter friends went through similar scares. Of course, investigative reporters never doxed people the way pseudonymous internet nazis doxed us, but you wouldn't know it from certain currents of discourse.

On May 8, someone on VDARE using the name Rosa Luxembourg, after the revolutionary Marxist, published an episode of *Doxing the Doxers* about Jared Holt, who worked for the Atlantic Council. Jared and I had become good friends, united by harassment like this, and talked almost every day. I'd gone to his wedding. We often leaned on each other for support.

VDARE published photos of Jared's partner. They accused him of being antifa. Jason Kessler reached out to him for comment, as if this were a legitimate attempt to do journalism, and VDARE printed his response.

"You pathetic bitch," Jared wrote back in a direct message. "Not only dumb but cowardly."

On July 6, VDARE published something similar about another friend of mine, Chris Mathias. Chris wrote for HuffPost and covered the movement. Chris had also been to my house. He had been through his share of abuse from white supremacists too.

The Rosa Luxembourg person inserted an acrid twist into the post about Chris. They included photographs of his father, a doctor from Pennsylvania. One of the screenshots also included the address of where his father worked. It was gross.

Jason Kessler called me, and I was working on an investigation about a man named Charles Bausman, who had disappeared into Moscow after entering the Capitol on January 6. As soon as I heard Jason's voice, I knew what this was going to be. But I never turned down an opportunity to speak with someone in the movement when they voluntarily asked to speak to me.

Jason made it clear that he knew I had a wife and a sister. He also wanted me to know that he knew where my father and mother worked. That seemed to be his focus—just letting me know that the movement had an eye on me and my family. As soon as I got off the phone, I started lifting weights to release the tension I felt.

At the start of August, my family traveled to Rock Hall, Maryland, on the Chesapeake Bay, with its little beaches and views of the blinking lights on the water. It was our version of a pandemic vacation, but, as usual, I struggled to enjoy myself. I was still climbing out of the FBI scare, and the fallout from my separation with Aadya was still raw.

Jason kept texting me, almost every day. He asked me why I had recommended to a journalism podcast that people use a "diversity of tactics" in reporting and claimed that this had some connection to left-wing anarchism. In the most literal sense, I had no idea what he was talking about. The man was just riding unicorns around in his mind.

Then, on the morning of Monday, August 23, after weeks of Jason texting me, I emailed Peter Brimelow and pleaded with him to establish some boundaries. I tried to get across that if VDARE and I were to be enemies because of what we did, certain things should be off-limits, like family.

Within a few minutes of having sent it, I noticed that Peter had already published the *Doxing the Doxers* post about me and my family. It looked like he had done it close to midnight. VDARE's tweet promoting the post referred to me as "Antifa's propaganda minister."[7] Jason Kessler's byline sat at the top, not Rosa Luxembourg's.

My immediate concerns with the post were not its claims about my political leanings. VDARE linked to my sister's social media accounts, published pictures of my parents, and even linked to a photo of my son. These were not things I wanted the movement to see, particularly with the FBI calling me about murder threats.

One other thing enraged me when I read it: "Sadly, Hayden seems conflicted about his parentage. He writes glowingly about his mother as an immigrant, but mentions his father only in passing and never by name."[8]

The implication was that I hated my white father because he was white. Not only did I love my dad, but he, more than anyone else, had helped me see men like Jason for who they were. In my house, when I was growing up, my father was not white. My mother was not Arab. We were a family.

A man going by the name Edward James responded to VDARE's post, saying, "Disgusting, demonic slime. Let his way be dark and slippery, with the angel of the Lord pursuing him! Let destruction come upon him when he does not know it! And let the net that he hid ensnare him; let him fall into it—to his destruction!"[9]

On that same Monday, August 23, a federal appeals court in Denver ruled against VDARE in its case against the City of Colorado Springs for purportedly getting in the way of its Cheyenne Mountain Resort conference.[10] Remember, it was the purported injustice of that moment in the aftermath of the 2017 Unite the Right violence in Charlottesville that inspired the Brimelows' relocation to Berkeley Springs.

I spoke with Ted Stein—who had tweeted about the Brimelows' supposed role in the counterprotest against the second Berkeley Springs Black Lives Matter event and been threatened with a lawsuit—a few times that summer. I told him that lawyers at the SPLC had agreed to look at his situation, which was true, and reiterated to him that this did not guarantee that they would take any substantive action.

Ted held firm and refused to retract his statements. That was his choice. I gave him no advice. On August 19, Peter formally sued him. When I spoke to Ted, the terror he felt after his first encounter with Peter's legal team had returned.

"I'm working to see what we can do, okay?" I told him. "Hang in there."

On August 31, the town canceled the Apple Butter Festival for a second consecutive year. When staff members announced the cancellation through the city's Facebook page, they turned off comments to avoid the backlash.

On September 3, a middle-aged woman with blonde hair named Denise Trent Selby started publishing photos to her Facebook page from the Berkeley Springs Castle.

"Where's Waldo?" her first post read.

People started to gossip that Denise had gone to work for the Brimelows. She had a reputation for being a hard-line reactionary, like a local version of the conspiracy theorist and congresswoman Marjorie Taylor Greene of Georgia. Denise sometimes posted pics of herself on Facebook wearing costume dresses from the nineteenth century or firing big guns.

On September 29, Paul and Trey went into arbitration with Charlie Curia over the imploding biergarten project. What had started back in June 2020 with the stripping of the Pride flag had dissolved into an atmosphere of pure acrimony that now hovered like a fog across Fairfax Street.

Both sides had accused one another of trespassing. Both sides had called 911 on one another after tense encounters. Because of the trespassing accusations, Trey and Paul hired a security guard to oversee propane delivery into the coffee shop.

As this was happening, a man named Hunter Clark started preparations for the Bath Christmas Project, a beloved feature of the town's yearly tourism cycle. The Bath Christmas Project mostly focused on beautifying the town as the holiday season approached, making it as Christmassy as possible. People who knew Hunter before he connected with the Brimelows described him to me as a simple man with a gentle disposition. Conservative. A religious Christian. But kind.

Hunter's 501(c)(3) attracted families with kids from around Morgan County and beyond. He leaned heavily into Berkeley Springs' quaintness. Hunter's project seemed like the least offensive thing happening in town to people like Trey, but that changed overnight in the run-up to the 2021 Christmas holidays. That's when contributors to his project slowly began to learn that Hunter had given Peter and Lydia Brimelow an award for their generosity to the Bath Christmas Project.

As in any town as small as Berkeley Springs, gossip traveled. What people heard was that the Brimelows had donated $2,500 to the Bath Christmas Project. (I attempted to confirm this total a year later and Hunter hung up the phone on me.) The sum sounded meager, but, as Trey told me, that amount went a long way in Morgan County.

Trey and Paul had taken over the Star Theater earlier in 2021, raising their profile in the community and filling the void left behind by Jeanne Mozier's death. Paul went to work revitalizing the building's elegant interior. Trey had agreed to loan out the Star Theater to the Bath Christmas Project, which meant that her own name appeared on its website alongside Peter's and Lydia's.

When Trey discovered it, she felt nauseated. She later called Hunter on the phone to tell him, "If the VDARE people are involved in this, I don't want anything to do with it." A local nurse who contributed to the Bath Christmas Project also felt shocked to learn that VDARE had become involved in it. When she saw her name next to Peter's and Lydia's on the website, she told a volunteer about it.

"A lot of people have been complaining," the volunteer said.

From her mushroom farm, Lisa Marie noticed what she perceived to be VDARE's infiltration of the Christmas holidays. The Brimelows were now permitting tours of the castle as part of a "Christmas at the Castle" segment of the Bath Christmas Project.

The Brimelows also hosted a Christmas dinner at the castle for the first time. Castle owners had hosted people for Christmas in years past, but this was different. What bothered Lisa Marie most about it was the fact that people had bought tickets to this affair with no warning that they were traveling to a building owned by "Nazis." If a Black family bought tickets, they would have no clue that a great-replacement-focused activist group owned the space.

"Fascist activity alert," Lisa Marie posted to Twitter on December 5. "The official event for Berkeley Springs' Christmas Dinner will be hosted in the neo-Nazi compound owned by VDARE. This is an overt attempt to normalize VDARE in Berkeley Springs."[11]

On the morning of December 7, 2021, Lisa Marie told people on Twitter to call Matt Omps, a manager for the Country Inn, to urge him to stop associating with VDARE. Buses were taking people up to the castle for tours from the entrance of the historic inn. Lisa Marie also defended her embrace of the Second Amendment.

"So tired of middle class white activists telling marginalized groups that we should not have guns," she wrote. "We are tired of being hunted in the streets. We have the right to exist. And we will defend ourselves with extreme force if that is what it takes to stay alive."[12]

Then she responded directly to Peter Brimelow. He had written, "This is treason #IMPEACHBIDENHARRIS," while linking to a VDARE post about five hundred Afghan refugees resettling in Nebraska.[13] "Everyone I know in West Virginia thinks you are a racist bigot from the city," Lisa Marie wrote. "If you hate immigration so much why don't you go home to the UK, where you are from, city boy. You will never be accepted into our community. Don't let the door hit you, where the good lord split you."[14]

That afternoon, Lisa Marie arrived at the inn with a gun at her hip and signs that said things like, "There is Hate at the Castle."[15] She confronted participants to tell them that the people who ran the castle were white nationalists.

Some reactionary types tried to cough on Lisa Marie, implying they had COVID. After nightfall, a person allied with the Brimelows allegedly pulled up along Route 522 in her Jeep. Lisa Marie said this person started shouting at her, using a derogatory word for a trans woman.

No one could deny now that the Brimelows had built connections in town, including with people who would fight in defense of their name, if need be, Lisa Marie thought. Denise. Hunter. How many more people were like this?

"It is our hope to deny VDARE access to the local tourism industry . . . as well as convince VDARE to move out of our state," Lisa Marie announced on Twitter after her protest at the Country Inn.[16]

One day later, VDARE posted on its website that the castle was "a sign to the world and to ourselves that American patriots cannot be shouted down, cannot be shamed, and cannot be canceled into defeat." Emboldened by her confrontations at the inn, Lisa Marie posted a screenshot of this and wrote a response.

"Wanna bet?" she wrote.[17]

Lisa Marie continued to post about VDARE in the days that followed. She also seemed to take aim at their collaborators in town. She wrote, "Nothing is more insidious or disgusting than how nice and kind bigots are . . . when surrounded by people who look, act, and believe as they do."[18]

Lisa Marie's mom came to visit from Kentucky for the Christmas holidays. Lisa Marie decided to take her mom to Mass at St. Vincent de Paul Catholic Church on the morning of December 19, fully understanding they could run into Peter and Lydia.

She and her mom drove through the winding roads along Route 9 in cool but not frigid weather. The interior of the church was decked out in violet and rose advent decor. When they settled into their pew, they sat three rows away from the Brimelow family and off to the side.

Lisa Marie could see the Brimelows very clearly from her pew. They were no longer detached characters from articles. They were human, flesh and blood. Peter, with his poofy white hair. Lydia, a head taller than her husband. Their daughters, smartly dressed for church, wearing what looked to Lisa Marie like coordinated outfits.

The Reverend Michael Lecias, the pastor of St. Vincent de Paul, had emigrated from the Philippines, and he spoke with a pronounced accent. He had also spent time in Mexico, learning Spanish. One might think that an immigrant priest could present a challenge for Peter and Lydia, but he was the man in town then.

Lisa Marie remembered Father Lecias speaking in his homily about how another priest back home had blamed him for the destruction created by a powerful typhoon, saying, essentially, that God had responded to him being abroad by killing people in the Philippines. Lecias also said that someone had severed his Christmas lights with scissors and that someone had stolen money from the church safe, but it wasn't him.

Lisa Marie told me her mom called it "the strangest Mass" she had ever been to.

Lisa Marie waited through the stages of the Mass. Then Father Lecias announced the Rite of Peace, where parishioners turn to one another, shake hands, and say, "Peace be with you." A few beats after it began, Lisa

Marie left her pew and moved over to where Lydia stood. Lisa Marie's gun sagged at her hip.

Lisa Marie reached out her hand. Lydia shook it. Then her face collapsed into a mask of horror.

"Peace be with you," Lisa Marie said. "Black Lives Matter."

PART II

THROUGH HELL AND CREATION

15

Next Stop, America

I skipped watching football with my sons on Sunday, November 13, 2022, rented a Pathfinder from Newark Airport, and drove down to Berkeley Springs. It was just shy of a thousand days after I'd met Trey for the first time, and the air outside felt too warm for the season. I took a moment to catch up with VDARE's latest activities before I made the trip.

VDARE had hosted its first conference at the Berkeley Springs Castle in April 2022. They subtitled it "Uncancelled." Peter and Lydia Brimelow did what they said they would when they'd bought the place: They gathered thinkers of the movement together to discuss the fate of the "historic American nation." Andrew Torba of Gab sponsored the conference.

VDARE publicized video footage of the event, selecting particular aspects of the conference to show off. When managing editor James Fulford announced his presence, he joked that he used his real name, unlike other attendees. Then the camera stayed off his face. And the footage also missed the faces of the guests who attended.

Kevin DeAnna, whom VDARE announced to the audience using his James Kirkpatrick moniker, sported a black jacket with a gray pocket square and a checkered tie. He combed his oily hair tight to his head like a man from the 1950s. Kevin opened his speech by referring to the Biden administration, saying, "It seems we have a government that is dedicated to the destruction of the nation."

Kevin then defended the movement against the notion that its proponents were more dangerous than Black people. He also said that Germans had been "brought up from birth to regard their national history as something to be ashamed of"—coming as close as VDARE would come to publicly apologizing for Adolf Hitler.[1]

"While I think America, and the West, is doomed, I think we in this room are *not* doomed," he told VDARE's guests. "And on that note, I am more optimistic, more enthusiastic than ever. Because every single person who enters this movement now knows this isn't a game, knows they're going to have to pay costs, and they're willing to go through with it until the end."[2]

On May 14, a teenage consumer of movement propaganda named Payton Gendron performed his version of going "through it to the end" when he shot ten Black people to death in a Buffalo supermarket. Gendron targeted a Black neighborhood in Buffalo because he thought he was doing something to stop the "great replacement," the same narrative Peter and his friends hyped through VDARE.

To blunt the spread of the great replacement, Gendron executed eighty-six-year-old Ruth Whitfield on her way back from caring for her partner in a nursing home.[3] He gunned down fifty-three-year-old Andre Mackniel as he picked up a birthday cake for his three-year-old son.[4] He also killed seventy-two-year-old Katherine Massey, who had advocated for federal legislation to curb the spread of gun violence.[5]

Peter Brimelow posted a response to the massacre—which, in addition to deaths, also produced horrific injuries—on VDARE. He asserted in all caps that he was "OPPOSED TO VIOLENCE" before noting that the great replacement was actually a pretty big deal in Buffalo. In his post, he embedded a chart of the white population in the city dropping relative to other races.[6]

"According to what appears to be his manifesto, Gendron was motivated by serious racial concerns, particularly by what he saw as the displacement of his race by anti-white government policies, above all mass non-traditional immigration—the 'Great Replacement,'" Peter wrote.

I fixated on the phrase "motivated by serious racial concerns" when I read it.

Lydia Brimelow was still sending out fundraising letters citing the great replacement in the aftermath of that Buffalo attack.

As this was happening, Peter continued to punish Ted Stein, the man he had targeted with a legal threat over two misleading tweets. At the start of June, nearly two years after Ted had published his first tweet about the Black Lives Matter event, Ted quit fighting and paid VDARE $20,000 to end the nightmare. Peter stated publicly that he made no profit from the lawsuit.

As part of his punishment, Ted had to write an apology that was published in *The Morgan Messenger.* The case underscored the point that this was about more than money. It read like a warning to the entire town. Neighbors of Ted's described it to me as a humiliation ritual.

> To Peter Brimelow and the VDARE Foundation:
>
> I apologize to Mr. Peter Brimelow and the VDARE Foundation for my unfounded tweets of August 22, 2020 and March 19, 2021, which in substance accused them of organizing an armed, racist counter-protest of the Black Lives Matter rally in Berkeley Springs, West Virginia on Friday, August 20, 2020.
>
> The allegations were especially egregious, coming in the wake of the January 6 protest, when the federal government was investigating people for alleged armed protests. I regret the harm my false charges caused to Mr. Brimelow or the VDARE Foundation, and will endeavor to accord those I perceive as political opponents with greater respect and dignity.
>
> Yours truly,
>
> Ted Stein

Ted stopped talking to me after that and moved out of town. He wanted nothing to do with Berkeley Springs, nothing to do with VDARE, and nothing to do with the SPLC.

People in town who opposed the castle pitied Ted but learned from him, a little. When speaking about VDARE, they understood they needed to avoid hyperbole and stick to what was verifiable. They learned that if they weren't careful, Brimelow would use lawyers to dogwalk them.

Peter bragged to his readers that he had also pulled his Ted Stein trick on Bibi Hahn. Her husband, Matthew Hahn, was the man who had run for office as an anti-Trump Republican and attended my first talk.

Peter alleged that Bibi had made a claim similar to Ted's on Twitter. Hahn's Twitter account had just a few hundred followers. The overwhelming majority of her posts generated zero engagement—no likes, no retweets, no comments—nothing. Bibi, who chose as her Twitter moniker "Hillbilly Fairy," deleted whatever she wrote and issued an apology cut word for word from Ted's.

"But what was going on in Berkeley Springs was in some ways a microcosm of how the Left subverts Red State America," Peter wrote following his local legal triumphs. He then clarified what he meant by subversion: "Morgan County, of which Berkeley Springs is the seat, voted 75% for Trump in 2020. But casual tourists are often deceived by the proliferation of Black Lives Matter and gay banners and slogans aggressively pushed on local businesses by local Leftists, themselves usually weekenders or migrants from Washington, D.C." In addition to that likely reference to Fairfax Coffee House, Peter named me. He claimed that my Twitter followers "made open plans to firebomb" the castle.

"Whatever the local Left was up to in Berkeley Springs, WV, we have disrupted it. We have even successfully held our first conference," he wrote. "Next stop, America."[7]

Peter may have succeeded in terrifying everyone who opposed him in rural Morgan County, but his big-picture legal endeavors, the ones that with better luck might have reshaped our country for the history books, failed. VDARE's suit against the City of Colorado Springs had collapsed in August 2021, but his attempt to sue *The New York Times* had ended in an even more insulting fashion.

A judge agreed with the paper's argument to dismiss in December 2020. Now, in April 2022, the paper filed an anti-SLAPP suit against Peter and his group, a maneuver permitted under New York state law intended to defend against aggressors who abuse the legal system to stifle free speech. When the anti-SLAPP suit failed, thrown out by a judge on a technicality, Peter attempted to spin it as a victory while asking his donors for more money.[8] This debacle happened two years after Peter had written in grandiose terms about his legal ambitions, painting what he was doing as an attempt to reimagine *Times v. Sullivan.*

An even bigger legal problem crept up on VDARE at the same time, although I knew very little about it. In June 2022, the New York Attorney General's Office, headed by Letitia James, issued the first of what would be a series of subpoenas requesting records from VDARE as part of a mysterious investigation. Because James, an outspoken Black woman, targeted the "historic American nation," Peter and his cohorts framed her actions through the lens of race. They portrayed James as "an anti-white racist" and a "racist in reverse."[9]

Peter and Lydia didn't understand the magnitude of what was happening at first. They couldn't figure out what James was trying to find. Although VDARE operated out of West Virginia, and previously out of Connecticut, Peter had registered his nonprofit in the state of New York in 1999, a time that roughly overlapped with his work in financial journalism. That meant New York held the power to peer into VDARE's business practices.

The Brimelows hired a lawyer named Frederick C. Kelly to push back against the inquiry. I knew Kelly's name because it appeared at the top of the cease-and-desist letters that two separate neo-Nazis had sent to me in 2019. Both letters rambled incoherently and accused me of being "antifa," so I didn't think highly of his work.

VDARE later hired a lawyer named Andrew Frisch, a more accomplished figure than Kelly. A bald man with glasses and experience as a federal prosecutor, Frisch's resume stood out. Few decent lawyers jumped in to work with accused white supremacists. Given the choice between taking on a client who had become notorious for peddling great replacement propaganda and one who had no such baggage, most lawyers preferred the latter.

Frisch and VDARE turned over six thousand pages of documents to the Attorney General's Office between September 2022 and the time I visited Berkeley Springs that November.

I pulled over to piss in Maryland, threw water on my face, and sat in the Pathfinder for a minute, staring at a big white semitrailer. I made a few calls to check in about my stay and fought off a pull to turn around, drive home, and crawl into bed.

I turned my second visit into a much bigger production than the first one. The author and documentarian David France had started making a film that included coverage of my work at the SPLC. David wanted to capture the fight against the movement following January 6. So I used his project to convince my managers to let me return to Berkeley Springs and fulfill the promise I'd made to Trey to keep reporting on the Brimelows. David brought a camera crew. They had gotten into town before me that Sunday.

I also convinced the SPLC to fly Tanya Gersh down to speak with people there. Gersh, a Jewish real estate agent living in Whitefish, Montana, had sued the neo-Nazi website Daily Stormer and its editor Andrew Anglin through the SPLC in 2017 after they had terrorized her and her family in a coordinated campaign. After I dined with Tanya at a conference in Pittsburgh in September 2022, I thought she might be of some help to Trey. I used David's film as the excuse to make that happen too.

Berkeley Springs might get a rosy look at the SPLC through my little talk with Tanya, but in reality, the atmosphere at work had unraveled. Work culture had deteriorated so much that I fretted about David and Tanya seeing it. It was like living in a dysfunctional family and not wanting to bring people into your home.

Earlier that year, bargaining unit members of the SPLC's Intelligence Project had pulled together a collective action in the form of an internal letter criticizing the job performance of that department's senior leadership. Our staff monitored relentless cruelty, including grisly terror attacks like that Buffalo shooting. Many of us worked for very low wages across long hours. Our impression was that Huang's team did very little but go on lavish retreats.

The week before my trip to Berkeley Springs, leadership sent our editorial team on a retreat at a wine-themed hotel in downtown Atlanta. It was the day of the 2022 midterm elections. The organization's branding centered around voting rights and saving democracy, and there we were, no clear agenda, gawking at wine bottles encased in illuminated glass. Some of us literally assigned ourselves monitoring work around the election while we were there because it felt so icky to be doing nothing.

I brought up our need for better mental health care to the SPLC's lead union steward, Esteban. Esteban was well built with long hair and a beard. He looked like a distant cousin of Che Guevara, probably on purpose. He told me I should become a steward.

"I'll think about it on my trip and let you know," I said.

I thought about it. Mental health challenges and detached supervisors were one thing. This perceived signal from the top that we shouldn't work, probably in part out of a fear of risk, was another. Our output had slowed down. No one in the org seemed to want us to write.

Dusk fell as I crossed over the Potomac into West Virginia. I recognized the clean white and red marquee of the Star Theater as I passed it. People had already put up some early Christmas lights along Route 522. When I pulled into the parking lot of the Country Inn, I looked up and saw the castle.

I jogged up to room 20, carrying a duffel bag. The air in the inn felt thin and stale. Everything was old and drafty. I hated it.

I threw a navy blue sweater over a dress shirt and walked down to the dining area to meet David. He had round wire-rimmed glasses and an intellectual demeanor. There were a few crew members with him and everybody was pleasant.

"You know," David said at some point during the meal, "a million four isn't very much money."

"Sorry?"

I ate from a plate of fish and vegetables without really tasting it.

"That's what they paid for the castle, and it isn't very much," he explained. "Compared to New York real estate prices, that's practically nothing."

"Right," I said. "I hadn't thought about it that way."

16

Strange People on the Hill

Lights from the windows of Fairfax Coffee House glowed through the gaps of the white gazebo as I crossed through the park. When I got a little closer, I saw that Trey was still running her Halloween lighting effects. Shadows of ghosts and pumpkins rotated around the walls.

As I crossed onto Fairfax Street, shapes moved in the shadows. The blur appeared to be a person, or people. One of the people-shapes crouched down away from the lights of the coffee shop as I passed them, folding into that biergarten area where I had first met Paul. I couldn't make out an age or gender. I resisted an impulse to chase the person down until I could see his or her face.

When I entered the shop, I saw that a small crowd had gathered. There were enough people to stage a talk, but the crowd was smaller than at my first appearance. I waved to Paul, who wore his customary bandanna around his neck. I spoke to David as his crew set up.

"Is someone outside?" I asked him.

"It certainly *seems* that way," he said. "Doesn't it?"

I found Trey wearing a black turtleneck with a maroon dress pulled over it. We hugged. She was as I remembered her, maternal, solid, but I sensed that something had sapped her spirit.

"I'm so glad you're here," she said.

"I know. And in person."

Trey and I had talked on the phone roughly a dozen times over 2022, sometimes for over an hour. I would leave my home office when she called and go for a walk past the maple trees around my neighborhood as they changed from spring to summer and fall. She would tell me the latest VDARE gossip, and catch me up on drama like what had happened with the Bath Christmas Project.

Tanya Gersh, an attractive woman in dark clothes and red, thick-framed glasses, exuded an energy that felt oversized for the Fairfax Coffee House. She had just finished a run of speaking engagements about anti-semitism with some wealthy groups that included CEOs. When Tanya spoke about hate, she was loud, but she was also effective at conveying urgency. She reminded me of one of the energetic pitchwomen from QVC.

"You never know when to expect it," I heard Trey tell her. "It's a side-walk, they're allowed to be on the sidewalk."

They were talking about the people who shifted around outside to spy on us.

"And did these people know this meeting was—"

"I have no idea how they found out," Trey said. "And it just creeps me out."

"Well, it's a small town," Tanya said. "Everybody knows everybody."

Trey abruptly started to cry. The sparkle of raw emotion broke the facade she'd kept up when she greeted me. She wiped away tears by curling down the finger of her left hand into a hook and pulling them away from her face. She had tattooed that hand with an arrangement of flowers during the run-up to her marriage to Paul.

"I'm not in danger of violence now," Trey said. "But it's just always there's . . ."

"Do people support you in town?" Tanya asked.

"We have *wonderful* people in town supporting us," Trey told her.

"More supportive than not?" Tanya asked.

"No, no, no, no," Trey said. "I wouldn't say that."

"How long have you been in town?" Tanya asked her.

"About six years," Trey said. "Paul has been here for about seventeen."

Tanya grabbed Trey's hands more tightly.

"You're gonna outlive whatever is happening up there."

"I may or may not," Trey said.

"Let's focus on the 'I may' tonight because... I want to inspire you. You'll hear my story and it's not fun, but... we are part of a *bigger* picture," Tanya said. "Do you believe the true lesson that God doesn't give you more than you can handle?"

Trey sniffed up her tears.

"No, I do *not*," she said.

When we got set up, Tanya and I sat across from one another in a space a few yards away from the shop's window, which was obscured by neon. Whoever had been scurrying around outside seemed to have moved on. Trey set up video conferencing on her laptop for a few people who wanted to attend virtually, and I addressed the room.

"Last time, I was here two years ago, right before the pandemic took over the news," I said. "I promised Trey that I wouldn't stop reporting on the VDARE situation, which all of you guys found yourselves in for no reason. You didn't ask for it... but all of this is a long game, and you guys are going to *win*."

The people at Trey's shop looked very serious and sincere. I suddenly felt like a complete and total bullshit artist while standing before them.

When Tanya started to speak, I sat down, feeling relieved to shut up. She told the story of how her Jewish family had moved from Brooklyn out West as part of the hippie movement. And Tanya said that it felt like home popping in and out of the small shops along Route 522 in Berkeley Springs, relative to Whitefish.

And then Tanya talked about the harassment she had endured at the hands of the movement. How neo-Nazis had targeted her twelve-year-old son with threatening messages. Some of the messages sent to her child intimated that Tanya had been involved in depraved sexual acts.

Tanya talked about how the pain never left her, even after she'd won that lawsuit. The SPLC ultimately never retrieved the money for her.

Tanya's lead tormentor, Andrew Anglin, had fled somewhere abroad with his cryptocurrency.

"They really are the scum of the earth," Tanya told the room. "They use the term white nationalists, white supremacists. You know what I call them? *Maggot scumbags*. Because you know what they are? *Murderers*. They don't dislike us. They don't want us *alive*. I don't beat around the bush with them. I can be that one person that can call them the *slithering* slugs that need to stay under the ground. And they don't deserve to be in our coffee shops."

I cringed. I tried to avoid dehumanizing movement people. Movement people took words like that, wrapped them up, and used them to present these gnawing false equivalencies to outsiders. "We're just harmless white advocates but they are the ones using the language of extermination!" I could hear these activists responding in unison as soon as that "maggot" left Tanya's mouth.

Jim Hoyt, a man with bespectacled Steve Martin looks paired with an affable Mr. Rogers demeanor, talked about how he had been stalked and threatened by someone over his position as chair of the Morgan County Democratic Party. A man named Charles McBee had left him threatening voicemails in September 2021: *Fuck you, communist Democrat. Go suck a big pack of fuckin' dicks. Motherfucker. Trump won the election. Fuckin' go to hell. You're gonna go down. It's not gonna end well for you motherfuckers.*

It was the type of message that only a person capable of making extremely bad life choices would send. Larry Schultz, the lawyer who had helped stage the Black Lives Matter rally, urged Jim to make McBee face accountability. But Jim didn't want to see McBee go to prison. So, after the court convicted McBee, Jim pushed for him to receive counseling instead of imprisonment.

Originally from the deep red Putnam County village of Ottawa, Ohio, Jim had moved to Berkeley Springs in 1983. He had then worked for companies that sold software until his retirement. It was only then that he committed himself to his duties with local Democrats. Jim had a long history of supporting Democrats on Republican turf but said he had never seen things unravel the way they had during the Trump era.

In June, a pro-Trump group called the 1776 Restoration movement had set up in Berkeley Springs for an event that coincided with Juneteenth, essentially undercutting it. Jim showed me a photo he'd taken of a boy about ten years old holding a flag that said, "FUCK BIDEN."

"Think about what you're doing. That's a little kid," Jim told me.

Liberals in town regarded Jim as being too soft-hearted. They thought he settled for being polite in defeat, like the trope of the Washington Generals staging a self-effacing collapse to the Harlem Globetrotters. But at their monthly courthouse meetings, Jim reminded the dozen or so Democrats who attended that, like it or not, the party had no roads in front of them leading to short-term success in Morgan County.

"In the electronic pages of VDARE they are repeatedly talking about a civil war," I told the room. "And that we are in a *cold* civil war. Well, I am not in a civil war. I am not fighting a civil war. Okay? I'm not at war with *anyone*. No one here should be at war . . . with *anyone*."

What I'd said might calm people's anger at VDARE, but I realized after I said it that it was misleading. Just because I didn't want to be in a civil war didn't mean I could avoid it. It was like saying, "I don't want to be mugged." I had rather obviously been living in something like VDARE's "cold civil war" since James Fields had murdered Heather Heyer at the Unite the Right debacle in Charlottesville back in 2017. Was it inevitable that everyone else would eventually feel as damaged as I did, given America's trajectory?

After we finished, I met Dan and Cynthia, a pseudonymous married couple. They lived above town behind the castle in a gorgeous house with a postcard view of the woods and hills. Dan preserved buildings of historical importance in Morgan County and Cynthia wrote books.

I also met Abby Chapple, an eighty-year-old who worked in the museum in town. She was a fighter, but with the softest possible demeanor. I was immediately drawn to her kindness.

And I met Lisa Swanson. Lisa was a retired nonprofit worker whose love of nature enabled her to rattle off the names of plants and flowers that she found by the region's hiking trails. She worked part time at the Ice House, a cultural center in town, and volunteered for progressive causes.

Although I didn't formally meet them until later, "Amy" and her husband, "Doug," also attended. Amy was a psychologist, with bright blue eyes and big, blonde, 1980s-looking hair. She had started to grow tired of the divisions that had subsumed Berkeley Springs and was developing ideas about how to repair them.

Before I left the coffeehouse, I took a selfie with Tanya and said goodbye to David. I trotted down the stairs into the dropping temperature outside. I wore only my sweater, so I tucked my hands inside the sleeves to keep them warm. From my peripheral vision on the left, I saw it again. A moving shape. As I drew closer, I caught that the shape was a woman. She seemed to be young. She scrunched down behind the front right wheel of a car.

Was the woman photographing me? When she realized that I saw her she got up and ran across the street toward another human shape.

"The fuck are you doing?" I yelled at her in my best Queens–Long Island voice.

I watched as the woman scampered to a darkened shop with a tan awning: Mountain Laurel Artisans. I turned toward the Country Inn and laughed.

"The fuck is wrong with you people," I said to no one.

The next day, I met with a photographer hired by the SPLC. He was a tall, handsome young Black man—I'll call him Kevin. Kevin pulled me aside at the front of the inn. He looked alarmed. I tried to project some empathy.

"I'm gonna wear a mask. I don't want anybody to see my face. I don't even feel comfortable being *in* this town," he said.

"Okay," I said.

The urgency of his tone made me flinch.

"It's nothing against you or anything you're doing with the reporting, but I just don't like being here," he said. "I'm going to do the job, get whatever we need and then go. I don't want my name in the story."

"Of course," I said.

"Sorry," he said.

"Don't be sorry."

I had never considered how a Black person might feel about Berkeley Springs. It seemed obvious to me only after he said it. I resisted an impulse to defend the town and tell Kevin that it wasn't all that bad. But was that even true? Deep down, I wasn't sure anymore.

Kevin snapped his pictures in a face mask. He walked right up to the castle and took one there. He took portraits of Trey, Abby Chapple, and Lisa Swanson. Then, having finished, he left. He gave up a paid hotel stay that night.

David and his crew also left town, which was fine with me. I liked David, but I disliked always being filmed. From the inn, I pressed Trey about who she thought had been sneaking around outside of her shop.

"It's Charlie Curia," she told me over the phone.

Charlie Curia, the neighbor who had butted heads with Trey and Paul over expressions of Pride back in June 2020, had become an outsized presence in their lives. He was a topic of constant conversation as a result of the growing conflict over the underdeveloped biergarten space next to Fairfax Coffee House. I knew nothing about that yet. I had never even heard of him.

"Charlie? Charlie who again?" I asked.

"Charlie Curia."

"Who is he?"

I heard Paul behind Trey trying to interject a description. The two of them spoke over each other. What I pulled from it was that Charlie ran that Mountain Laurel Artisans shop on the corner of Fairfax Street, where the woman ran after I saw her. Charlie had recently unveiled a drawing of a swastika at a meeting for Travel Berkeley Springs, a group that worked to boost the travel industry in town.

At the meeting, a consultant was recommending new branding for Berkeley Springs to put some separation between liberal tourists and this rolling, negative story about the alleged white nationalist castle in town. The consultant suggested that the town use an image of a rainbow. That's the context in which Charlie reportedly whipped out his swastika drawing. It was apparently his go-to argument against Pride.

I called Charlie that Monday evening and he barked at me. He spoke critically of the SPLC, which didn't bother me. I told Charlie I found the whole scene on Fairfax Street that Sunday night a little too weird. I managed to keep him on the phone long enough to impress upon him my desire to understand him better. Charlie had someone trying to speak for him from behind. It was his partner, Sue Evans, the woman who, according to Trey, had called her an "abomination" at the biergarten meeting.

"I would like to hear your side of the story too," I announced.

Charlie told me to come to his shop the next day around midday. When I stepped into Mountain Laurel Artisans, I met Sue, a heavyset woman with silver hair, and then I met Charlie, who came out from the back of the store. A bald, portly guy with a silver goatee, as he moved around the shop he kind of dominated the space. I sensed that he had some adrenaline running through him.

Charlie started to talk about Trey and Paul and the legal action he'd taken against them. I listened to his story. What I didn't learn was that a judge had ruled to dissolve the biergarten project. And since the time that Charlie, or someone in his company, had removed the Pride flag, the two shops had devolved into a mess of combative legal maneuvers. Both sides had taken legal actions.

I pressed Charlie to tell me about his swastika. I said I wanted to include it in a story I was writing. He pulled out a folded-up piece of paper and handed it to me over a glass case containing crafts he had for sale. I saw a lot of text.

"I'll read it," I said. "What about the Brimelows?"

"What about them?"

"Have you ever met with them?"

"They're very nice people," he said. "Yes, I have."

"When did you meet them?"

"Around the Christmas holidays, last year," he said.

Charlie picked his chin up defiantly when talking about the Brimelows. He described a gathering in town where he had conversed with Peter.

"Are you bothered at all by any of the stuff Peter believes?" I asked.

"He's a journalist and a writer. Isn't that the same as what you're doing?"

I thought about answering the question and then thought better of it.

"Have you read his site?" I asked.

"He writes about immigration. Some people may disagree with it. But he's not a hate group like BLM and *antifa*," he said. "Or Pride."

"What about the great replacement stuff?"

"He writes about *immigration*," he said. "He's a journalist."

"Okay," I said, waving his paper. "I'm going to read this. Thank you very much. It's really nice to meet you."

Over a veggie burrito and iced tea at Mi Ranchito, I read Charlie's rant. He had written out five full paragraphs using around five hundred words about the swastika meeting. He described how he had drawn "a symbol" on the back of a piece of paper. It was absolutely true that a swastika was a symbol, no denying that. He said he had done it to object to their idea for a new decal to be displayed by businesses in Berkeley Springs.

Charlie noted that "the symbol," a swastika, "was also used as a symbol of evil during a relatively short time in history," but that he himself didn't mean it that way. He wrote that it had also meant "well-being, good fortune, and/or honor" in another context.

"I am using this symbol to show that symbols have different meanings to different people," he wrote. "It is my opinion that using the 'pride' flag colors exclusively on the new decal/sticker could potentially deter 97% of businesses, as from what I have read/seen, only 3% of the population identify with this symbology."

Charlie also wrote that he had heard people say negative things about the town after that first Pride event in 2021. He claimed that Pride was a "hate group," "similar to good old boys, antifa, BLM, etc." In conclusion, he wrote, "Hate has no place here in Berkeley Springs, and we should work towards eliminating the hate."

I ordered a refill of my iced tea and read it again.

The next morning, I wandered downstairs at the inn to eat French toast and found a young woman with dirty-blonde hair working the desk. She might have been a college student or just out of school. She was alone. No visible bosses.

"Hey, I'm in room 20," I said.

"How can I help you, sir?"

"I'm just curious about the people living in the castle," I said. "Do people here seem to be bothered by them at all?"

She leaned forward and dropped her voice.

"You mean the strange people on the hill?" she asked.

"Peter and Lydia Brimelow," I said.

"They come down here." She pointed to the restaurant area. "I've never talked to them. But they sometimes get large groups of people in there. I used to go up to the castle when I was a little girl, but I wouldn't go now."

"You're from here?" I asked.

She nodded and looked over her shoulder.

"Morgan County born and raised."

"Why don't you want to go to the castle now?" I asked.

"It's because of all the weird stuff people say is going on up there," she said.

"What are they doing that's so weird?"

"All kinds of weird stuff," she said. "But I actually don't know."

"Thanks," I said.

Abby Chapple, the older woman who worked at the museum, told me that a group of movement people had waltzed into her workplace one day. The museum was a small space, filled with little charts about the makeup of the healing water and the history of the baths. It was hard to avoid unwanted conversations there if someone chose to instigate them.

Abby said that a man with an English accent had leaned over the desk to ask, "Ma'am, are you a patriot?" and that she understood the word to be a euphemism for white nationalism.

"You think it was John Derbyshire?" I asked.

"I don't know who he is," Abby told me.

I showed her a photo from my phone, but she still wasn't sure.

Late that night, I walked along 522. Mist covered the street, dampening the swinging traffic lights on the corner of Fairfax Street and making the headlights refract off of the few lonely cars that whizzed past. Outside of the Star Theater, Trey and Paul kept the lights of the marquee running.

The Stranger played on two-buck Tuesday, but now everyone was gone. A vintage recording of "Puttin' on the Ritz" played from a speaker outside the theater to an audience of only me. On the misty, empty road, it gave Berkeley Springs a hallucinatory quality.

That Wednesday afternoon, I reserved a session at the Old Roman Bath House to sample those much-advertised healing properties. When I opened the door, my glasses fogged up so much that I accidentally walked into a bench. I cleaned them on my shirt and asked a woman named Kelly about the Brimelows.

Kelly told me she'd heard they were racist, and that they'd bought the place with cash. She said she lived in Maryland, just over the border, and drove to Berkeley Springs to work. I asked if the Brimelows came there to get baths.

"Not that I've ever seen."

Kelly asked if I liked my bath very hot and I said that I did. She brought me to a white, skinny room with steps leading down into a steaming pool and closed the door so that I was alone. I undressed and submerged myself.

The pulsing heat crawled up into my head. I closed my eyes, watching the insides of my eyelids projecting shades of red, purple, and navy. I convinced myself that the water was alleviating a pain in my shins and back. I never wanted to leave.

17

You Need to Apologize to My Wife

I met the Brimelows in person for the first time that December. The New York Young Republican Club, NYYRC, held its annual gala on Saturday, December 10 in Manhattan. The club advertised alt-right activist Jack Posobiec and Congresswoman Marjorie Taylor Greene as co-headliners. Although it wasn't the type of event the SPLC typically took on, it featured two rising MAGA celebrities with ties to the movement. I wanted to go.

My colleague Hannah Gais loved covering big events, and she was good at it, so she took the lead in plotting out how we would do it. If anyone from the NYYRC recognized who we were, they'd block our entry. So Hannah decided to buy tickets under her mother's name, Johnson, as in "Hannah Johnson." She said I would be Hannah Johnson's plus one. We were a married couple, the Johnsons. Mike Johnson and Hannah Johnson.

I suggested that if we got inside, we could hang back until the end of the gala. If we succeeded in getting to the end of the night, we could ask people questions. Hannah and I could then try to continue talking to guests until they extracted us from the event by physical force or threat of legal action.

We hashed out who would be there. Gavin Wax, the NYYRC's president, openly defended the Proud Boys. A doughy schmoozer-type, Wax's social scene was filled with Putin-apologists in bowties. His lieutenant,

Viswanag "Vish" Burra, served as the executive secretary. Burra stood out for being brown in a scene that mostly attracted white faces. Physically, he resembled a bulldog. He was a convicted former drug dealer.

The NYYRC boasted that Steve Bannon, Roger Stone, and Rudy Giuliani would attend. They bragged that representatives from Alternative for Germany, or AfD, and from the Austrian Freedom Party, FPÖ—founded by a former Nazi SS—would come too. Representatives from Hungary's Fidesz party also planned to attend, to the delight of this scene's many Viktor Orbán worshippers.

The NYYRC mentioned that newly elected members of Congress would come as well. One of them had won the district where my parents lived. When I looked him up, I read that he was an openly gay, Latino Republican who also claimed Jewish heritage. His name was George Santos.

On the night of the gala, I took an Amtrak train to New York from Philly, where I had just spent time with my sister. By coincidence, I sat ten seats behind Jack Posobiec and his wife. I had written over a dozen stories about Posobiec by then on his links to the movement and the lies he told in service of Trump's ambitions. I put on a mask and snapped a few pictures of them as I stepped off the train into Penn Station.

I walked to the Upper East Side and found Hannah watching *Point Break* in her hotel room. She drank cough syrup to fight back a cold. David France showed up to film us dressing up and I struggled with the buttons on my tux while he did. Then a driver took us to the edge of 583 Park, the huge, classy venue where the NYYRC was staging the gala.

Hannah and I took a breath before we walked in. Antifascist protesters booed us outside. Inside, Hannah and I found the name Hannah Johnson printed on a folded white card on a long table in a reception area. A young woman in a shiny dress staffing the table, nobody familiar, ignored us.

We grabbed the card and scrambled down the stairs into a big room with mirrors and lights. The space was nearly empty, and we snatched up some hors d'oeuvres and champagne to give ourselves something to do.

After we had spent a few minutes chatting up the bartenders, who seemed suspicious of the event and the people there, a happy-faced woman in her early thirties approached us to ask questions. She worked as a coordinator for the NYYRC, or something like that.

"So, are you members?" she asked.

"We just bought tickets," Hannah explained.

"Really?"

"We were interested in the speakers," I said.

"Are you interested in becoming members too?"

"Possibly," I lied.

She explained the benefits of becoming dues-paying members and asked us where we lived. I blurted out "Long Island." Hannah and I hadn't practiced much of our cover story and I'm not sure that we had picked a place to live.

"What do you guys do for a living?"

My eyes darted to Hannah's and back. I thought about it.

"We're journalists," I said.

"Who do you write for?"

I felt the weight of a heavy pause fill the space between us and then sit there. I knew I couldn't tell the truth. I thought about making something up but decided that I couldn't sustain the bullshitting that would follow without being exposed. I'm not a particularly gifted liar.

"It was really nice meeting you," Hannah told the woman.

We walked off. New people kept flowing down the stairs.

"Okay," I said. "So, you're my wife and I'm going to take pictures of you."

"Okay."

"I'm going to point the phone at you. Just let me take it over your shoulder."

I showed Hannah a picture I grabbed with my phone. The picture missed Hannah's right ear, grabbing the face of a guy standing behind her instead. I set up other photos of Hannah and then leaned to the left or right to capture more people's faces. I took pictures of almost everyone there that way.

Through the lens of my camera phone, I saw two heads hovering. The woman had to be a full head taller than the man, but I recognized him first because of his dramatic poof of white hair. It was them: Peter and Lydia Brimelow, blending in among the other paying attendees, bobbing and weaving. Yes, it was very obviously them.

Decades earlier, when Peter's ideas were still considered viable by *The National Review*, the NYYRC would have likely made Peter a VIP. And as I saw him chatting it up with guests, I suspected that he had fallen into some bad luck. Why did the NYYRC treat Jack Posobiec and members of ultranationalist European political parties as guests of honor, while herding Peter into the event space with the regular attendees? Were these figures really considered more respectable? More legitimate?

The NYYRC shuffled us into the main hall, and I lost sight of the Brimelows for about fifteen minutes. We were seated at random tables for dinner, and there they were again. Peter and Lydia Brimelow sat at a table in the center of the hall. Hannah and I watched as person after person approached Peter to talk. The Republican Party ignored Peter, but its activists didn't.

I wanted to get photos of the men who leaned over at Peter's table to talk to him, but I couldn't do it, because the hosts might have thrown me out if someone identified me. So Hannah and I sat at our table with some local Republicans, trying to keep from being seen.

Someone asked us about our wedding. Hannah and Tom had gotten married a few months earlier in Pittsburgh, and I'd been there, so we stole our details from that. No one seemed to notice how out of place we seemed. They were too fixated on war.

"We want to cross the Rubicon. We want total war. We must be prepared to do battle in every arena. In the media. In the courtroom. At the ballot box. And in the streets," Gavin Wax told the room when he spoke.

Wax looked like the kind of guy who would do the homework for lacrosse players in high school to avoid getting beaten up. Posobiec also spoke, delivering a cluster of platitudes. Donald Trump Jr. pumped out some clichés too. I had forgotten that he was there until he started speaking.

Later that night, I walked right up to Junior's table and took a picture of his long, hairy face. Up close, he had dull eyes and a foolish-looking grin. Everyone like this, every MAGA celebrity, smiled and hammed it up when I approached to take their pictures. To me, this posturing seemed expressive of their vanity. I think they assumed I was a fan.

Steve Bannon seemed different from the other MAGA celebrities. When I got close enough to take his picture, he smiled with an unfabricated confidence and joy. Everyone loved Bannon and everyone wanted to be near him. He never spoke on stage, but he always seemed to be at the center of the event, like a king.

When Marjorie Taylor Greene gave her keynote, I stood at the back of the room, outside the corner table where Posobiec sat with his wife. He was sitting across from Josh Hammer, who edited the *Newsweek* opinion section.

"I will tell you something. If Steve Bannon and I organized that, we would have won," Greene said of January 6. "Not to mention, it would've been armed."

I looked at Hannah from across the hall when Greene said this, because I understood the comment to be the kind of thing that would sound insane outside of the walls of the gala. People clapped for it. Then I noticed someone staring at me later on in Greene's speech. It was Tanya Tay, Posobiec's wife. It wasn't a good stare. She whispered something to her husband.

The first thing we did after the speeches broke up was follow the Brimelows. Now we could be bold and take a chance of getting tossed. We watched as Peter and Lydia waited in a line to speak with Bannon. I took pictures of them talking but couldn't hear anything they said over the din. It looked like they talked for a while.

When they finished, Hannah and I fell back to try to talk to them. Peter walked by first.

"Peter, it's Mike Hayden," I said. "We've exchanged some emails."

He smiled and replied with something semi-coherent through his accent. I thought I heard him say, "How's it going?"

It sounded like Peter had pebbles in his mouth. Lydia passed me next. She moved through the crowd looking like an elegant telephone pole.

"Lydia, Mike Hayden from SPLC," I said. "I just emailed you about the Bath Christmas Project in Berkeley Springs. I wanted to—"

Lydia's eyebrows sharpened into two sharp triangles. She soured up her lips.

"You've been hounding me!" she shouted.

After Lydia faded into the crowd, I dropped my head into a laugh—the kind of laugh that just hits you hard from nowhere. I don't know why it was so funny. Maybe because I had emailed her only one time and she referred to this behavior as "hounding." Maybe just because the entire thing was so surreal. Hannah and I started to feel a goofy high from the whole thing, like we were sixth graders who had snuck into a movie theater.

Next, we caught up with Josh Hammer of *Newsweek* and introduced ourselves. He was a rotund, hirsute guy who had an expression on his face like that of a child taking in Disney World. I told him directly that we were with the SPLC, but I guess his brain didn't process it, because the grin never faded from his face.

"Did you know that Peter Brimelow is here?" I asked him.

"He's right *here*, right now?" Hammer asked about the VDARE founder. "I'm going to say hi to him!"

You'd be forgiven for thinking I told Hammer that Martin Scorsese had shown up. He stopped short and asked again where we were from. I told him a second time that we worked for the SPLC. In fact, I had written a few stories about Hammer that year, and I had put pressure on *Newsweek* to look closely at him. Hammer's face dropped. His date said something insulting to me and they ran off. Hannah and I resumed laughing.

We moved over to Posobiec, who stood on stage next to Tanya Tay with a line of fanboys waiting to shake his hand. I noticed that he had a stray buzz mark on the side of his head where someone had botched his haircut.

Right before I got a chance to speak to him, Hammer ran up, red faced and out of breath, pointing at me and whispering a series of indecipherable words. Posobiec's body visibly tightened up when he saw me.

I had a bunch of questions for Posobiec, but every time I started to ask them he plowed through what I said and made the conversation about me. Among other things, Posobiec claimed that I had ruined his wedding to Tanya Tay because I'd reached out for a comment about a lie he promoted back in 2017, apparently while they were getting married. I had no memory of this event. Jack told a lot of lies.

"You need to apologize to my wife!" he shouted.

"No," I said.

Tanya Tay looked at me with the same dour face she'd made at her table. Of all the things I knew in this world, I knew that I wasn't going to apologize to Jack Posobiec's wife. The two of them had a conversation in a foreign language. She was from Belarus. I couldn't tell if they were speaking in Polish or Russian.

A crowd of people gathered around me when Posobiec started shouting. I knew someone would kick us out. Burra, the bulldog, volunteered. He grabbed me by the arm to drag me off the stage and out.

Burra barked nonsense into my ear across the length of the venue. He had foul-smelling breath and kept intimating that he wanted to fight.

When we left the venue, Hannah and I walked out to the anti-fascist protesters, who were sectioned off behind a police barricade. A policeman pushed me back, but I leaned past him and waved at a friend. When the protesters understood who we were, they cheered.

18

May You and Yours Get Everything You Deserve

Charlie Curia purchased the biergarten space at the end of 2022 through an auction. In a futile effort, Trey and Paul fought the decision to dissolve The Source but only wasted time and money. They dragged the spectacle of losing a property battle into the new year and beyond.

Geoffrey Wendel, the purple-clad wizard who ran Portals Metaphysical, turned on the Johansons over the course of the dispute. Once an ally who celebrated Trey's coffee, Geoffrey made it his mission to warn the town, and the metaphysical healing community, against the Johansons.

"I am really not fond of folk who are grifters.... [I]t does not matter to me what 'side' they are on," Geoffrey wrote of Trey and Paul on December 19, 2022, months after he started to hammer them publicly. "In the battle for the [biergarten] property, the grifters present as being progressive/antiracist/liberal stalwarts. They might dress-up/camouflage/identify as such...but this does not make them honorable or good people."

Geoffrey once held a small stake in the biergarten project, but by the time Charlie and Trey summoned lawyers, he no longer did. His displeasure seemed to relate to property lines being disrespected, rules about where and how and when workers could deliver propane to Fairfax

Coffee House, and where Trey could lawfully park her car. I read through his grievances and found them to be inscrutable. He ignored my email asking that he explain what exactly happened to make him feel that way about the Johansons.

Back on October 12, 2022, Geoffrey had shared legal documents from the dispute over the biergarten project on Facebook, urging Berkeley Springs residents to read them. And then, for the following twenty-two months, Geoffrey posted publicly about the Johansons on Facebook at least 136 times. Frequently, he imbued his posts with a withering tone.

Geoffrey's mockery of the Johansons made up nearly 75 percent of his Facebook writings across that span. He referred to the Johansons repeatedly as "The Fairfax Grifters." He also called them "The Fairfax Trespass League." He photoshopped Wile E. Coyote's head onto Paul's body in one post.

When the Johansons opened a new ice cream shop in town, called the Lazy Sundae, an effort to showcase Trey's ice-cream-making ability, Geoffrey labeled it "The Crazy Sundae." He told his neighbors that they would be crazy to eat there. He mocked the popcorn they popped at the Star Theater too. He posted a picture of microwavable popcorn and declared it favorable by comparison.

Trey claimed not to pay attention to Geoffrey's posts. She found him to be "not a very good wizard." But in a small town, everyone always heard about everything that was happening, and Facebook amplified everything nasty that everyone thought.

Trey's father jumped into a Facebook chain after Geoffrey, Barb Wolfe, and others publicly chastised his daughter.

"That is exactly what you have been doing to Trey," Trey's dad wrote. "Ganging up to crucify her with words, about a parking lot issue. I hope the Lord forgives you for this abhorrent behavior, because I would find it hard to do so."

Geoffrey responded.

"Enablers tend to defend their wayward children," he wrote. This was, he alleged, "not just a parking lot issue, sadly. Your ill raised daughter and son in law have broken court orders repeatedly, owe [Charlie Curia] thousands of dollars, and continue to be overall the sort of people who hide behind enablers like yourself. May you and yours get everything you deserve. And no others are harmed by your ilk."

Not content with leaving the comment in a place that would limit its visibility, Geoffrey screenshotted his "may you and yours" response. Then he posted the screenshot to his own Facebook feed and showed the world how he'd put Trey's dad in his place.

The Johansons told me that they'd lost money on the biergarten and owed no one. Curia stopped talking to me after I visited his shop, and he declined an opportunity to speak about the Johansons.

Trey's detractors didn't necessarily support Geoffrey during his feud. Some Christians believed that this wizard convened with Satan. The Brimelows held Geoffrey in particularly low esteem. Peter labeled Portals Metaphysical a "WITCHCRAFT STORE," in all caps, around the same time that Geoffrey told liberals he wouldn't spare the Johansons because of their politics.[1]

Berkeley Springs' reputation fell under scrutiny as the calendar turned toward a new year. First, defenders of local police, including the young man Bill who had hosted the first Black Lives Matter event in town, woke up feeling embarrassed after learning that, on December 3, members of the Morgan County Sheriff's Office had manhandled two Latino men who had been involved in an altercation at The Troubadour.

It was the same bar where a small group had met to follow up on the initial meeting about VDARE. Footage of the arrests circulated on TikTok before it became a story.[2] Local news covered the violent encounter both on TV and in print.

Then, a month later, on Wednesday morning, January 4, 2023, *The Washington Post* exacerbated the tensions in Berkeley Springs by publishing an article highlighting the town's now undeniable divisions. The biggest paper in the region published Ellie Silverman's "A 'Hate Castle' or Welcome Neighbor? VDare Divides a West Virginia Town" and placed it on the front page of its local section.[3] It was the most attention Morgan County had received in decades.

Around the start of 2022, Ellie had contacted me asking what she should write about on the radical right beat. It was common for reporters to dig for stories by asking for the SPLC's help. Ellie was courteous, and she sounded sincere about making an impact with her reporting, so I urged her to report on the local response to the castle. I pointed her in that direction hoping to bolster Trey and put some pressure on the Brimelows.

Influencing the media to care about what was happening in Berkeley Springs was something I'd promised Trey I'd do back in 2020. It played out with mixed results. *The Washington Post* ultimately did draw more attention to the struggle in Berkeley Springs, but it also made that struggle worse.

I had published two investigations myself by that point, including a longer one in December that covered the issues around the Bath Christmas Project. But a story from a national paper carried serious weight. It forced Peter to respond to questions, among other things.

Peter described the labels of "white supremacist" and "white nationalist," which the SPLC and others had ascribed to him, as being "devil words" in his responses to Ellie. I laughed when I read that. I thought that maybe Peter should ask a Black person whether those were devil words. They might agree from a different angle.

In her reporting for the piece, Ellie also spoke to Jeanne Mozier's sister, Barb Wolfe. "They are not white supremacists. They're anti-immigration. They don't like people just coming over the borders. There's a lot of people like that. Whatever they want to do, it's not my concern," Barb told Ellie.

The people in town who opposed VDARE recoiled at Barb's quote. One liberal told me, "I bet Jeanne would reach down from heaven to choke her." Barb had a reputation for being both simpler and more reactionary than her sister. I thought what Barb said was something that only a white person who had lived a long time only with other white people would say.

Disgusted with the poisonous vibe of the town, and ready for retirement, Barb closed her souvenir shop and moved to Florida not long after her quote went public. She continued to reply to Facebook discourse about the town after that, aligning herself with the reactionary, pro-castle crowd when she did. When I emailed her in 2024, she said she didn't want to talk to me and cited *The Washington Post* article as a reason why.

"I don't trust that (truthful) things I say will not be distorted as I have experienced in the past," Barb wrote in an email. She said that her experience talking with Ellie Silverman had made it clear to her "that 'journalists' cannot be trusted" to "print what was said."

Then she mentioned the lawsuits, saying that too many conversations had ended up in frivolous lawsuits, and that she did not want to be involved in them.

Liberals and queer people expressed shock when Ellie quoted Scott Collinash, the chef at the Country Inn who had led Berkeley Springs' first Pride celebration, weighing in about the Brimelows using a sympathetic tone. Scott called Lydia "a delightful woman" in the story.

"I'm sure they both know that I'm gay, and they have not said anything to me. They have caused me no trouble at all. And they have caused Berkeley Springs Pride no trouble at all either," Scott said.

When people asked Scott what he was thinking when he said such things, he claimed that Ellie had taken his quote out of context. But I had my doubts about that. What would the missing context be? If Lydia was delightful, she was delightful. So Scott would have to believe that Lydia was delightful either because of her racism or despite it. Some people never forgave Scott for saying that.

Around the same time Scott spoke to Ellie, Lydia joined a podcast as a guest and said something that didn't come across as "delightful" to her critics. She laid out her point of view about race in as succinct a way as a person could.

"Diversity is weakness," she declared, offering an inverse to the liberal platitude "Diversity is our strength."[4]

VDARE's operations showed signs of wear in 2023. Although I didn't know it, the New York Attorney General's Office had ramped up pressure on the Brimelows at this time, making life very stressful for Peter and Lydia Brimelow. In 2023, the Brimelows worked a balance between complying with the AG's demands for documentation and filing unsuccessful appeals to block the reach of this mysterious investigation. Specifically, Peter and Lydia wanted the real names of pseudonymous people linked to VDARE to remain unknown.

In April, they enlisted Marc Randazza, a lawyer who branded himself around free-speech issues and accepted clients from the movement. Randazza, a balding man with dark, deep-set, probing eyes and a scrunched-up face, had unsuccessfully represented the neo-Nazi Andrew Anglin of the Daily Stormer in the SPLC and Tanya Gersh's lawsuit against him. Randazza brought his history of ethics violations—which included soliciting bribes from porn sites—with him onto VDARE's increasingly expensive team.[5] VDARE's legal team started to look like a revolving door of oddball characters.

Amid the investigation, which seemed to center around the legality of VDARE's ownership of the Berkeley Springs Castle, the group wandered into some of the SPLC's reporting again. On May 6, a neo-Nazi named Mauricio Garcia gunned down a random collection of innocent people who had exited a mall in Allen, Texas, at the wrong time, killing nine and wounding seven. Peter's group used Twitter to stress that the killer was Latino, implying that his race had been a factor in the crime and that the mainstream media wanted to cover that fact up.[6]

But we discovered that Garcia was a VDARE reader, Latino or not. The killer even posted a link to one of VDARE's posts on a Russian social media site called Odnoklassniki. There were four of us on the byline, and I wrote my part from a Pittsburgh hotel across the street from where the death penalty trial of the Tree of Life killer was taking place. Grisly video in the morning, grisly video at night.

VDARE held its second conference in the aftermath of that shooting. And from what I saw, matters of cancellation and persecution were becoming more important to the Brimelows than immigration. They obsessed over what they saw as their maltreatment. It was as if they'd lost their core identity in Berkeley Springs and settled for a new one built on the notion that certain people who lived outside of the castle walls wanted to harm them.

Lydia spoke at the conference, and when she did, she wasted time talking about me and Hannah. We weren't even in Berkeley Springs or watching it live. A tipster sent me a video of the speech after the fact.

"It's easy to donate blood to the Red Cross. It takes a little more bravery to donate money to the VDARE Foundation," Lydia said, praising her donors. "And I get to see it every day. And that's something I will always be grateful for."

She smirked and leaned back from the podium.

"How could I keep from celebrating, *Michael Hayden*?" she taunted.[7]

In the warm-weather months of 2023, Trey told me that Supreme Court Justice Ketanji Brown Jackson had passed through town and stopped at her shop for coffee. It was a welcome distraction from the feud with Charlie Curia and Sue Evans, which had become too big to contain.

Charlie ran a Facebook page called "HLI, LLC," which purported to update people on the construction of the new, Johanson-free biergarten. But he and whoever else ran it spent almost as much time hashing out grievances with the proprietors of Fairfax Coffee House.

Sue Evans also opened a YouTube page to post security footage videos showing Paul and Trey doing various things as evidence of the liberal couple's nefariousness. Each time she posted footage of them, she wrote "Owner of Fairfax Coffee House and Star Theater" in the description. It looked like she was trying to drive down traffic to their businesses. Some of these videos managed to get over a thousand views, which was a high number for silent little snippets of a small town's drama.

In early May, Sue posted three YouTube videos to Facebook purporting to show the Johansons engaging in abusive behavior. In the first video, "Owner of Fairfax Coffee House and Star Theater Attempts to Run Woman over in Parking Lot," Paul pulls his silver pickup truck out from a parking area behind a cluster of shops. The truck slowly backs up, moving in Sue's general direction.[8]

Everyone knew Paul's truck because it popped up all around town. It was a quarter-century-old manual transmission Toyota Tacoma King Cab. Paul had acquired it in June 2000 because his previous truck, a 1978 Datsun, had died. It took him three years of working as a gardener to pay it off. Sue, who referred to herself in the title of the video as the "woman," sat in a chair at the perimeter of the parking area.

After backing up his truck, Paul turns the wheel and pulls forward; then he backs up again in a different direction and pulls forward out of the lot. The truck had hovered near Sue for about a second. She appeared to yell something at him. It ended.

In the second video, "Owner of Fairfax Coffee House and Star Theater Throwing Glass onto Neighbors['] Parking Lot," everything is dark. I faintly made out something being thrown without knowing what and by whom. Trey told me she'd had a glass of wine and, feeling like hell, took the wine glass around back and threw it.[9]

In the third video, Sue alleges that Trey moved a surveyor stick, although it's unclear to the viewer whether that actually happens.

"She seems rather satisfied with herself upon completing her work, does she not?" Sue wrote in the description. "Some people think they are above the law."[10]

These videos served as Rorschach tests for Berkeley Springs. If you felt sympathy for the Johansons, you probably believed that Sue was lying, or at least exaggerating, to defame them.

If you believed that the Johansons were thieves, grifters who rammed Pride branding no one asked for down everyone's throat, you probably saw a man deliberately pulling his truck close to a woman to intimidate her. You probably also thought the concerns about VDARE amounted to a bunch of hysterical shrieking.

On May 15, Sue Evans pushed her feud with the Johansons further into public view. HLI, LLC posted a video of a translucent brick embedded in the foundation of the biergarten space. Through the translucent exterior, it was clear that the Johansons had once stuck a happy-looking photo of themselves inside the brick. The idea would be that long after they were gone, their memory would live on inside of the structure of the building they left behind.

Sue seemed to dislike this idea.

"Okay," Sue says in a mocking, singsong tone. "Let's say goodbye to Paul and Trey."

Sue then pours what looks like caulk into the hole, smearing it all over their faces.

"For those of you who see this as petty, and uncalled for—you have not walked in my shoes the past five years. Sit down and have a conversation with me before you judge me," Sue wrote.[11]

Barb Wolfe responded in the comments.

"Bye bye bad energy," she wrote.

Charlie Curia delivered the ultimate humiliation to Trey and Paul later in 2023, when he painted over their love mural.[12] The love mural was that colorful artwork I'd noticed on the side of Fairfax Coffee House back in 2020. The image of the sun with creatures circling around words for love made an impression on Morgan County, and many people had grown fond of it, including some conservatives. Matthew Denton, a Martinsburg-based artist, had painted it. Nothing about the mural signaled an alliance with queer culture, other than perhaps the emphasis on universal love.

Charlie wanted it gone. As the weather in town grew chilly again, and the country settled in for another Trump-dominated election season, Charlie's crew started painting over the love mural on the side of Trey's shop, replacing it with a bland tan background dotted with patriotic-looking red, white, and blue banners and vintage lettering that proclaimed, "The Town of Bath: 1776."

"I hate to see the existing mural go away (I personally loved it) but am excited to see what you have in store for that wall and the space," a woman named Kathy wrote under a video that HLI, LLC posted of workers caking the love mural in a foundation that at first looked like big smears of gray.

Losing the mural devastated Trey, which I assumed was the point. Charlie must have known it would hurt Trey. They knew each other and understood what would hurt. The repainting of the mural dragged on over the course of weeks. Charlie's supporters, and the VDARE apologists, rejoiced over the symbolic liberal subjugation.

In another Facebook video, Charlie shared images of the completed repainting, including the detail about 1776. Denise Trent Selby, the woman who now worked at the castle for the Brimelows, crowed, "This new mural makes me HAPPY! We ARE the Town of Bath. We ARE in Berkeley Springs. We ARE in West Virginia. Just perfect and welcoming to our locals and our visitors from out of town!"

19

Friends and Enemies

Because Peter and Lydia Brimelow had made a surprise appearance alongside prominent Republicans at the event Hannah and I had attended that December night in Manhattan in 2022, when Jack Posobiec tried to make me apologize to his wife, our NYYRC story made a bigger impact than anything else the SPLC did around that time. The coverage culminated in me describing Posobiec and Marjorie Taylor Greene as the Korn and Limp Bizkit of the MAGA movement on Chris Hayes's MSNBC show. I also warned the audience about the civil war rhetoric.

"They're not talking about making your pocketbook more full, they're not talking about getting your kid health care, they're talking about separating the country between friends and enemies and punishing the people they perceive to be enemies," I said.

That moment became the last time my job felt tenable. Around the same time, I finally agreed to become a union steward, because I wanted to fight for better mental health care and because our shop was a dysfunctional mess. It was filled with angry workers who believed that the SPLC's management no longer wanted to fulfill the SPLC's mission. I knew very little about union-breaking tactics then, but I learned fast.

The shift started in January 2023, when I filed a grievance against our director for mishandling Hannah's security at an event that took place in November 2022. On the weekend before Thanksgiving, Hannah had trekked down to Burns, Tennessee, to report on the American Renaissance Conference, AmRen, a sister group to VDARE.

Run by Jared Taylor, AmRen featured Peter Brimelow and Kevin DeAnna, going by his other pseudonym, "Gregory Hood." AmRen also hosted Laura Loomer, the woman Lydia had awarded a maximum donation in her failed run for office.

Hannah embedded with anti-fascist protesters outside of the event and things got edgy. A group of Proud Boys, acting as muscle for AmRen, attacked. They later chased after a car that had Hannah in it. As this happened, our leaders at work were nearly absent.

The grievance succeeded because of the potential scandal that would befall the SPLC if an extremist killed Hannah. Then our union delivered a letter with about 80 percent of the bargaining unit signed on, calling for our human resources department to investigate our senior leadership. The SPLC reviewed our claims and put our director on what sounded to us like a performance improvement plan.

After that, the SPLC had apparently seen enough of me attempting to reform the shop. In February 2023, management issued a verbal warning about my tone in a meeting that had taken place an entire month prior to issuing the discipline. I had never received discipline before, and each of my performance reviews had been layered with praise. This warning had fabricated quotes in it. The fake quotes were too crazy a thing for me to accept. I was livid.

"They're lying about what I said," I told Esteban, the union steward. "They literally fabricated quotes."

"It doesn't matter, because they can't do anything with a verbal," Esteban told me. "They just want to scare you."

But the retaliation continued. A month later, my friend Luke O'Brien and I worked together on a story surrounding the trial of Douglass Mackey, a cause célèbre of the movement embraced by figures like Tucker Carlson. In 2016, Mackey, going by his alias "Ricky Vaughn," posted fake internet flyers hoping to get Black Hillary Clinton voters to text their votes to a fake number, essentially wasting them. Feds charged him with election interference, and the MAGA right portrayed him as a political prisoner of the Biden administration.

During jury selection for Mackey's trial, Andrew Frisch, his lawyer, the second guy who represented VDARE, pointed at me with his long finger suggesting that I had published biased reporting about his client. He shouted to the judge, "*This man!*" And I responded by putting my hand to my heart, shocked that I had offended him so greatly.

Luke found connections between an expert witness for Mackey's defense and the movement. More specifically, we had emails between this witness and VDARE's Kevin DeAnna. After Luke reached out for comment, Frisch pulled the witness, but Clare Locke, a high-powered defamation firm, sent the SPLC a legal threat. The SPLC responded that it wouldn't guarantee Luke any coverage in the event of a lawsuit. He could have been screwed in a defamation case without our support.

Rather than working it out with our legal team, as we had in past situations, the SPLC killed the story, caving to Clare Locke. Our director told us that the decision came from Margaret Huang. They chose not to let the DeAnna emails see the light of day. It was the exact type of story that the SPLC's donors expected us to publish, I thought, and running from it signaled an unwelcome shift in the SPLC management's attitude toward risk.

Faceless extremists resumed threatening me around the same time. A guy wrote to me from a burner phone telling me to watch my back. The combination of legal threats, physical threats, and a feeling that the SPLC no longer supported our investigative work built up a cloud in my head.

One morning in April, I had a panic attack in the shower and collapsed. Aadya had to fish me off the tiles, wet and nude. It must have been a pathetic sight. I had never had a panic attack before. Everything got very bright and very empty in the shower stall, and then I was looking up from the floor, absorbing the reality that my head had banged into something on the way down. The hot water hit me. I sniffled mist into my nose, which left a pinching sensation on the roof of my mouth.

In a meeting with our director, her boss, and the managing editor, I confessed to going through a tough time and having that panic attack. The SPLC responded to my confession by pulling me into an hour-and-a-half-long investigatory meeting, accusing me of trying to "compel" my bosses to give Luke a contract. It was Kafkaesque.

"They're just trying to bully you into quitting," Esteban told me.

"Well, unfortunately for them, I have two sons in elementary school to feed," I said.

I wanted to calm things down after that, but my colleagues continued to message me about their disenchantment with leadership. Drama erupted when the SPLC delayed the release of its annual "Year in Hate" report for nearly half a year. We were told this was done at the behest of Democratic lawmakers. The Dems apparently had said that if we held back the report, Nancy Abudu, an SPLC attorney, would be more likely to be confirmed as a judge on the Eleventh Circuit of the US Court of Appeals.

My colleagues admired Nancy, but not enough to shake off the impression that SPLC workers were now taking orders directly from the Democratic Party. The SPLC had partners at the local level who depended on these hate reports. If you were an activist from the queer community living in rural Florida, and the SPLC labeled a group creating problems in your area a hate group, you now had to wait to use that material in your fight, because the Dems felt the report was too controversial. Plus, the SPLC's direct cooperation with politicians raised serious ethical concerns for the reporters and editors working there.

Two people quit the SPLC's Intelligence Project around the time of this internal scandal. The SPLC then started to integrate paid mediators to smooth out the tensions with workers, but that only made things worse. The workers got much angrier and then signed on to an entirely new letter calling attention to worker dissatisfaction with the department's leadership. The environment was untenable and everyone knew it.

Over the summer of 2023, I traveled with Aadya and our sons to Heidelberg, Rome, and Delhi. At the end of the trip, Aadya and I separated again. We decided to share the house to make things as easy as possible for the kids. When we got back, I moved downstairs to the TV room. The foldout couch bothered my back, so I slept on the floor. Dr. K had me taking Zoloft to manage symptoms of depression. The medication destroyed my stomach, giving me daily gastrointestinal distress.

As the new school year rolled around, David France told me that he likely wouldn't complete his documentary, a result of his dealings with the SPLC's leadership. I was walking through the parking lot of a supermarket near my house when he said it, pacing around and getting air.

"A documentary about incompetence isn't very compelling, unfortunately," he said of our leaders.

"Yeah. Look, I get that," I said.

I had France's camera equipment in my home office sitting around doing nothing for over a year after that. In late September, I traveled to Gothenburg, Sweden, for a journalism conference with Hannah and my editor, Rachel Janik. It rained every day. At the end of it, Rachel and I took vacation time and went off to Copenhagen. Maybe for the first day in a year, not including some lucky moments with my kids, I felt happy.

We took a boat ride out on the harbor, and I watched Rachel, with her auburn hair, take in the setting sun, the factories, and the shoreline bars. The vessel rocked a little and the air had a pleasant chill to it. Whatever either of us had going on in our lives outside of that boat, we succeeded in leaving it onshore for a few hours.

I bummed a cigarette that night outside of a bar in Vesterbro and felt like life itself should just end right there. I felt like I should stub out the butt and that would be the end of everything, with the streetlights and phone screens just melting away into black space and stars, taking me with them. Of course, this didn't happen.

On Friday, October 6, I went to Brooklyn, and on the train ride home I spaced out on X. That's when I saw that Hamas had killed a bunch of people in Israel. It looked like a major attack on civilians, in addition to military personnel.

Egyptians on my mom's side had come from Palestine, and the issue was fraught for us. We actually had a Palestinian nationalist, or a resistance fighter, in our family. Terrorist, if you prefer. This surprised me when I first heard about it from my sister, because everyone I knew on my mother's side held moderate, bourgeois views. This man killed people. When police came looking for him, he hid in a crawl space.

As Israel started to mount a response, American culture locked into a tilted discourse around antisemitism and the devaluation of Arab life. The Anti-Defamation League, or ADL, which shared the field of extremism research with the SPLC, pushed a line that seemed to conflate empathy for the Palestinians and criticism of Israel with the kind of antisemitism embraced by the movement. It made me feel horrible about everything.

In reaction to that, the SPLC's union posted a statement to social media condemning genocide in Gaza. My only contribution was to add one line mentioning antisemitism. I felt like we couldn't do it without acknowledging that this was also happening. But it didn't matter. Conservatives portrayed the union statement as being terroristic. Pro-Israel donors threatened to pull their money from the SPLC.

In late October, Hannah passed me an open letter from various writers calling for a ceasefire in Gaza. The letter called Israel an "apartheid" state and described the country as being "ethno-nationalist." My freedom to sign it was protected by the SPLC's contract, so I signed. I felt like that would be my lone contribution to the Palestine discourse.

I had forgotten about the letter until November 4, when The Washington Free Beacon, a conservative website, published a post titled "Southern Poverty Law Center Spokesman Signed Letter Blaming Israel for Hamas Terrorism." Instead of using a picture of me, the post used an image of Hamas militants carrying heavy weaponry.[1]

I was out playing soccer in a field with my six-year-old son when I read it. I got so mad that my hand shook.

I emailed the author, and the website added a note. It said, "Hayden responded to the Free Beacon after publication, claiming that the article was a 'racist attempt' to target him. He said any 'attempt to conflate my concerns about Palestinian rights with supporting Hamas is cowardly and vile,' and added that he has 'made considerable sacrifices to undercut the activism of American antisemites.' "

Four days later, the SPLC dragged me into another investigatory meeting. This time, they issued a written warning, claiming that I had violated some vague protocol for spokespeople when I'd defended myself by stating that I wasn't Hamas and that I wasn't antisemitic. Again, the written warning featured provable inaccuracies, such as claiming that I hadn't sent emails that I had indeed sent, and portraying a June 2023 meeting—one that I had scheduled myself for purposes of clarification—as being disciplinary in nature.

When the union showed these mistakes to the SPLC, the org responded by coughing up a skeletal version of the same warning, this time focused narrowly on the fact that I'd tried to defend my reputation against the racist article. Of course, it had little to do with our contract and everything to do with silencing speech about Gaza. Maybe I had alienated a wealthy donor. Maybe I had angered the ADL. Whatever it was, I believe both parties knew it, but the SPLC's leaders still had to go through this charade, pretending to justify the discipline with different words, because they knew they couldn't talk about what they were doing out loud. They were a civil rights group, after all.

One of the SPLC's stewards pointed out that they had disciplined me, an Arab American, but hadn't disciplined Hannah, a woman with Jewish heritage. The steward said this was a violation of Title VII of the 1964 Civil Rights Act, the act's section on employment discrimination. I didn't know what to make of that at first. Hannah called me and told me the same thing. Another steward told me to file a complaint with the National Labor Relations Board about the ongoing retaliation.

In a trance, I did everything everyone told me to do. I called the Arab American Institute for help. They recommended lawyers. I called the American Civil Liberties Union. The ACLU's lawyers very badly wanted to take the case on and go after the SPLC, but they encountered conflicts of interest with our legal team. The ACLU recommended an outside lawyer and wished me luck. I ended up speaking to six lawyers in a week.

In November, some of the members of SPLC's leadership team were out of the office, and a longtime SPLC researcher, let's call him Andy, co-led an online meeting in their place. I considered him a good friend.

Andy boasted in the meeting that the SPLC hadn't lashed out at workers who spoke out about Gaza. I corrected him in the chat. I said this was happening to *me* right then, at that moment. Andy said nothing. He actually shut the meeting down after I wrote it, as if he were trying to stop me from telling people about what had happened. I never felt as alone as I did after the meeting blinked off my screen. I closed my laptop and put my head down on it. I lay like that for an hour.

20

Room-Temperature Vodka

On Friday, December 8, 2023, I drove a silver Kia Soul down to West Virginia. The Berkeley Springs Castle Foundation had advertised an event called "Christmas at the Castle" that night. It was a toothpick food and cocktails type thing. The ads didn't mention who owned the castle or what they believed in.

I had just started sketching out this book and I wanted to know what the castle looked like on the inside. When I told Hannah about it, she got annoyed that I was planning to go alone.

"I wanna go too," she said.

It takes a very particular person to feel left out on a trip like this.

"Okay," I said.

I figured we would freelance a little story to help cover the cost of Hannah's travel, since the trip had no direct relationship to her job. We planned to pull the same act that we did at the NYYRC gala. She bought tickets as Hannah Johnson, and if anyone asked, I was her plus one and husband, Mike Johnson.

We grabbed rooms at an Airbnb above the Lazy Sundae, Trey's ice cream shop. It was across the street from the 7-Eleven and a funeral home. I climbed into a sweater. We stepped out into the frigid air along Route 522 and turned left toward the park.

Even on a Friday night, we encountered nothing but silence. From the park below, the castle glowed white. It looked celestial. An illuminated inflatable cartoon dragon rippled against a battlement on the castle's northeastern side.

I took out my phone to call Trey. I hadn't mentioned we were coming, because I didn't want to get caught. Trey said to call Paul because she was out of town. I called him.

"Where are you?" he asked.

"At the park, basically."

"Oh wow, already there. Okay."

"So, the main thing is if something weird happens with the police or anything, can I give you a call?"

"Of course," he said. "I'm right here."

"Thanks, Paul."

Hannah and I walked up the hill and through a wooded area before popping up on Route 9 in front of the gates. Someone sat there in a dark SUV. Hannah passed along our information to whoever was inside it. We walked up to the castle's grand doors and went in.

Oversized, ornamental silver presents sat on a table at the center of the foyer. Hannah and I put our coats in an alcove decorated with a knight's suit of armor. Next to the alcove, a grand fireplace propped up candles and glittery cut-out angels.

A massive tree reached the high ceiling of the foyer beside it. White lights, translucent white ribbons, and a glowing angel adorned the tree. A matching wreath hung above the fireplace. Hidden speakers played Bing Crosby's "Do You Hear What I Hear?"

As we had done at the NYYRC event, Hannah and I decided to maximize our time before getting thrown out. But I saw no Brimelows. I mentioned to Hannah the possibility that they might not even show up. We grabbed champagne and moved through the space.

The people talking around us didn't seem like active VDARE readers. I assumed they were probably Republicans. Maybe some of them had heard about some controversy around the castle but tuned it out. We picked up a few appetizers from an adjoining room with a long, opulently laid table and then headed up a red carpeted staircase that split the big stone walls of the foyer.

On the next floor, we found a pristine phonograph next to a painting of green hills and a white sky. They also had a print of the Karl Ludwig Friedrich Becker painting *Othello Tells His Story to Desdemona*. It showed Othello in front of a row of columns, his Black skin draped in Renaissance garb, gesticulating as he speaks to an older white man and a young white woman who is demurely peering up at him.

We walked down the halls and found a few untouched bedrooms. They looked like part of a fancy hotel. Then we ducked into another room with a Christmas tree. It was empty and we hung out there for a minute to take a break.

When we moved on to the next room, we found that it was a scullery. There were no Christmas decorations in it, just framed pictures of Civil War generals. General Robert E. Lee was there. So was Stonewall Jackson. They also had a portrait of General Ulysses S. Grant. I wondered whether the Brimelows had put them up or the room came that way.

Hannah and I jumped up another small flight of stairs and stumbled into the room where VDARE held its conferences. At the center, we found the dais marked with VDARE's circular emblem, an outline of a white doe surrounded by blackness. Behind it was an oil painting and what looked like Chinese sculptures of white, red, and black guard dogs. I found it bizarre that they had left the room accessible.

"Let me take your picture," I said to Hannah.

Hannah posed and then took my picture next. I opened my palms in a shrug at the dais when she snapped it. From that angle, I was looking at a giant illuminated wreath and VDARE's conference tables. There were only a couple dozen chairs.

Next to the conference area, facing west, I saw two doors. Someone had put up signs telling people not to access them, and I wondered if people lived there.

We exited through a door on the eastern side of the room, stepping into the cold. We took selfies with the illuminated battlements behind us. I looked down on the silent town from there. Traffic lights were changing colors, but there was no traffic.

When we went back inside, some other people had come into the conference room, and Hannah volunteered to take pictures of a couple who wanted a photo of themselves standing in front of the wreath. Then we walked back downstairs and got new drinks. We sat down together along a plush loveseat at the back of the foyer.

I contemplated interviewing the people milling around and then making an abrupt exit. The trip wasn't wasted. I had seen the castle. But then the doors opened, the wind and cold air blew in, and Peter and Lydia stepped forward with their three daughters.

The bench Hannah and I were sitting on angled along the stone walls in a way that obscured our faces from most of the room. We turned our heads to the side and looked at our phones so it would be harder to notice us. The Brimelows talked about the weather when they came in, and some people walked over to be closer to them.

I was about to suggest to Hannah that we make a move back up the stairs when Peter walked directly toward me. Dressed in a brown corduroy blazer and matching pants, he came closer and closer and then marched past me. Behind my back, Peter fiddled with something and muttered to himself. Hannah and I shared a glance.

Peter returned and hovered in front of us. He looked directly at us.

"I need to turn the heat on," he said in his gravelly British accent.

He left. Someone pulled Lydia into a conversation, occupying her, so Hannah and I got up from where we sat and moved back to the table with the hors d'oeuvres. Two of Brimelow's daughters, the older ones, dressed in plaid and white, were thumbing through a book that had pictures in it. Hannah and I communicated only with our eyes. We saw an opening, headed back up the stairs, and found an empty space in the room with the second Christmas tree.

"I gotta talk to them," I said.

"Once you do they're gonna throw us out," Hannah said.

"What's left to do here?"

"Up to you. It's your book."

We walked back over to the top of the stairs, near *Othello Tells His Story to Desdemona* and the phonograph. There were a few guests wandering around. I composed myself before approaching.

Before I could descend the stairs again, the Brimelows' youngest daughter bounded up to them, radiating the kind of energy kids get when they're at an adult function after bedtime. The girl said a few things to me and Hannah. She spoke like a child unfrozen from the 1840s.

"How is it living in a castle?" I heard myself asking, amid her monologue.

"Oh, it's wonderful. And, there's a dungeon!" she said.

The Brimelow girl detailed the time she'd visited the dungeon. My gaze hung over her shoulder, on her parents, who were chatting with someone in the center of the foyer. I decided to end the conversation and started moving down those carpeted stairs. I took no more than two steps before Lydia looked up at me.

I saw the stages of Lydia's recognition in what felt like slow motion. First, her eyes opened in shock. Then, her brows furrowed. Her frown sucked in to cover a row of teeth that clenched visibly beneath the curtain of her lips.

Lydia led Peter into a private conversation, presumably warning him about our infiltration. I saw Peter straining to look for where we were. His general cluelessness was almost charming. Hannah and I went to the bar and I got another drink while the Brimelows talked. When I got my drink, I turned around to approach them. Hannah flanked me.

Lydia stared at me like she wanted to jab a stake into my heart. She closed her eyelids around her dark irises and held them that way, letting them twitch with contempt.

"Hey Peter, how are you doing?" I said.

"No pictures of the children," Peter said quietly.

Hannah and I erupted with crisscrossing expressions of "no" and "of course not" and "we would never do that."

"No pictures of the children," he said again.

"You had your phone out, and if you took pictures of my kids . . . ," Lydia said.

"I wouldn't do that," I said.

"*You* would do whatever you can," Lydia said, raising her voice.

"I would not, I would not," I said. "I'm not even here on behalf of SPLC."

"What are you here on behalf of?" Lydia asked.

"I'm writing a book," I said, trying to project a little defiance.

"About what?"

"About the *town*."

"Not about us?" Lydia asked.

"Well, you're part of the town," I said.

I told them they had a wonderful home, referring to the castle. I thought it was the thing to say at that moment. Lydia leaned forward, towering over her husband.

"It's not our *home*," she said. "It's our office."

I wanted to ask about the doors that they'd roped off adjacent to the conference room but I thought better of it.

"I mean, you've spent nights here, right?" I asked.

"It's not our *home*," Lydia repeated. "That is a very important distinction. We have a house with our family, which is not this house."

I told Peter that I wanted to interview him. He told me to send an email. Then he looked at Hannah directly.

"What's wrong with room temperature vodka?" he blurted out.

For years, Hannah and I had made watching VDARE's holiday fundraising livestream an annual tradition. We would inevitably post screenshots and videos to Twitter and poke fun. In one of them, Hannah had mocked Peter for drinking room temperature Tito's vodka. We laughed at Peter's joke. At that moment, it felt like a peace offering.

"As a Slavophile, I simply think it should be cold," Hannah said.

When I laughed about the vodka, I involuntarily put my hand onto Peter's left shoulder, as you would do to a friend. After I realized what I had done, I drew my hand away. I watched Peter's eyes monitor the movement of my hand as it left him. I continued to feel the corduroy of his jacket on my fingers long after touching it.

"You traveled all the way here? For this?" Peter asked, his tone shifting to one of displeasure.

Lydia leaned forward in my direction.

"As soon as you come into town, I get a string of text messages," she said.

"Well," I said and stopped short.

"And I get recordings of your meetings."

I searched myself for what she might be talking about. I remembered the night with Tanya Gersh and her comments about maggots.

"Well, it was certainly nice to meet you finally—," I started.

"These people are *normies*," Peter said in a low voice, putting emphasis on the word "normies."

His eyes flitted to either side, referring to the people there. "Normies" had a particular connotation in the movement. He meant that they were people who had no connection to radical politics. Hannah and I were not considered normies because we were perceived to be in the fight—in the "cold civil war."

"No, we're not—," I said, starting to explain that I wasn't writing about the guests.

"And unblock me on Twitter," Peter said.

I squinted at him after he made the comment and then looked at Lydia, who continued to watch me intently. It caught me off guard because of how stupid it sounded coming from Peter's mouth.

"I don't want to get in any public back and forth," I said.

"Then why do you attack?" Lydia asked.

"I don't attack," I said. "I never attack."

"You're writing a book called the *Strange People on the Hill*, what do you call that?"

"It's from a quote," I said.

"It really should be called Strange People in the *Castle*," Lydia said.

Her youngest daughter arrived at her side. She looked at Hannah and me like we were her new best friends.

"That's not bad, but again, it's from a quote," I said and forced a smile.

"It's disingenuous to say that you don't want to get into a back and forth, so you're going to *mock*," she said.

"Well—"

Peter raised his hand.

"This is enough," he said. "Merry Christmas."

"Merry Christmas to you," I said.

The energy shifted from a pantomime of collegiality to something harsher, darker, and colder than the air outside. When we picked up our coats, someone who wasn't the Brimelows followed us to make sure we left. He was an older middle-aged man wearing black fleece. As we stepped into the cold air, he looked down on us from the big doors.

"You're not welcome here," he said.

Hannah and I walked the long driveway to the gates. They were closed. It might not have been more than a minute but it felt like half an hour before someone opened them for us. We crossed Route 9 and hiked down the hill to the park. The only place still serving food was a bar on 522 called the Naked Olive.

"These people are *normies*," I said to Hannah, imitating Peter's voice.

21

The Billion-Year Plan

Peter fired off a tweet that night—Friday, December 8, 2023—around 11:30 p.m.

"So SPLC enforcers Michael Edison Hayden and Hannah Gais used fake names to infiltrate a community Christmas charity fundraiser at the Castle and creeped on our children."

In a second tweet, he added, "This is the creep who interrogated my eight-year-old," and he linked to that VDARE post with photos and descriptions of my family.[1]

Jason Kessler, the guy who had authored that previous post, replied in the comments.

"Explore your legal options with an attorney," he wrote. "Restraining order at the very least. Then write about it."

Hannah and I filed a dispatch for the Daily Beast about the Christmas party. We described Peter and Lydia as looking like "Boris and Natasha" in it. As soon as the dispatch was published, the SPLC interrogated us separately over Peter's accusation.[2]

"You didn't interrogate his children?"

"Obviously not."

"So, did you interact with his child?"

"The girl approached us on the stairs. We obviously didn't want to talk to her. Obviously not. Men like Peter say stuff to make it seem like you did something bad when you did nothing. I myself have two sons in elementary school, okay? Right?"

Emails fired back and forth on the night of December 14. Aadya and I went to Barclays Center to see Madonna. It was a bizarre separated "friend" date. The next morning, I was supposed to head back to West Virginia for more research, but as I packed my bag, I got an email from the SPLC, disallowing me from going.

"Aren't you using vacation time?" Aadya asked.

"Yes."

"And they're saying where you can travel on your own vacation now?"

"That's right."

"They can't do that," she said.

"Well, they are."

Esteban explained in a phone call that the SPLC wanted to get me on insubordination. They needed to catch me disobeying an order, because they would lose in arbitration if they fired me with no discernible grounds for doing so. He said to cancel my trip. I said I wouldn't because it was too unjust.

The SPLC could only find out that I went to West Virginia in three ways. One way would be if they tracked my laptop or work phone. This was technically possible, so I left those devices behind in New York. Another way was if someone snitched. I only told Hannah, Rachel Janik, and Esteban that I was going. I told everyone else I was visiting my uncle Raji in Fort Lauderdale. The final way was if anyone from the movement recognized me and posted about it on social media.

I rearranged my trip to avoid detection. I switched to an Airbnb in Martinsburg, the city forty minutes over, in Berkeley County, on West Virginia's northeastern side. I could hover near the town, and then at night sleep outside of it. Later, I would stay at Trey and Paul's. I trusted them to keep a secret.

Late at night on December 15, I pulled another rented RAV4 into a housing complex. Peanut M&Ms spilled out of my car and rattled against the black pavement of the parking lot when I grabbed my bag. Martinsburg was frozen solid.

My rented room was the basement of a duplex in a cookie-cutter housing complex. The owner had set up a security system, and the cameras and lights made loud whirring sounds as I approached. When I got inside, I called Hannah to complain. I sat on the edge of the hard bed and dropped my head into my hands. My voice was scratchy.

"I'm really not feeling so good, Hannah," I said.

"You'll be okay, I think. I *think*," she said.

Everyone told me they thought I would be okay. Then they'd qualify it by adding "I *think*." I hadn't eaten anything but the M&Ms. I searched for places where I could get some food. I found the roadside strip club called Lust, the place that sometimes hosted "Dwarf Toss." The menu featured alligator meat. It was next to the Airbnb, and I figured I could stop by and learn something about the meaning of life.

Lust had a white plastic Christmas tree at the back of its illuminated dancing stages and drunk men stumbled around it, ripe to have their wallets drained. Gaudy pink and teal neon shot across the mirrors that reflected the dancers. In between dances, the DJ played a snippet of Kid Rock's MAGA anthem, "Don't Tell Me How to Live," as transitional music. A man would announce "Give it up for Candy!" and then the guitars would kick in and Kid Rock would rap for a bar or two, on repeat.

I sat down at the bar and ordered a giant buttery pretzel from a glowering woman. The Knicks were playing the Suns on West Coast time. Jalen Brunson scored 50. One of the dancers asked me for some of my pretzel discreetly. She reached out a soft hand from the shadows and I gave her half of it. She ate it and then reached out for napkins with her neon yellow manicured fingers.

My second Jack Daniels and Coke arrived in front of me with a hair in it. That was my limit. I got up to leave without either finishing my half of the pretzel or complaining. There was no dwarf toss that night. Such a sight would have left me feeling worse.

The next morning, I bought a West Virginia University hoodie from Walmart, along with a matching hat. It was not a disguise so much as camouflage to make someone less likely to look closely at me on the street.

I drove to the nearby Cracker Barrel to get some French toast. Depression physically seeped into my stomach. I had to chew Pepto Bismol tablets just to get through the meal. In the men's room of the Cracker Barrel, I noticed that someone had carved the letters "RWDS" into my stall. RWDS meant Right Wing Death Squads. It was a movement-centric meme focused on extrajudicial violence, anticipating a day in a fascist America where vigilantes would slaughter opponents of the movement in their homes. I took a photo of the RWDS graffiti.

I drove into Berkeley Springs and then out to Prospect Overlook, that view of West Virginia, Pennsylvania, and Maryland across the Potomac, flanked by the B&O Railroad line. I killed the engine and waited ten minutes in silence for a call from a lawyer. The view had seduced me when I'd first seen it back in 2020, and it was still one of the most beautiful things I had ever seen. Now I wanted it to swallow me. I wanted to die right there and let my body fall into the river below.

After the call, I drove down to the Brimelows' church. The parish hosted a midweek event there, and the few people who attended were leaving as I came in. I went through the motions of a prayer, touching the holy water and genuflecting.

Father Michael Lecias, the Brimelows' Filipino priest, walked along the hallway behind the basins of holy water.

"Hey, how are you, Father?"

"Good, how are you?"

"Good, I'm actually writing a book," I said. "And that's why I wanted to talk to you."

"About here? You're visiting?"

"Yeah, about here."

"Okay," he said. "You're writing... good things?"

He said it in a way that immediately felt loaded.

"Well, I really love it here," I said. "So, did you recall any, uh . . . conflict over the Brimelows? I heard they had a security detail or something for them."

He squinted. "No conflict," he said coldly.

"I know there was like, um—"

"Nothing. Thank you."

The priest dipped into his office. The story I wanted to follow up on was that armed security had allegedly started attending Mass every week to protect the Brimelows. If this happened, it may have started after Lisa Marie, the trans woman who farmed mushrooms in her holler, said "Black Lives Matter" to Lydia at Mass that day back in December 2021. Lisa Marie and others told me that a local chapter of the Knights of Columbus provided the help.

I realized that I'd taken the exact type of risk I'd told myself not to take. Now this priest could call the Brimelows and that could be it for me.

The next day, I woke up having only slept two hours. It felt like I had sand in my eyes. I drove an hour to Harpers Ferry in that condition.

Kevin DeAnna supposedly had a place out in Harpers Ferry, but I wasn't going to go looking for him. So did Cassandra Fairbanks, a reactionary known mostly for pushing a Russian line, tweeting out objectively stupid, racist things, and dressing her pet monkeys in little baby clothes. I hiked around the trails and watched the freight trains rumbling over the bridge. I took in the site of John Brown's raid.

I raced back to Berkeley Springs, wrapped in my college clothing, and barely made my appointment at the Roman Baths on time. There, I held my head under the scalding water and kept it under there. I waited to see how long I could hold it until I popped up to breathe. When I got out of the bath, my mother called me.

"What's wrong with your voice?" she asked.

"What's wrong with it?"

"You sound sick."

"Oh? I didn't notice, Mom."

"I'm praying for you," she said. "God will protect you."

On December 18, I pulled up a long, steep hill into a wooded area where Paul Johanson had built his house by hand. My voice had almost completely atrophied for reasons beyond my understanding. The air around Trey and Paul's house felt crisp and clean in the cold. I showed up with a bottle of wine I'd bought at a restaurant in Martinsburg.

I did whatever I could to make my outside look better than I felt inside before I stepped into the house. Trey and Paul hugged me and made me feel important. When I told them what had happened to me, they expressed shock.

"Well, no one will know you're here," Trey promised.

Trey showed me the trees that Paul had built through the center of the house, the wine bottles he'd built into the walls, and the sauna they'd installed in the basement, which had what looked like a crash test dummy inside of it. She introduced me to her old cat, Violet, and an old dog named Charlotte. She showed me the old-fashioned wood-fired furnace and how she filled it with firewood, and said the warmth would travel up to the top floor, where I would be sleeping.

"I was in the buckle of the Bible Belt," said Trey, speaking about her childhood. "I was outed for being a Jew. I'm little. Like I'm a small woman—I was a little shrimpy kid! I remember being in the cafeteria and I had just moved to this new school and I just made this new friend. And then she finds out I'm Jewish."

Trey looked up at me from a crouched position on the cold floor, holding the wood. Her blue eyes widened as she told her story.

"And she comes up to me and says, 'Oh my God, you're going to hell! You must accept Jesus Christ as your savior!' I didn't know what to do. I had never experienced that before," she said.

"Right," I said.

Trey pointed to her eyes.

"Well, look at these blues," she said. "Remember, I have a Swedish dad. I could pass. Which as an adult I felt some shame about. But as a kid I'm just being a kid. I'm just trying to get by."

"Sure, I know what's up too, because, like, I have my Arab background, which has only gotten me into trouble recently. But my name is Hayden. And I similarly have light eyes. Green eyes, I guess."

"Right, right," she said. "And then there is also—and I didn't talk about this until I'm old—I'm also queer."

"Oh really," I said. "I'm bisexual."

"I didn't know," she said. "Because frankly it's nobody's business."

"Right, no—"

I coughed while trying to pull more sound from my failing throat.

"Because I was always like this is nobody's business," Trey said. "I'm not part of this fight. Several years ago, this young person comes to the coffee shop. I'm probably gonna cry now because I can still think of this person. Hey, I'm looking for a job, blah, blah, blah. We're doing an ordinary interview."

Trey got choked up, as she said she would. She physically swallowed down some of the feeling as she spoke.

"Because I met this person as Vincent. But this person says, 'If my parents come into the coffeehouse, could I, like, hide in the back? Because they don't know I go by Vincent.' And we had just bought the Star Theater. And we were hosting a drag show in the summer. COVID had just started."

Trey took a breath to reset and then finished the story.

"And that's when I came out to the public as bisexual. Because this kid needed to know that they weren't alone and that there are adults who understand them," she said.

"And it's a big deal," I said. "In a red state and everything."

"It's a very big deal," she said.

That night, we drank the wine I brought. We finished it and then we dipped into another bottle. Their yellow cat, Violet, climbed all over the tables and countertop. I asked the Johansons if they worried about people harming them because of everything that was happening with VDARE—not through legal actions or on social media but physically. Trey told me they had a crawl space. Paul mentioned he had a shotgun. Despite these things, the Johansons didn't even lock their doors.

During our long night of talking, we deemed Lisa Swanson to be a safe person for me to hang out with at this moment. The dark-haired Scandinavian American passionately supported the labor movement and could be trusted with secrets. Lisa and I went hiking the next day in a place where no one would see me.

Nearly two decades older, Lisa outpaced me. She told me all about how she and her husband had bought their place when it was the remnants of a meth lab. Their relationship fell apart and she stayed in the refurbished building alone, sorting out her feelings about living in Berkeley Springs.

Later in the afternoon, I followed Trey around the house and continued to record her thoughts.

"I keep asking myself, what is wrong with our species? We supposedly have consciousness," she said.

"Maybe we're not meant to last," I rasped.

"And then there's the billion-year plan. Our sun will die. Ordinary. Very ordinary. Right? I have a friend I hope you'll meet one day, Reverend Bob Emerick. He thinks on that scale. And he believes that what humans must learn is *well-being* love," she said.

I tried to think about the sun dying but couldn't get a handle on it. It sounded bad.

"We need to care for the *well-being* of all humans," Trey continued. "Because we don't know who that one human being will be that will take us closer to being able to escape our solar system, when our sun dies. His thinking is so... broadly universal. What are we doing if we really are supposed to be working toward the survival of our species?"

Trey eyed Violet. The blonde animal walked precariously along the counter where Trey made tea and coffee.

"Like my cat," she said. "Violet's good with her survival of *her* species-thing."

The next day, Trey drove me out to Paw Paw, through the winding roads along Route 9 that crisscrossed over river water. Dan, a historian who had attended my 2022 talk, had begun restoring a Gothic Revival Catholic Church there.

"I think geographically, the fact that West Virginia is largely these hollers and hills keeps families, kin tribes, extended families, whatever you want to call them, pretty isolated from one another," Trey said as she drove. "So, there's a cultural sense of mistrust of the outsider, mistrust of the other, that comes naturally from living in this geography."

Paw Paw had very little to it that I saw, just a Liberty gas station, a corresponding convenience store, and a Dollar General. But right in the middle of those businesses, Dan showed us this beautiful church, which builders first erected in 1876.

The guts of the place were in disarray, and Dan and another man moved from room to room showing us what they intended to fix and how. Dan talked about Paw Paw's unlikely antiracist past. A Black school was set up behind the church in 1928 and the students intermixed with whites who lived there. Paw Paw residents once ran a man out of town because he refused to release his slaves.

Trey drove me back thirty minutes into town to show me the inside of the Star Theater, pointing out where Paul had worked to restore its ceiling and the popcorn machine, which was built in 1949.

"The popcorn isn't from 1949," Trey assured me.

Trey showed me a gorgeous pianola up near the stage, and an original Star Wars poster in the men's room that had been donated. She poured me soda from the concession stand and showed me the racks of candy boxes in storage.

"When I came to Berkeley Springs, I wanted to be just a positive member of the community. I wanted to make friends. I wanted to be a good neighbor," Trey confessed. "And I didn't realize I was part of a group of people you could accuse of trying to change the culture of Berkeley Springs. That was *not* my intention. I was more naive about how radical my behavior would be perceived."

From the Star, I walked with the UWV cap over my eyes and tucked myself inside for yet another appointment at the Roman Baths. It was their last shift of the day. What happened next came upon me without warning, but only because of how deeply I had fallen into denial about the deterioration of my mental health.

I stood in the heat and steam and immediately felt lightheaded. My heart hammered in my chest. I saw spots in my vision. Very clearly, I imagined slamming my head full force onto the sharp corner of the bath. I would arch my head back, gather my full strength, and then bash my head at the maximum possible speed.

Given that I already felt lightheaded, I could surely knock myself out, if I didn't kill myself on impact. I just needed to bash my head as hard as I could against the corner of the bath. Then, I'd drown.

The bad thoughts came naturally to me and it was pleasurable not to repress them. I let myself think them, imagining the blood pouring into the pool as I floated.

Then I thought about my sons and I felt perverse and selfish. I wanted someone to give me permission to be selfish. I wanted someone to say to me that everything would be okay if I died.

I sat in the bath until someone knocked on the door to say my time was up. Then I left, walking out into the freezing cold with my body temperature still hot.

In a trance, I returned to Trey's place to interview a young historian, Zach Salman. The erosion of my voice had become so pronounced that I struggled to be understood. As Zach spoke, my mind flashed to what had happened in the bath and I had to pinch myself in the thigh to keep my mind focused on work.

"It was kind of a resort town from the beginning. It's hard to put a date on when Berkeley Springs drew the attention of the elite from DC and Baltimore, but the word was already out about it from the founding of the country," Salman explained.

That night, I decided I needed to switch my brain off and relax, but it was impossible. I drove all the way back to Martinsburg to watch the Knicks at Buffalo Wild Wings. About fifteen minutes after hitting the dark turns on Martinsburg Road, I started to imagine accelerating and just obliterating the RAV4 against a tree.

I switched the music off. It was a rap album, *Voir Dire,* and it had a black and white cover showing the skeletal specter of Death as a judge, banging a gavel. The image registered on the dash. The violent thoughts came back, stronger. I pulled over on a gravelly spot at the side of the road because I felt like I shouldn't drive. I didn't think about anything, I just cried for ten minutes under the moonlight, periodically hearing an SUV or a pickup truck rip past me.

I didn't make it to Martinsburg until after halftime. It took me that long to get back into a place where I could drive. I had a miserable meal of cauliflower wings in hot sauce and Coke Zero while watching the Knicks pull away from the Nets. I made it back to Trey's and took trazodone to fall asleep.

The next morning, Aadya called me. I hesitated before answering, but I knew that I had to do it. I looked down from Trey's guest bedroom on the top floor, looking through the window at wood and dead leaves.

"I've been having thoughts of suicide," I told Aadya.

I had a feeling of defiance when I said it. I was defying myself because I knew I didn't want to tell anyone. Aadya gathered her thoughts on the other end of the call before speaking again.

"Okay, so your mother and I are looking into places where you can go to get help," she said.

"What do you mean, like a mental hospital?"

"We're just looking into some places where you can get the help that you need. Because I really think you need around-the-clock care right now," she said.

"You and my mother want to put me in a mental hospital. Is this something you're talking about while I'm down here?"

"You're going to get better," she said. "But you have to admit that this isn't great, what's going on. Right? It's too much. So, I think we need to get you home."

Fifteen minutes after I hung up, Lisa Swanson drove me to Cacapon Resort State Park for another hike. We turned into the mouth of the park and the trees spread out everywhere. We hiked up the base of the hill.

Hannah called me and I picked up.

"They suspended me," she said.

"What? You don't even have a disciplinary record."

"Well, they suspended me without pay. I don't know what to tell you."

When I clicked off the phone, I continued to follow Lisa, but then I stopped to stare at nothing, maybe a fern. I looked at nature without seeing it. Lisa started talking to me but I heard nothing. She kept talking anyway.

"Hey," she said loudly, to cut through my rushing thoughts. "You look really . . . you look upset."

"I am—not doing great, Lisa," I admitted. "Sorry."

Lisa and I hiked up the Ziler trail at Cacapon to a small landing with a bench on it. We both understood that I couldn't go any farther and just needed to leave town. We walked down the hill, and she drove me back to Trey's. Lisa's tone was perfect. She said nothing in particular, but I felt safe with her, and it later hurt me to leave her.

"Whatever it is, whatever it is that happens, it's going to pass," she assured me.

She dropped me off and both of the Johansons were out. I packed my bags, put them in the RAV4, and drove to Abby Chapple's house. Abby was the lady in her eighties who worked at the museum in town. Her house sat among small green hills with only a few farmhouses around it. It looked like an Edward Hopper landscape painting. She made me green tea and told me how offended she was when VDARE bought the castle.

"The falseness of their whole demeanor. Of their presentation of themselves. Of them even *having* an organization. And it goes back to the symbol of this castle, right? That gives them *prominence*. And that gives them supposed *respectability*. And the town is agreeing to it without any kind of analysis. What can you say about it?"

I barely made it through the forty-minute chat with my head upright. At the end, I said goodbye and she hugged me for a long time. I don't know if Lisa had told her anything, or if she just understood from looking at me that I was hurting, but when I started to move away, she looked at me squarely.

"Hey there," she said. "Are you okay?"

22

In a Dark Place

When I pulled up in front of my house, I had a strong feeling that time was thinning. I tossed my bag on the bed and then ripped everything from my work laptop onto an external hard drive in case the SPLC cut off my access. Then I sent an email to the SPLC requesting family and medical leave of absence paperwork.

I wanted to go to a psych ward about as much as I wanted to spend a month in dental surgery, but I had no argument against it. I told Aadya that I would submit to an evaluation if I could wait until a few days after Christmas. In the event of a lengthy departure, it wouldn't disturb our boys as much. Maybe I'd even be able to receive treatment from home.

I survived Christmas in a numb state. The SPLC expected us to return to work on December 26, and that wasn't happening. At 10:09 p.m., I sent an email to the managers. "At the urging of loved ones, I'm pursuing emergency psychiatric treatment and will not be able to attend work this week. I'm in a dark place right now and I need help," I wrote. "I'll update you as soon as I have more information about my return. I'm cc'ing Rachel because we are collaborating on a few things." Then I signed it, "Thanks, and I'm sorry."

Thirty-six hours later, on December 27, the SPLC emailed me a PDF of a sloppy, typo-laden termination notice. It claimed that the cause of the firing was that I was pursuing writing a book, which had no basis in our contract. Other SPLC employees had written books with no issue, including me. Columbia University had published a guide I'd written on Open Source Intelligence in 2019, and the SPLC had congratulated me about it. Plus, I'd told them about the book nearly two months before the firing and no one had said anything then.

Nothing mattered. All of this had started because those in leadership at the SPLC wanted to destroy our union. It ended because they wanted to lash out about Gaza. I had risked my life and spoken to the press on behalf of the SPLC. Now they were siding with Peter Brimelow and VDARE against me. It was a profound betrayal.

My mother took a cab with me to the 168th Street entrance of NewYork-Presbyterian Hospital the next day. When I got to the desk, a Black woman with a tough demeanor called me up to the front desk.

"Why are you here today?"

"I—"

"Ma'am, can you please take a seat?" the woman yelled.

My mom sat down, still close by.

"Over there," the woman ordered.

She pointed to the back of the waiting room. My mom walked off. I waited for her to sit down again. She looked very small in the sterile and otherwise empty space.

"I'm suicidal," I said.

"For how long?"

"A week? Maybe over a week now."

"Did you have a plan to kill yourself?"

"Sort of. Yes."

"What was the plan?"

I lowered my voice.

"I was gonna bash my head in and then drown myself in a Roman Bath. Then I was gonna slam my car into a tree. These weren't deeply thought-out plans."

"Where was this?"

"West Virginia."

"West Virginia?"

"Yes."

"And what did you say about a bath?"

"That was in West Virginia too."

"What was that?"

"It's a thing they have in Berkeley Springs. Which is in West Virginia."

"It's like a public bath?"

"You go in alone but yes."

The woman wrote something down and yelled someone's name out. An orderly came over to put me in a wheelchair. He took my duffel bag. My mom came running.

"Ma'am? Please respect his space."

"It's my mom," I said.

"It doesn't matter who she is. This is a hospital."

I looked at my mom from the wheelchair.

"It'll be okay," I told her.

My mom watched as her forty-four-year-old son got wheeled off through an imposing set of doors into the psych ward. The doors closed and then sealed me off from the waiting area. There was no way out now for anyone without a badge.

The orderly took me to a room. I stripped in front of him and another man. One of them rifled through my duffel bag. The other one observed me getting naked. My bare ass was so cold. The guy with my stuff turned my phone over in his hands like it was something much more than a phone. Then he pointed into the bag.

"What are these?" he asked.

"My books."

He put them aside with the things he had confiscated, which was everything I'd brought.

"Can you put this on, please?"

They handed me a gown.

"Hey, I need the books," I said.

People had told me that I'd get "plenty of reading done in there" when encouraging me to check into the hospital. Not quite. All five books were books related to my interests in West Virginia, and I wanted them. One was a history of Berkeley Springs authored by Jeanne Mozier. One was a history of the B&O Railroad. One was a book about ghosts in Morgan County that Trey had given me as a loaner when I'd stayed at her house. The other two were books by the progressive West Virginia writer and commentator Joe Bageant, *Rainbow Pie* and *Deer Hunting with Jesus*.

They didn't give me my books. Next, they dumped me into a big ugly open space next to two bathrooms and a row of black public phones. The phones had extra-short silver cords attached to them. Patients were splayed on recliners that were covered in forbidding blue vinyl. I reclined and watched patients watching a television set attached to the ceiling that played a PIX11 news broadcast. They gave me graham crackers and apple juice. I was the only patient there who wasn't Black.

After an hour in the common space, an orderly led me to a tiny empty room with bad lighting. Something clanked. A woman started shrieking. I sat there for about ten minutes listening to indecipherable voices.

A tall, skinny doctor in slim-fitting pants arrived. He looked like he was probably pretty young under his COVID mask. He had the energy of someone who had just finished wowing the parents of his girlfriend at a holiday dinner. We talked about thoughts of self-harm.

"Always dealing with people who want to hurt me. Getting into *confrontations* with people who either already hate me or will rapidly learn to hate me. Guys who wanna sue me, guys who wanna kill me," I said. "And then people around me who were tasked with supporting me turned on me.... I mean, they sided with reactionaries, with a guy they describe as a white nationalist, actually, against me."

"How do you feel right now?"

"Not great."

"Do you want to hurt yourself?"

I thought about it.

"I don't know," I said. "I can't really do it because I'm trapped in here, right?"

"Thanks for this," he said.

He kept writing notes. I watched him for a bit.

"Doc?"

"Yes."

"May I have my books?"

"What books?"

"They took my books when I came inside. I have five books in my duffel bag. Oh, and I had a marble notebook. And a pen to write with."

"If they don't have any hard edges, you *should* be allowed to have them. But I'll mention it. As for the pen, you can't have that. But I'll ask that you be given crayons."

When he said "crayons," I froze up.

"So, do you think I can get out and be an outpatient?" I asked.

"I think you need to be here for a while," he said.

"Really?"

He rotated his loafers on the tiled floor.

"So, this here? Where you are? This is not where you will be treated. This is the emergency psychiatric facility. People go off to different places after being evaluated. Unfortunately for you, you came during the week between Christmas and New Year's Day. Gonna be slow going."

The nurses put me on a good amount of clonazepam to numb up my brain. I sat in the common area glazed, barely watching a game show with the sound too low, and a tall, skinny Black guy in his early thirties leaned into my plane of vision. He held out my books and a packet of eight generic crayons.

The man then led me past the toilets and the phones with the suicide-proof short cords. There was a sealed glass nurses' station. A woman with a fair complexion and long lavender nails scrolled through Instagram on her phone. She looked up at me when she saw me staring at what she was doing. The man opened the door to a small room with a cot in it. The TV was running on a low volume, showing an ad for people who suffer from moderate to severe plaque psoriasis.

"I get my own room now?" I asked.

"You tested positive for COVID. They want you to stay here now. You can't be out there without a mask on. Just the nurses' station and the toilet. That's why you got a room. This is isolation."

"COVID?"

"If you need to change the channel, you need to ask at the nurses' station," he said.

I glanced at the TV.

"Wait, the TV only gets one channel at a time?"

"Correct."

"Why don't we just get a remote?"

"Because a remote can be used as a projectile. Think about it."

I thought about it. I felt like I could definitely throw a remote against the wall at that moment.

After he left, I sat staring at the ugly cream walls of my little room, wondering where I got COVID. Did I have it before I got to Berkeley Springs? Did I get it from the stripper who ate my pretzel at Lust? It was impossible to nail down.

The trazodone and clonazepam couldn't put me to sleep. I kept watching the shadows moving past the jumper-proof window. I gave up, turned the light on, read some of the Bageant, tried to sleep, and then started the process over again.

I had no idea what time it was. I had already forgotten the date. I walked to the nurses' station and told a handsome, slightly balding guy, Italian or Greek, with a Queens accent, that I couldn't sleep. He said not to worry. He joined me in my room a few minutes later with a small bottle of water and a pill in a cup. After that, reality disintegrated.

I lost track of everything. The hospital crew worked understaffed during the holiday week, and I think they compensated for it by giving me pills. I enjoyed my books, the Bageant in particular, and tried to write in the marble notebook with a crayon. I drew pictures of the emergency ward. I drew an entire map of Berkeley Springs.

My parents visited me while I ate my bland meals, which often involved only the vegetarian parts of the trays intended for those who ate meat. I ate things like mashed potatoes and green beans with salt and pepper. I would cram the food into my mouth and wash it down with the apple juice I hoarded from the nurses' station.

When my father showed up, he wanted to talk about sports, the easiest topic for men who want to avoid bumping into something heavy. Dad referenced a pitcher without saying his name. I knew the pitcher he meant—he threw for the Cleveland Guardians—but I couldn't remember his name. Not only that, but I also couldn't imagine his face. When I tried to picture the player, I saw a flesh-colored blob.

When I brought this incident up to a doctor who attended to me later, I insisted that it felt like something far worse than everyday forgetfulness. He told me that I was suffering from memory loss, partly as a result of the medication, but also because of the trauma I had experienced plunging into suicidality.

"Well, I don't like this," I said. "Can you fix it?"

"It may take some time to get your memory back, unfortunately. Once we get you out of the emergency area and isolation, they can do a better assessment."

Aadya came to visit me and sat in a hard, ugly chair at the foot of my cot. I could tell that everything about the situation made her profoundly sad.

"I'm sorry," I said.

"About what?"

"About everything."

"It's okay," she said. "Just focus on getting well."

Time slid in and out. I watched the Jets losing to the Browns one night, and without knowing how the game ended, I woke up in the morning to someone handing me a fresh cup of pills. Pills, pills, pills. They made time disappear.

The hospital admitted a young, fairly pretty, and extremely uptight-looking Korean American woman into the ward who spent a lot of time standing by the phones with the short cords, waiting for a call that never arrived. She sometimes mobbed the nurses' station, shouting that she needed to be somewhere else.

"Call my father," she said. "Call my brother!"

Nobody let her do anything. She spent most of the time that I saw her walking through the halls with a Bible in her hands, talking to herself. She stood outside of my room, waiting for another showdown with the nurses' station, and I wrote down what she was saying in crayon.

"It's not going to be like this," she said. "And you need to get used to it. That's just how it is. I'm not going to be treated this way. Not anymore. Do you understand me? My father will not believe it."

On New Year's Eve, I had the balding, handsome nurse put CNN on so I could watch the ball drop. When he visited me, we talked a little about Queens. We had lived close to each other when I was in Jackson Heights.

"Hey, do you want me to get you some ginger ale?" he asked me.

He said it like he was treating me to some cocaine he'd acquired.

"Yes," I said.

He left and came back in a few minutes carrying a paper cup and a two liter bottle of White Rock Ginger Ale. He handed me the cup and started to pour.

"It's not champagne but it will do, right?" he said.

I drank the ginger ale. It was ice cold and I savored the bubbles as they tickled my throat. At that moment, it was the most delicious thing I had ever consumed.

"May I have some more?"

He started to refill my cup.

"I don't want people to think I'm giving you special treatment," he said, laughing.

Drugs put me under before the ball dropped on TV. The next day, a woman came to my room to tell me they were transferring me to their facility in Westchester. I could only see her eyes over her mask.

"We are transferring you to Five South."

"What is that?"

"It's in our Westchester facility. The transfer itself can be a little scary. *Most* patients prefer to take something before making the trip. Did *you* want to take something?"

"Of course," I said, following her cue.

A nurse gave me a pill around noon and told me it would take about half an hour to take effect. Around then, orderlies came by and strapped me to a gurney. Then they tied me down with some straps across my body, kind of like a straitjacket. They pushed the gurney. We moved fast through a crowded corridor filled with sick people. Everyone stared at me.

The gurney hit the open air and I breathed it for the first time in five days.

"It's so cold!" I shouted.

My speech slurred and I struggled to get the words out, like when you try to shout out loud in the middle of having a nightmare, but your jaw feels like molasses. The gurney slammed into the back of an ambulance and an orderly popped his head in.

"Go to sleep."

I disappeared from reality again. I woke up in the dark in a clean, spacious room with white walls. The sun had set while I was unconscious. I studied this new, much bigger, much cleaner, much darker-looking room, trying to understand where I was.

I eyed a big window and went to it. The window overlooked a grand courtyard. I could see the black sky. For a moment, I sat in that feeling of not knowing anything.

I turned to the door of the room. It was heavy and I opened it slowly.

"Hello?" I said to no one.

"He's up," a woman's voice said.

In Westchester, the staff kept me in COVID isolation—something about New York laws that I didn't understand. They gave me an iPad, heavily restricted in its capabilities. I had access to email and Google Docs for writing. I wasn't allowed to use the short-cord phones or go into the hallway at first, but each floor had a flip phone, and when no one was using it, a nurse would stand by while I made a call.

I had my own bathroom, which I liked. It had a foam rubber door over the shower that could be torn off with Velcro. The food improved and I even started to like it.

On January 3, 2024, Hannah and Rachel forwarded me an email from the manager from leadership who had first punished me over the Gaza stuff. Abruptly, the manager had resigned from her post.

"The timing of that is VERY sus. Especially considering the potential legal threats. I singled her out repeatedly in the discrimination claim. They also rushed my exit without HR because they were all on holiday. The letter was filled with typos. I'm just saying it is very sus," I wrote back to them from my bed.

"Oh it's so sus," Hannah replied.

An orderly came past the window at my door every fifteen minutes to peek at me and make sure I hadn't figured out how to end my life. This made it challenging to masturbate, which was the activity I most wanted to do while stuck in isolation. Sometimes, when I desperately needed privacy, I would remove the Velcro door of the shower and block entry to the bathroom.

A doctor in a face mask with big yellow straps on it dropped by in the mornings. She started communicating with Dr. K, who was traveling in France. They traded info and collaborated on a diagnosis.

"You have bipolar two," she said.

Her idea was that I had been a very high-functioning person, producing lots and lots of work, but that I'd had these manic episodes. I'd suffered from insomnia most of my life, like the time I'd stayed up for ninety hours straight in the summer after my senior year of high school. But then the pressures related to my job became too much for me to withstand, and the manic energy gave way to the depressive side of the disease that I normally repressed.

They switched me off the antidepressants and put me on lithium instead. The memory loss and cognitive damage proved to be an ongoing challenge. When I tried to write on the iPad, I ended up writing and rewriting the same sentence. It started to scare me. I couldn't move on from my sentences. My mind couldn't get around the order of the words.

A portly Black man who sometimes brought my meals started chatting with me about sports, music, and sci-fi. I told him that I was a writer.

"You know there was a guy who wrote a book about staying in this place?"

"Oh yeah?"

"Famous dude," he said, and picked up his phone to look it up. "Well, a little famous. Barely. William Seabrook. *Asylum*."

"Have you read it?" I asked.

"No, I haven't yet," he said.

I had heard of Seabrook, mostly that he had some scandal involving cannibalism. I decided I would read *Asylum* if they ever let me out of the facility.

I got closer to that goal on Saturday, January 6, when they announced that my isolation had ended and I could roam the halls of the psych ward at my leisure. I couldn't walk far. It was two long corridors, one cut short because of an off-limits section containing people with a history of violence, but I could move.

Snow fell. It fell heavily on the courtyard outside my window. I thought about Trey and Paul. I thought about Lisa Swanson, and Abby Chapple. I even thought about the Brimelows.

On January 8, Hannah sent me an email with no body, just a subject line, which said, "Can you call me when you can." I kept her and Rachel's numbers written down in crayon in the marble notebook so I could access them. I squatted down to meet the short cord of the public phone and called her. Hannah told me that the often-absentee director of the Intelligence Project we had targeted with union campaigns, who had spearheaded some of the retaliation, had abruptly resigned.

"What do you mean?"

"She's gone too."

"Resigned?"

"Yep," she said.

We laughed a deep laugh. Other patients looked at me, scrunched down with the short cord, reacting like I had received news of a war ending. Now everyone in my management chain up to Huang had abruptly resigned.

I reached out to the lawyer the American Civil Liberties Union had recommended. Her name was Deborah, and she was an older Jewish intellectual type. She talked very fast, but she chose her words carefully. I always felt at home with fast-talking New Yorkers like that.

"Listen to me," she said. "And this is very important. When do you think they're going to let you out of the hospital?"

"I don't know."

"You think they're going to let you out in a week?"

"I hope so."

"Pay attention to this. I want you to call me at 2 p.m. on January 18 and then send me the documents we discussed. And for now I don't want you to do anything. Just focus on your health. Can you do that for me?"

"Yes."

"If they want you at the group sessions, go to them. If your doctor suggests something, follow it. You're not going to be able to do anything in this process if you don't focus on your health," she said. "I need you to get better."

The hospital asked me to go to group sessions. I felt guilty because it seemed like everyone had it worse than me. One young woman lived with her parents and had what seemed like debilitating obsessive-compulsive disorder. She flinched like a gun had fired every time someone moved in her vicinity. She kept her arms slightly raised at all times, like she was scared of what would happen if she rested them on her chair.

The doctor moderating the group asked a wiry, middle-aged Black man with a thinning patch of gray hair a question about what he could do to de-escalate an unpleasant situation. He had graduated from the off-limits section where they kept people prone to violence. The man held out his hands to look at them and show them to us.

"I would stop to think," he said. "Before I laid hands on the man from my building that was troubling me. I would count down so that I didn't react with my hands and beat on him."

A young trans woman from Venezuela approached me after one of the meetings when I was standing in a line to get my pills. She was early into her transition and spoke limited English. She cut into the line to speak very close to me.

"You look so nice," she said.

"Thank you!"

"I want to hug you," she said.

"Okay."

She hugged me.

"I love you," she whispered in my ear.

"Thank you very much," I said.

"No, I *really* love you," she repeated. "I'm in love with you."

One of the nurses raised her voice from down the hall.

"Hey, hey, hey. No, no, no. You know this! You don't do that! You don't do that!"

Two nurses guided her down the hallway. One of them spoke Spanish. I never saw her again. Selfishly, I wanted to hear more about how much she loved me.

A few days before they discharged me, my colleagues posted a letter to Teams, the office message board. More than half of our bargaining unit signed on in solidarity, including many people I didn't even know personally. The letter addressed my situation, citing the "long campaign of harassment and intimidation" I had endured after becoming a steward and taking on the job of submitting "collective complaints from our bargaining unit about the substandard and negligent leadership." The letter said, "Over the last few months... management's retaliation against Mike became more targeted, especially after he and our colleague Hannah Gais exercised their free speech rights as private citizens to sign on to a letter calling for a ceasefire in Gaza."

It went on to say that "Mike, [the Intelligence Project's] only public-facing Arab American employee, was singled out for discipline and stripped of his spokesperson title. Mike was terminated for working on a book on his own vacation time, and Hannah was given an unpaid suspension.... Not only is this an egregious abuse of employer power and an unacceptable encroachment on staff's private liberties, we believe this excessively harsh discipline is directly related to management's desire to punish them for private pro-ceasefire speech."

Hannah replied to the statement with a personal comment, explaining that watching what happened to me was, "without a doubt, the hardest moment of my entire professional career." Tears fell from my eyes as I read it from my hospital bed.

When they let me out of the hospital, the staff gave me a card with a drawing of carrots and greens growing from the ground up into a blue sky. Roots of the plants stretched deep into the soil. "Good Luck, We're *Rooting* for You," it said.

Underneath, one of the nurses had printed a handwritten note: "Wishing you much luck, Michael! You got this.—5 South."

When I got back into my office, I pinned the "Rooting for You" card onto the bulletin board above my desk.

23

Tropical Fish

Kate Lehman, the woman who had given the ill-fated prayer at the Berkeley Springs Black Lives Matter rally in August 2020, published a letter to the editor in *The Morgan Messenger*'s January 24, 2024, edition. Lehman expressed concerns that coverage in the *Messenger* of Trump's win in the Iowa caucus flattered him. She compared Trump's movement to ultranationalist, authoritarian parties abroad.

"I hope that 40 years from now, our grandchildren will not have to apologize for our silence and resignation," she wrote.

I pulled a rented Jeep into the gravel yard behind the Lazy Sundae on Friday, January 26, dropped my bag off at the same place Hannah and I had rented for the Christmas party, and hiked up the hill to the Berkeley Springs Castle. It was a little after 9:30 at night and everything was silent and cold. I snapped a picture of the long driveway, with floodlights smearing grainy shadows over the sandstone.

I sent the castle photo over Signal to an SPLC researcher named Jeff Tischauser. Jeff worked the white nationalism desk, and he followed VDARE closely. For whatever reason, I wanted to show Jeff that I was still alive. Out of the hospital, into the hills.

"Back on my bullshit," I wrote.

"Hell yea," he wrote back. "This is good to hear."

I walked back down the hill thinking about William Seabrook and *Asylum*. That was the book the orderly in Westchester had told me about, by the writer who'd stayed at the same institution back in the 1930s.

"Never having cared for suicide, and doubting I would like being dead any better than being alive, if as well, the only stupid, decent thing to do seemed to be to make the best of it," Seabrook wrote of his future after hospitalization.[1]

The hospital had admitted Seabrook because of alcoholism, which manifested in him as a kind of slow-motion suicide. I found what he described familiar, even if some treatments they gave him amounted to light barbarism. But then, as I looked further into Seabrook's life, I learned that, rather than "making the best of it," he had actually killed himself. The guy took an overdose of pills ten years after *Asylum* was published. When I learned that, I had to fight back despair.

Two weeks prior, a brunette social worker who wore white fluffy sweaters had drawn up a plan for my life after hospitalization. The most appealing part of it was that I would attend therapy sessions with a Westchester-based practice. I got excited to finally get regular, affordable therapy, but it never materialized. The termination notice that ended my employment in 2023 also took my insurance from me. Aadya could pull me onto hers, but the month-long disruption undercut whatever deal the hospital made.

In Berkeley Springs, I walked into 7-Eleven and picked out a packaged croissant infused with peanut butter and jelly. I was going to pair it with a tepid can of V8 I had back at my room in the hopes of achieving a balanced meal.

A South Asian guy worked the counter, and it was rare to bump into anyone of color in Berkeley Springs, so I decided to talk to him.

"May I ask where you're from?" I asked.

"Delhi."

"Oh yeah? I lived in India for five years," I said.

He relaxed his shoulders.

"You're Indian?" he asked.

"My wife is."

"Where'd you live?"

"Six months in Delhi and over four years in Mumbai."

He nodded and then spaced out.

"What do you think of Morgan County?" I asked. "Buying this too, if you don't mind."

I handed him a prepackaged soft pretzel from the counter.

"Morgan County is nice," he said.

"Does anyone ever give you shit for being Indian? Sorry if that's a weird question."

He thought about it as he put my stuff in a plastic bag.

"No."

"That's good to hear," I said, moving to the door. "My name's Mike, by the way."

He spoke up as I started to turn away.

"Some people call—and say things."

"Say things?"

"Mean things."

"Oh, they do this on, like, the phone? Like, prank calls?"

"Yes."

"Does it happen a lot?"

"No," he said.

I fell asleep trying to imagine how stupid a racist prank call to the 7-Eleven might be in practice.

When I woke up, I ordered a coffee and bagel from Fairfax and criss-crossed the town without my Walmart costume, doing the exact types of things I would have done in December if I hadn't had to hide myself. I loved the town.

That Saturday night, I drove from Berkeley Springs to Washington, DC, and met a group of reporter friends at Lyman's Tavern for drinks. It was damp out, and the group, which included Hannah, her husband, Tom, and Luke O'Brien, lined a bench under a heat lamp to stay dry.

Everyone bought me drinks. One thing about graduating from a psych ward: People who have never been in a rush to buy you drinks will suddenly step up and buy you three of them. They also wanted to hear about how I was going to sue the SPLC. The SPLC employees there especially wanted to hear about it.

We also talked about the coming presidential election. While in the hospital, I had almost forgotten it was an election year. Everyone seated at the table thought Trump would lose because of the criminal investigations, but no one felt great about it. These were journalists, ultimately. Nobody really felt great about anything.

I texted Trey on January 14, soon after I left the hospital. When I did, I was responding two weeks late to a Happy New Year's message that I'd had no ability to access. When Trey replied, I got her on the phone and told her that I was working solo and had just spent time in a psych ward. It was a difficult thing to say to someone who had served voluntarily as my writing subject.

I drove from DC to Trey's house on that Sunday evening and Trey sat me down at her dining table. She invited Paul to join us. It had the feeling of an intervention. She leaned forward and directed her light blue eyes at me squarely.

"I think you need to know," Trey said. "I've had experience as a therapist. Okay? Maybe not for a very long time, okay, but I do have experience with that. That was my job, once. And Paul has moderated group discussions around mental health. So, if at any point that you are here, and you don't feel well, you need to speak up. Come speak to *me*. You're family. And I don't want to see you suffer. The way you were last time... it broke my heart. You need to speak up and understand that this . . . ? Is a safe place. You don't need to hide what you're feeling."

Trey had left her therapy practice after she'd developed a relationship with one of her patients. He was a younger man and he became her second husband. She told me that story more than once, and both times, it came out with what sounded like a sprinkling of shame.

"Well, I appreciate that," I said. "But I'm a lot better than I was. I don't feel very much pain at this moment. I think the worst is behind me."

"Okay, but you understand what I'm saying," she said. "Because things can change."

"I do understand."

"Do you? Because you need to speak up if you're in pain. If you're feeling *anything*."

"Okay."

"I'm serious about this."

"Yep. I got it."

We ate dinner and that was the end of it. I went back to work. The Johansons gave me stability, responding to the needs of my recovery process. Trey even started to use the word *love* when describing how she felt about me. It was an intimidating thing to hear, and I started to feel a sense of responsibility around that word. In my mind, I was a random New York writer who kept blowing in and out of town. Now I had to be worthy of love too.

I carried on interviewing people all over town about 2020, when Peter and Lydia had first bought the castle. One thing I heard repeatedly from people was that tourism had fallen after VDARE bought the place. No one could prove it, because the local government provided no resources or records to do so. They pointed to restaurants closing and empty locations never being filled as evidence, although this happened throughout the country following the COVID-19 outbreak.

I visited Lisa Swanson at her house. We relished the experience of talking, and me hearing her cleanly, without my head drifting into darkness. Her house had a simple warmth to it. Lisa's primary decor consisted of paperbacks with frayed spines and a navy and gold protest sign depicting a coal worker emerging from the shadows:

> SOLIDARITY with all coal workers. It's time for a JUST TRANSITION.

Lisa's house overlooked the castle, and if you walked onto her deck, it was impossible to avoid the view. Every time she stepped outside, the castle was the first thing Lisa saw. It appeared before her as clearly as the Empire State Building would from Boulevard East in Weehawken, New Jersey. Next door to Lisa's place, I noticed that someone had scattered junk and toys across the lawn of their house. The family that lived there had hung up a giant Trump 2024 flag that said, "Take America Back."

"The father is on the sex offender registry," Lisa said, raising her eyebrows.

Lisa wanted to hear everything that happened after we left the Ziler trail that day in December, and I brought her up to date. I told her I had secured a lawyer who seemed very talented, and that, in the meantime, I planned to focus on Berkeley Springs.

"You seem better," she told me.

"I'm trying."

"You didn't seem very good before. I'll tell you that."

"Well, I'm on a lot of medication. It's impacting my memory. Obviously, I take pictures and take notes, but now I'm doing it to remember what happened yesterday."

"Okay."

I met with food activist Patti Miller for the first time in Fairfax Coffee House—before that, I had only heard about her from Trey and Paul—and she told me that when the Brimelows had moved in she had opposed their beliefs, but she had never feared them. Patti had an undeniable grit. She was the exact type of person I would want to hide behind if something utterly insane happened in town.

"The fear was palpable. I couldn't understand the level of fear that some of my gay and lesbian friends were feeling.... What is the *threat*?" Patti said. "But they didn't live through the 70s, 80s, and 90s like I did. I thought, *Why didn't I share that fear?* It was because I didn't feel any threat. And maybe that was because I understood what a threat used to feel like."

As the calendar flipped into February, I drove fifty minutes east of the town to walk across Antietam National Battlefield. It made me think about VDARE's intimations of a second civil war. On September 17, 1862, as fighting had broken out in that Maryland town, men fired cannonballs that ripped bodies totally open, exposing spinal cords to the open air. Wagons dripped sheets of wet blood as they transported the dead.

Beyond the staggering death toll, three-quarters of all surgical operations performed during the Civil War, or roughly sixty thousand of them, were amputations. The war left behind a nation of disfigured men. Doctors sometimes left behind piles of limbs underneath operating tables, casting them aside like orange peels.[2] Clara Barton's Missing Soldiers Office answered nearly seventy thousand inquiries in the three years after the war ended as families searched for men who vanished.[3]

When I left Trey's place, I holed myself up in a cabin on the edge of town to write. I kept myself going with a few groceries I picked up from the Food Lion. Bread, cheese, mustard, peanut butter, a bag of carrots, apples, coffee. The cabin had weak internet and limited phone service, but it had a working fireplace. Woods surrounded it on every side.

One time, when I stood up from the cabin's tiny desk to stretch my legs, I decided to take a picture of my meds in their gallon-sized Ziploc bag sitting on the bed. There were so many bottles. Lithium, trazodone, clonazepam, and risperidone, a mild antipsychotic. That didn't include the vitamins. As I snapped the photo for posterity, I realized I would need a little luck to dodge the path of William Seabrook.

When I got back home, VDARE announced some bad news on X: "In the midst of our mortal struggle against NYAG Letitia James' lawfare, our long-standing payment processor just announced that it will end our ability to accept credit card donations on Sunday, Feb 18. PLEASE GIVE—WHILE YOU CAN—Peter Brimelow."

The statement included a VDARE post featuring a picture of Peter. He was staring directly into the camera in what I found to be a comical pose. I think VDARE was trying to make him look defiant in the face of lawfare, but it looked like the cover image of a pamphlet informing people about Alzheimer's.

"Stabbed in the back," the caption read. *"By payment processor."*

"Lydia is scrambling, but at this point, we simply don't know if we'll be able to accept credit card donations next week," Peter wrote. "Many thanks to our friends who are supporting us in this terrible time for us—and for America."

The next day, Lydia appeared on Tucker Carlson's heavily trafficked online show, which streamed on X. I watched it from my couch while eating granola. Without question, the moment represented the peak of Lydia's visibility as a public figure.

It may have been VDARE's peak too. Tucker started the segment with a mini-monologue that described VDARE's history in such absurd language that the organization I'd been covering for years sounded utterly foreign to me. "In the late 90s Peter Brimelow started to ask questions about our immigration scheme," Carlson said:

> Is this a good idea? Is it helping America? And of course, nobody could answer those questions because the answer is obvious. No, it's destroying America. As it destroyed California. As it will destroy your state. That's certain. For asking that question, Peter was fired from his jobs and shunted off into what we call the *fringes*. But he didn't stop. He started a website called VDARE.com. He runs it with his wife, Lydia. And for the crime in our supposedly free country of opposing the immigration system... powerful forces have tried to destroy their lives. Not just their lives, but the lives of their family. Using the justice system to do it. And you probably guessed this, using something called the Southern Poverty Law Center, which has nothing to do with the South, or poverty. It has to do with shutting down free speech in this country. They have descended on the Brimelows and really kind of tried to destroy them. That's not an overstatement, but you judge for yourself.[4]

The screen then split and Lydia appeared in a cream-colored top with a tassel around her neck and dry, recently straightened hair falling across both sides of her shoulders. Lydia talked about Letitia James and the subpoenas her office had issued. She called the labels "white nationalist" and "white supremacist" "scare words" and emphasized that she avoided talking about violence.

"We're even careful to talk about the national divorce, because of what implications that might have," Lydia said.

"Yes," Carlson responded portentously.

Marjorie Taylor Greene had talked about a "national divorce" exactly one year earlier in a tweet calling for the permanent separation of red and blue states.[5] In some circles of the movement, people used the phrase as a stand-in for violent civil war. You could understand it to mean an event where liberals are brought to heel through acts of extreme violence. I thought maybe that was what Lydia meant by "implications."

Lydia told the story of why they had bought the castle and how they had struggled to hold conferences without it. She said that Letitia James insinuated that there were issues with how they'd purchased the castle. Lydia accused James of lying in her pursuit of VDARE. Tucker showed a picture of James's Black face on the screen.

"For those who don't know, she has an IQ of about 85," Carlson said. "I would guess."

Carlson then turned to talking about my reporting and accused me of stalking Lydia and her family.

"We live now in Berkeley Springs. It's a very small town," Lydia said. She continued:

> It's a beautiful town. There are natural mineral springs that bubble up out of the side of the mountain, all year round. It was originally surveyed by George Washington. And the people there are just incredible. But there are very few of them. Only seven hundred people populate the main town.... The reason I say that is once you live there for a little while... you know everybody.... When you live in a rural county and you have... a stone castle looming over a tiny little resort town, everybody wants to know

> what's happening to it. So, when we first bought it, people were nervous because of everything the media said. "Is this the Ku Klux Klan which has now descended on our precious landmark?" Over time, it became evident that, no, our main goal is to be good quiet neighbors.... The overwhelming number of people in the town are good friends of ours, but there are a few bad apples and the SPLC has really fixated on them.[6]

Lydia then broke off into something preposterous. She said that the SPLC had flown me out and embedded me in the town to coax the bad apples into saying things about them in the press. I wondered if she believed what she was saying or if she knew it was bullshit.

Lydia said we hosted "secret meetings" in "after-hours back rooms." But those two meetings had not been secret. Nor were they conducted in back rooms. She referred to Fairfax Coffee House as "the one leftist organization in town" and said you could identify it by the colorful flags they hung.

"Like tropical fish, the more colorful they are, the more poisonous they are," she said.

Lydia said that I wanted to organize a torch mob to pull her family out of the castle. Who would be marching with the torches here? Lisa Swanson? Patti Miller? Then she quoted Tanya Gersh's line about maggots, showing beyond a reasonable doubt that a mole had been sitting in that meeting to report back to them.

"When that didn't scare us off, Michael Hayden decided to write a *book* about our family," she said. "In support of this supposed *book* that he's supposedly *writing*, he spends a lot of time in town. He hangs around my church, and pesters my priest about what my faith habits are—"

"That's not true! I didn't get to ask him any questions," I said out loud.

Lydia said I had interviewed town council members about her, which I hadn't done. I didn't even know who they were by name at that point. Specifically, she said I'd asked town council members if they "had seen her children in town." More lies.

Lydia switched next to Lisa Marie, the trans woman who had approached her at Mass to say "Black Lives Matter." She described a "group of trannies who have decided to stalk my family" who had "multiple guns on the outside of their bodies."

"The main leader is male to female but one of his sidekicks is male to *goblin* identifying. Do goblins even have a gender?" she said.

Even Tucker seemed a little confused by that one. I paused the video and wrote down the timestamp. Half an hour of the most attention Lydia would ever get in her whole entire life, and she used it to rant about a trans goblin.

I started to wonder if Lydia might also be mad. I could easily imagine talking to Lydia about the goblin in that hospital up in Westchester—say, over lunch in the cafeteria there. Maybe the cold civil war had rendered both of us insane.

24

A Long Time to Die

On Saturday, March 30, 2024, VDARE issued an ominous-looking announcement on its website's landing page. A header image of the org's fawn logo circled by a crown of thorns appeared. The title declared, "IT IS FINISHED."

Below the logo, Peter told his readers that Letitia James had persecuted VDARE to the edge of murder and that the site would soon cease to exist:

> I launched VDARE.com on Christmas Eve 1999. So it is perhaps appropriate that, on Good Friday 2024, the anniversary of Christ's death, I must announce VDARE.com's crucifixion by New York State's communist Attorney General Letitia James.
>
> On March 27, 2024, in another of her lightning-fast NYAG James–compliant rulings, New York State Supreme Court Judge Sabrina Kraus held us in Contempt of Court because we have not yet complied (because we were fighting it) with her January 23, 2023 order that we meet NYAG James' massive and crippling subpoena demands.
>
> Judge Kraus did modify her earlier order to reflect the intervention (much appreciated) of the Institute for Free Speech. So now we no longer have to reveal, explicitly, the names of our

pseudonymous writers, some of whom would certainly be fired from their jobs if their identities leaked.

But we are still required to review 40 gigabytes of emails, an enormous amount. And of course these could in fact reveal the names of those pseudonymous writers, as well as our donors, privileged communications with lawyers, etc.

Judge Kraus has also now allowed us to redact these emails. But this is a huge task, which our lawyers estimate could cost as much as $150,000.

An observer tells us this order is more typical of major corporate litigation, not a tiny charity.

And, perversely, although Judge Kraus has now modified her January 23, 2023 order, she is *nevertheless now fining us $250 a day for not complying with it.*

We have fought NYAG Letitia James, at a cost of up to $1 million, for nearly three years. But now we are literally hanging on the cross.

REMEMBER, VDARE.com HAS NOT BEEN CHARGED WITH ANYTHING—BECAUSE IT IS NOT GUILTY OF ANYTHING.

There is no legitimate explanation for NYAG James' enormous fishing expedition—other than a desire to nail us to the cross with compliance costs. The process is the punishment.

NYAG James has claimed to be interested in our purchase of the Berkeley Springs Castle as a conference venue. But this transaction was expensively lawyered and is bulletproof. Significantly, NYAG James has refused to meet with our expensive lawyers to discuss it.

The victims of crucifixion typically took a long time to die. (Christ was an exception.)

All our resources are now focused on our death struggle. VDARE.com will continue publishing on a reduced schedule as long as it can, at least until after our April 26–28 conference.

But, as Christ said on the cross, "It is finished."

The suppression of VDARE.com's voice, at a time when the immigration debate is moving to a climax, is of course a political scandal.

But, on a personal level, I might also observe that VDARE .com was an entirely viable 24/7 opinion convenience store. I had hoped to leave it to my young wife and our children after I am gone. Now it appears, thanks to Letitia James, that this will not be possible. They will need some other means of support.

Nevertheless, I'm immensely grateful for VDARE.com's much loved readers and supporters over these many years.

We hope to see you on the other side.

Peter Brimelow[1]

A few words in particular caught my attention: "At a cost of up to $1 million." If VDARE had spent that much on legal fees, I didn't see how they could go on. An extremely rich benefactor would have to pick up the tab. And they'd had those before. But why would a rich benefactor invest in an organization that could be facing dissolution when so many new MAGA influencers threatened to upstage them? One thing about the movement: I haven't observed much loyalty in it.

Peter also said he paid $250 a day for noncompliance. That meant it would cost them a little less than a hundred grand in one year to keep defying subpoenas. Peter said he chose to pay this exorbitant rate to protect the names of those who had involved themselves in VDARE—authors, donors, et cetera.

The only people who used their real names on VDARE's site were men like Jason Kessler. And Kessler lived an unenviable life on the margins. Whoever it was whom Peter sought to protect would rather watch the movement itself disappear than live life as Jason Kessler, or even Peter Brimelow.

I sent an email to Trey, Paul, Lisa Swanson, and Dan the historian with the subject line "Very dramatic VDARE post," and then linked to it.

"Oh, my, golly-gosh," Trey wrote. "Are they comparing themselves to Jesus, on Easter? Can it be true that they are really closing up shop?? Maybe there is a god."

Peter made a passing reference in his missive to what would be the third VDARE conference at the Berkeley Springs Castle. I wanted to go. But if I bought a ticket, the Brimelows could take my money, ban me, and defend themselves from scrutiny, blessed with the foreknowledge that I would be in town. I drew up a more conservative plan. If it worked, I could scratch out intel about the conference without as much personal risk.

Before executing it, I had a detour I wanted to make. The guys at Enterprise upgraded me to a burnt orange Camaro, and the engine hummed in a way that pleased me. On April 20, I zipped it past Maryland, past Morgan County, and in the direction of Appomattox, Virginia, where the Civil War nominally ended.

I passed through a beautiful network of green hills, sparsely populated and frequently dotted with Trump flags. A local radio station played a song by the Christian group Mary McKee and the Genesis. The song was about how people's dreams fell apart and then Jesus came to fill the void.

To get into Appomattox Court House, I had to drive around Liberty University. A month prior, the US Department of Education had fined Liberty University $14 million for underreporting of sexual assault cases on campus under the federal Clery Act. There were also allegations that the school had punished victims of sexual assault for violating a campus rule against premarital sex.[2]

At Appomattox, Confederate flags hung off several buildings. A red banner hung over a dilapidated building, shouting, "HATE SPEECH IS COP KILLER RAP MUSIC LYRICS!" I stayed at a bed and breakfast where an ancient mattress broke down at an angle that nearly caused me to roll onto the floor. I had a miserable night's sleep.

The next morning, I ate lukewarm toast with an older couple who shared the table with me. The man, Earl, had a long white face that made him look like Droopy Dog. The woman, Chris, wore a sweatshirt with a big photo of a white kitten on it.

"I'm of Confederate heritage," Earl announced.

"He's Confederate all through," Chris said, nodding.

"All through," Earl said.

"You said you're from the Blue Ridge Mountains?" I asked.

"Yes, but I came from Alabama. Went to a small college in Alabama," Earl said.

Chris left with her dish. Earl watched her go. He whispered to me, "When I was in school, wanna know who was there with me?" he asked. "George Wallace's *daughter*."

Earl acted like he had just name-dropped Elizabeth Taylor or something.

"George Wallace's daughter," I repeated.

"And, I *really* got to know her. I got to know her *close*," he said.

"Oh yeah?"

"Yessir. She was very famous there."

Nobody said anything for a merciful beat, and then Earl piped up again.

"You said you were here for Civil War history?" he asked.

"Mm-hm."

"I feel like a lot of things get misunderstood about John Wilkes Booth," he proclaimed. "Booth was an actor but he was also a great man, in many, many respects."

I nearly choked on my coffee.

"He assassinated President Lincoln because he freed the slaves, Earl."

"He did. He did do that. But of course he was fighting for his *side*. Booth's life story requires greater attention. That's all."

"Sounds interesting. Really nice chatting with you."

I moved my unfinished meal to an area for dishes. I kept my back turned to Earl, but I could feel him still looking for my attention.

"Hey, you didn't tell me where you're from, what line of work you're in," he said to my back.

I pretended not to hear him and left.

I hiked around the Appomattox Court House National Historical Park and saw the spot where Confederate infantrymen had stacked their arms before the feet of federal troops. I visited the room where Peter's hero, General Robert E. Lee, surrendered to General Ulysses S. Grant. Then I passed a small cluster of graves and found them littered with little Confederate flags. There were dozens of them, burrowed into a small fenced-in rectangle, situated right where Grant would have passed to enter the town on the day the war ended.

I walked up to a uniformed employee, a later-middle-aged guy who looked like he had worked there for a few decades. He gave me a polite smile.

"Sorry," I said. "What's with the Confederate flags over there?"

"That area's maintained by the Daughters of the Confederacy," he said.

"In a place where people come to remember the end of the Civil War—the Daughters of the Confederacy can just flood the zone with Confederate flags?"

"It's close to the park, it's on the edge of the park, but isn't *owned* by the park."

"You don't find that messed up?" I asked.

"Well, I agree with you," he said in a low voice. "But it's just how it worked out."

In the run-up to VDARE's conference, one of my molars started to throb. It was in the back of my mouth on the lower left. I had a lot of time booked on the road in front of me and the pain was inconvenient. At first, I tried to gut it out.

I scouted out the three properties on Stucco Drive in Berkeley Springs that were visible on Route 9. People speculated to me that the Brimelows had lived in the castle previously but had relocated to a smaller home in response to Letitia James's investigation. If that was true, I thought they might live on Stucco Drive, which was short enough to be a driveway and angled slightly upward into the back of the castle grounds.

VDARE could have had access to all three of the houses on Stucco Drive, but only one of them looked livable from my view on the street. The first one resembled a dilapidated garage. The third one just looked small, hollowed out, and dark. The middle one, however, had a long staircase that climbed to the height of the trees. The skinny house at the top of the stairs appeared to be an active, lived-in home.

I knew that Lydia drove an Audi. I looked for one but couldn't find it. I wanted to prove that they did live in that middle house, but it was hard without staking out the property. Route 9 had no sidewalk, after all.

I spent the remaining days before the conference booking a tarot reading, hitting the Roman Baths, and doing a couple of interviews. I spoke to Larry Schultz about his ill-fated Black Lives Matter rally in 2020, and I talked to David Floyd DeGraw, the man the local police had jailed for making terroristic threats against the antifa radicals who never showed up.

When I found David at his home, he was riding his mower around the back of it. He was isolated and monitored by law enforcement. The government had taken away his guns in response to the threats he'd made on Facebook about the August 2020 Black Lives Matter rally. He said he'd started to make plans to leave Berkeley Springs, which was a refrain I heard more and more around town, regardless of political ideology.

When I told David who I was, he stared hard at me from the seat of the orange vehicle, nursing a look of profound incredulity.

"Boy, you got some huge balls to be coming around here, do you know that?"

"Maybe! Maybe I'm insane," I said.

David seemed to like that answer, for whatever reason. He talked to me for half an hour about what had happened to him in 2020. At the end, I asked him a question for my own pleasure.

"What do you think is gonna happen in the election?"

"You mean for president?" he asked. "Trump's gonna win."

"Even with the criminal stuff going on?"

"It's all a lie. I'm not *stupid*."

"But he may... he may get convicted, at least in New York. And he could serve time."

David sneered at me and started to speak slowly and emphatically.

"You want to see a civil war? Put handcuffs on Donald Trump. You want to see something go from cold to hot real fast? Put handcuffs on Donald Trump," he said, referring to a reference I'd made to a "cold civil war."

The anger in David's tone sent a little spark of fear running into my stomach.

"I'm not going near New York because now I'm a felon," he continued. "They will put me in jail for the rest of my life. But you don't think these motherfuckers are going to come out of the woodwork if you lock up their favorite president? Go for it. New York will burn to the *fucking ground*, dude."

I also hiked with Lisa Swanson along the lush, seemingly infinite Chesapeake and Ohio Canal Towpath and it quickly became my favorite hike in the area. At one point, a big, long black snake shot out from the grass in the general direction of my feet before changing course.

"Children can identify hundreds of brand logos," Lisa griped. "But they can't name ten species of plants in their backyards. Isn't that sad to you?"

"I can't name ten plant species in my backyard," I said.

I went to the town junk shop, littered with cast iron skillets hanging outside and old bikes. Inside, I found a Confederate flag folded up amid a pile of stuff. The junk shop had a couple of racist ceramics too. I saw a little Black shoeshine boy, or something like it.

A man named David Yost owned the shop, which had a wooden sign above the door that said "Yost Bicycles & Antiques." His daughter Theresa was the woman who had helped broker the sale of the VDARE castle.

"You interested in that?" Yost said of a racist figurine.

"No, I was just looking at it."

"It's nice. Very old item. It's authentic. Everything here is authentic."

Yost walked me to the back of the shop where, if anything, it got even more cluttered. Junk filled every corner of the space. If it hadn't been for two cramped aisles, it would have been impossible to access the back of the shop. I asked Yost about his daughter and about the castle sale.

"People started harassing her over that," he said. "Everybody was so mad. I don't know anything about white nationalism or whatever it was. Theresa didn't know either."

"Is that true?" I asked.

"Absolutely, it's true," he said. "And Theresa doesn't know what to do with this shop either. I guess everybody's just waiting for me to die and then they're gonna have to deal with all this stuff."

"I'm sorry," I said.

"Why are you sorry?"

"The way you said it, it sounded sad," I said.

"It ain't sad. It's just life."

My tooth throbbed. I picked up a cast iron skillet.

"How about this?"

"I just cleaned that one up. It's from 1916. You can look it up," he said. "Check the back of it."

I turned it around in my hands. It was beautiful. The words "Favorite, Piqua Ware" were etched into the back in a curly font. I wondered who had owned it first.

"1916?"

"Yessir."

"How much for this one?"

"Sixty."

"Okay," I said.

I started to take out sixty dollars and saw a pocketknife resting on a pile of old, disentangled telephone parts. The handle of the knife said "ALABAMA" on it.

"What's that?" I asked.

"It's an Alabama pocketknife."

"I'll take that too."

"Twenty."

"I'll give you ten."

Yost took my seventy dollars without debate and walked me to the front of the shop, where he showed me crossbows, old sleds, and camera equipment that looked like it could have once belonged to D. W. Griffith.

"So, you've been here your whole life? What kind of changes have you seen?"

Yost gave it some serious thought.

"Are you married?" he asked.

"Technically," I said.

"Okay, that's good. Because I don't want to offend. But facts are facts. There are a lot of gay people in the town," he said. "Just all of a sudden, one day, a whole bunch of gays and lesbians. It won't matter to me soon because I'll be dead."

"Got it."

"Some people might be offended by that. That's why I asked if you were married."

"Mr. Yost," I said. "Thank you very much."

"Pleasure doing business with you."

The next morning, I got a tarot reading from a queer-friendly shop next door to Trey's place. My seer used two tarot decks and also a small pendulum, which he told me would work in conjunction with the cards, pointing me in the direction of the truth. He asked me what I wanted revealed, and I thought about it for a moment. I had a legal fight against the SPLC, I had my marriage split, and I had the VDARE project.

For the legal fight, he said I should prepare for a dramatic change coming. A good change. For Aadya, I should know that she was at peace at that moment and would eventually find a place of stability with me. For VDARE, it was more complicated.

"I see a battle, followed by a celebration," he said. "A big celebration. It could be the town, relieved that they leave. But the secondary cards suggest a delay of some kind."

"What kind of delay?"

"These are indicators to help you to find out the truth. It's not an exact science."

"A battle, a celebration, and a delay," I said. "In that order."

"Correct."

I bought a pack of tarot cards on my way out. That evening, on the eve of the conference, I returned to the Stucco Drive properties and noticed a gray Audi out front. I also watched a woman with blonde hair pull in between the gates of the castle and offload something out of her trunk. I wondered if it was Denise Trent Selby.

On the morning of the conference, my tooth scorched with pain. I had breakfast with Kate Lehman, the woman whom counterprotesters had jeered during her prayer, fresh off of her letter to the editor questioning our willingness to accept authoritarianism. As she told me her story, I gripped my chin from below and winced.

"Are you okay?" she asked.

"I have tooth pain, unfortunately."

She texted me a phone number.

"Please give her a call," she said.

I read the name.

"Magic Miller."

"My dentist."

"Her name is Magic Miller?"

"She's very good."

I remembered where I'd heard the name. Magic Miller had sold the coffee shop to Trey in 2017. Before Kate and I wrapped up, I asked her why so many people in Berkeley Springs aligned themselves with VDARE when tourism was so important to the town's economy.

"Because the same people who hate immigrants in Berkeley Springs also hate the tourists," she explained.

25

All Kinds of Evil People

When I met Lisa Marie at the park, she had a gun holstered to her hip. I had met her a few times on my trips to town, but didn't recall seeing her carrying a piece. She might have had it for the VDARE conference, anticipating what could happen there.

Lisa Marie handed me a few sheets of paper with dates and timestamps.

"What's all this?"

"A timeline, so you have it."

She had dark hair with faint streaks of gray and wore big, circular glasses around her pale, probing eyes. We walked around the edge of the park and up the wooded path that led to the castle. We climbed past a single stone battlement positioned across the street. I leaned against a traffic barrier.

"So, I think we'll just hang out for a bit," I said.

"Maybe they won't come through here yet."

"No, I think they will. They gotta be in time for dinner. That means they have to be on time for cocktails and hors d'oeuvres."

I looked more closely at the typed pages she'd given me.

"Thanks for this," I said, shaking it in my hand.

Dec 20th, 2021: Went to St. Vince DePaul Catholic Church in BS for 9AM Mass with mom. Shook Lydia's hand and said "Peace be with you, Black Lives Matter" during the exchange of peace. . . .

Feb 20th, 2022: Received letter from "S Black" claiming to represent the Brimelows accusing me of harassment.

"So, again, they sent you a legal threat?" I asked.

"Sort of. They spelled my name wrong on it," she said.

"And is it true that the church started to provide armed security after that?"

"It was the local Knights of Columbus who provided security."

"Knights of Columbus?"

"They're heavily involved in the church and right-wing politics here."

Much of what she'd written on the other typed pages dwelled on an incident with Trey and Paul that Lisa Marie had first described to me over the phone. The incident took place in June 2022, when reactionaries staged a "Freedom Rally" in town and Lisa Marie showed up to counter it. Police pressured Lisa Marie at the event, treating her as a threat. The next day, Scott Collinash's Pride celebration went off. Everything happening in this energetic forty-eight-hour period downtown seemed to churn into one big moment for Lisa Marie.

Lisa Marie and some of her friends had gone to the Star Theater after Pride, where Trey sought to keep the celebration going, with a sing-along of *The Rocky Horror Picture Show.* But Lisa Marie got into a conflict with some of the people there. Or rather, she perceived them as being instigators. And then she said that Paul had interrogated her about her "intentions," insinuating that she sought to carry out violence. Maybe it had to do with all the attention the police had given her.

"What you have heard about me isn't true," Lisa Marie said she told Paul.

Lisa Marie argued with Paul and left the theater, and he followed her outside. She claimed that after that, someone from the Star had called the police on her, suggesting that she had terroristic intentions. The next day, someone from the Hampshire County Sheriff's Department served a protective order, referring to threats against someone who was inside the theater that night. Lisa Marie cried. She felt totally scapegoated.

"That sucks," I said.

"Yeah."

"You want me to talk to them about it?"

"Trey's gonna act like she has no idea," she said.

A white shuttle bus started coming up Route 9. I flipped on my phone and filmed the bus pulling up to the gates of the castle. It drove forward and then backed into the property. A door opened and about eight people emerged. It was hard to see their faces. The body types and gaits told me they were older men.

"Looks like *Dawn of the Dead*," I said.

After the bus pulled away, a skinny guy who looked like he was in his late thirties walked out on the castle side of the street, looking down on us from an elevated position. His unfortunate haircut demanded attention. Greasy strands of oily noodles dangled wildly over pasty, skin-shaved sides. It was a disgraceful look, maybe the worst haircut I had ever seen.

He cupped his bony hands and started yelling things at us.

"You are trespassing!" he yelled.

"What?"

"You are *trespassing*!"

"I can't hear a word you're saying," I lied.

"You are *trespassing*!"

"We can't hear you!" Lisa Marie added.

We could hear him. We just felt like dragging it out.

"You have been warned!" he yelled.

He turned to walk away, and I took a picture of his head from the back, all smeared with that hair. I later figured out that this was likely "Noah Arnold," the guy who had filmed both the Black Lives Matter event in Berkeley Springs and the January 6, 2021, stuff at the Capitol in DC for VDARE.

We walked down the wooded path. I called Larry Schultz to ask him about my potential exposure for trespassing. It hadn't occurred to me that the battlement across the street formed part of their property.

"As long as you abide by the warning they gave and there were no signs, you should be fine," Larry said.

Lisa Marie and I marched through the park. I tossed two Advils into my mouth. I waved a finger at the Country Inn.

"I've heard that they do deals with the inn, so I expect them to pick people up from there," I said.

"Deals?"

"Like you'd have with a wedding party."

Lisa Marie and I made a quick plan to buy drinks at the inn's bar and then split up slightly to grab as many photos as we could of whoever emerged. As we ordered, a shuttle bus appeared at the entrance to the inn. I grabbed my draft beer and sat in the lobby.

A group of men wandered about. A man with his wife and two other men took seats out front. I thought I recognized the man and his wife, so I put my beer down and walked outside to call Hannah, to make it look like I was preoccupied with something that wasn't them. I snapped pictures of them outside while I talked.

The man, Warren Balogh, was a movement lifer. His last activist group, National Justice Party, had ties to that weird guy named Charles Bausman who had dashed in from Russia in 2018 and vanished back into Russia in the immediate aftermath of January 6.[1]

Balogh loved Hitler. He'd grown up in the movement, because his father was squarely in the movement. His friends loved Hitler too. One associate, Greg Conte, left a voicemail for National Justice Party members around the time the group folded in which he shouted, "Are you for or against the Führer?"

Emily Youcis, Balogh's wife, was once known as "Pistachio Girl" at Phillies games before they fired her for being too racist. I knew that she and Lydia posted on Gab at the same time, and given the paucity of women on that platform, it wouldn't have surprised me to learn that they either became friends or deepened a preexisting friendship through that site.

What stood out to me was that VDARE seemed to care so little now about optics that they were having hardened Hitlerites over for dinner.

What point was there in denying that you were a white nationalist group if you were going to have people like this at your conference?

I sent the pictures to Trey along with examples of Youcis making racist comments in the past. In one social media post, Youcis endorsed making calls to hang Jews, Black people, and gays, though those weren't the words she used to describe those groups. Trey then posted these examples to Berkeley Springs Cares, a Facebook page she and Paul managed that was designed to express resistance to the VDARE castle and the culture around it.

After Lisa Marie and I spent about half an hour capturing the comings and goings of VDARE's buses, a woman working for the inn asked us to leave. Lisa Marie didn't take well to that request and sprung to her feet, arguing bias.

"You're taking orders from Lydia Brimelow," Lisa Marie said. "Is that right?"

"We're just getting reports that you guys are taking pictures of the guests."

"We're paying customers. Are we not allowed to take pictures of a place where we're drinking?"

I got a feeling that the woman didn't want to be doing this to us. Lisa Marie raised her voice, and I could feel the woman getting more and more nervous.

"It's just interesting that the inn gives preferential treatment to a white nationalist group," Lisa Marie said. "Where she's not even here but she's able to make phone calls to chase customers away."

"If you don't take pictures, you don't have to leave but—"

"It's okay," I interjected. "Really, it's okay."

Lisa Marie had reacted to the woman like someone who had grown accustomed to people treating her unfairly. The two of us headed over to Cacapon Brewery for another beer, where Lisa Marie calmed down. Along the way, we passed an oversized flag with Trump's mugshot on it. We drank more beer.

"They did *not* have many people there," Lisa Marie said.

"No, they did not."

"VDARE's not doing so well, I think."

After a few beers, we hiked up a small hill to the landing where Lisa Swanson lived. Lisa Swanson set up a spread of hummus, bread, salad, and quiche. Her friend Sue, a light-haired woman with glasses and a downbeat manner of speaking, came over. Sue ran an art gallery outside of town. The four of us sat on the porch, overlooking the castle and talking. Lisa Swanson handed me a pair of binoculars.

"Can you believe it? I found these on a hiking trail," she said.

I watched the lights and saw the first of the buses transporting people out. I passed the specs on to Lisa Marie.

"They're coming down the hill right now," Lisa Marie said.

"It looked like eight to twelve on every shuttle and maybe three shuttles. To be generous, I would say thirty-five people came off and on. Then there were the people who arrived early and might be special guests of the Brimelows. So, let's say they had fifteen people already inside. That would be fifty people. If I'm undercounting, maybe sixty, but I doubt it. My money would be on fewer than fifty people," I said.

"Either way, not too many," Lisa Swanson said.

The next day was Saturday. Through tooth pain, I gulped down some yogurt and watched online as Keith Woods, an Irish bigot whom Elon Musk had recently promoted through his app X, gave a talk called "Immigration and Democracy."

Meanwhile, VDARE gave away the content from its conference for free, after having previously talked about selling online packages through the VDARE website. Two guests who'd been announced in their ads—the embattled comedian Anthony Cumia, known for making racist comments about Black people, and a micro-influencer named Amanda Milius, daughter of the Hollywood writer and director John Milius—never posted anything online to indicate they attended and didn't speak on the broadcast.

The third VDARE conference looked like a flop to me. The dream of growing the movement under a big roof in Morgan County, West

Virginia, had sputtered, and in the content I watched on X, I saw that whenever Peter spoke, he sounded shaky and insecure.

"If you stand up the camera might catch you. As you know there are all kinds of evil people who want to get a look at your faces," Peter warned the room as the conference went to break.

I zipped the Camaro along the curves overlooking the Potomac to Lisa Marie's holler, which sat adjacent to a Confederate burial ground. Her home was completely obscured by a network of trees and green, cavernous dips in the land.

When I got there, Lisa Marie showed me the strange jars along her property where she cultivated new mushrooms for harvest. Her farm seemed isolated. The roads around it were labyrinthine. She told me she used that to get out of trouble's way when people followed her.

"How often are people following you?"

"It happens, actually," she said.

If someone followed you in the Berkeley Springs area, driving straight into those twisting branches, dips, and turns, she said, enabled her to get a lead, and then she could duck hard into a holler while she was still out of visibility and kill the ignition and the lights. Then she'd wait for the bastards to drive past her on the main road. I'd had other people, including a photojournalist named Dominic Gwinn, tell me they'd used the land to disappear when they were being followed too.

Cars got swallowed by the bushes all the time, either because you couldn't see ahead of you in the night and fog, or because people dumped them there. I pointed out a black Bentley buried in a mash of branches, and without skipping a beat Lisa Marie said, "Somebody stole it."

When we pulled into Berkeley Springs, rain was coming down on the streets, giving the place a gray sheen. Paul had set up a network of flags from foreign countries, part of their annual pro-immigration counterprogramming to the VDARE conference.

Under the gazebo, people had baked goods to sample from different countries. Trey introduced me to a woman named Judy Gubinski, a baker in her late fifties, who had moved into town to focus on her poetry and creative writing. For the occasion, Judy had made Dutch Almond Bars, with homemade marzipan filling. They were something she used to make as a pastry chef in Shepherdstown, West Virginia. I had to eat them around the pain in my mouth, but I found them exceptional. I right away wanted them with black coffee, which is the way I prefer to enjoy my pastries.

Judy had black hair and a pale complexion. She reminded me of an adult version of the women I hung out with at goth clubs in high school and college. Her personality seemed to be slightly different from theirs, and certainly more influenced by a small-town environment, but she had a brooding intensity that I admired.

"These are really good," I said.

"I'm glad you like them. You know, I've wanted to talk to you. About what you're writing and—," she said before lowering her voice, "—about some of the things that have happened in this town."

"Okay," I said. "Let's talk."

Jim Hoyt, the man who had been targeted with threats at his home as the head of the local Democratic Party, sat in a Biden/Harris-marked tent in the park with a big smile on his face. He half stood up when I approached and waved.

I started to say hello back, but before I finished speaking, a guy in a black truck slowed down at the edge of the park, cupped his hands, and yelled in Jim's direction:

"*Fuck* Biden! *Fuck* Biden! *Fuck* you!"

On the final day of the conference, VDARE streamed a highlight reel of Peter's old media hits. They'd grabbed most of the clips from the 1990s, and in each one, Peter defended his positions with a confident, naughty grin. The video clips had the feel of a farewell, like the way they honor older actors at awards shows.

I watched the final part of the stream from a table outside of Fairfax Coffee House, where with the other eye I watched Paul setting up for Zach Shrewsbury. Paul had introduced me to Zach back in January, and

I had seen them working together on some local radio spots. Zach was running for Senate on the Democratic ticket.

The thirty-three-year-old grandson of a coal miner and a Marine, Zach ran a Bernie Sanders–style campaign, selling progressivism in a self-consciously unpretentious wrapper. Physically, he resembled John Fetterman but with a ginger beard. He used his big body to create space and command attention.

Paul had set Zach up to give a talk in the park, but only five other people sat listening to it. I couldn't make out what Zach was saying. After he wrapped up, he walked over to the coffee shop and we shook hands. His T-shirt said, "Jesus was a liberator of the oppressed, not a mascot of the powerful."

The dentist, Magic Miller, got in my mouth on the Monday after the conference and prescribed an antibiotic for me that didn't work, along with a painkiller that wasn't strong enough. I met Patti Miller at Fairfax. She told me about a woman named Gail in town who was an environmental activist and had recently died.

"And her husband said during the eulogy that the tensions in this town played a big role in *killing* her," Patti said.

That afternoon around five, Trey called me down from my room at the Airbnb to the Lazy Sundae to try a new ice cream flavor. She told me the same story about Gail.

"Two days before the memorial, I was at the coffeehouse, and I saw Gail's husband there with his two daughters," Trey said. "He said, 'Are you coming to the memorial?' and I said, 'Of course I will, honey.' Then he said, 'Good, because I'm inviting a lot of people and I'm telling you, I got something to say. From *Gail.*' "

"Wow," I said.

"He said, 'Gail died of a broken heart because of all the division in this town.' "

I learned some other things about the town that day. Apparently, Geoffrey Wendel had disappeared to Costa Rica and started running his shop remotely sometime early in 2024. I learned that because I wanted him to give me a tarot reading and couldn't find him.

I also learned that Denise Trent Selby had brokered a visit between the Brimelows and a woman named Judith Shumate, as a way to try to destigmatize them in the eyes of liberals and "normies." As a lesbian, Judith seemed like an atypical target for recruitment, but she was white. The Brimelows believed in their ability to persuade white liberals that the nasty things people said about them wouldn't hold up if they simply met them in person. That's why I think they chose her, at least.

"There are a lot of people who won't support Trey and Paul's businesses because of the stances they've taken," Judith told me at the coffee shop. "I think it's very unfair."

Judith had a grandmotherly quality about her and a disarming smile.

"I think that what they're doing with the Bath Christmas Project is insidious," Judith said. "In a small Appalachian town, it's very easy to be swayed by money. But they have a castle, right? They have a castle."

Judith said that when they led her into the castle she was surprised by what it looked like. She found it shabby and in need of upkeep. Judith said she told them she was married to a woman and the Brimelows received the information warmly.

"Well, in addition to being queer, you're also white," I added.

"Yes, I am."

Judith said she felt like Peter had a warmer connection with Denise Selby than he did with Lydia.

"Well, marriage is tough," I said.

Back in Forest Hills, New York, I finally got a root canal. I saw that *The New Yorker* had run a profile of Zach Shrewsbury. It didn't matter. He lost the primary by ten thousand votes, enough of a margin to consider his campaign a disappointment.

Around this time, seven different people from Berkeley Springs sent me a link to the same website. It was a simple-looking design with an image of the castle on the homepage. The URL was "berkeleyspringscastle.net," a slight deviation from "berkeleyspringscastle.com," an official promotional site for the building.

The top of the homepage read "Berkeley Springs Castle Watchers," with "Watchers" highlighted in red. A banner proclaimed, "Keeping Our Community Safe," and below that, a statement said, "We are a collective of local business owners, residents, artists and concerned citizens. Since VDARE has moved to our lovely town there has been an increased amount of dangerous extremists who they have invited to Berkeley Springs to visit them in their castle. From open Neo-Nazis to Holocaust deniers, VDARE has done nothing but try to destroy what makes Berkeley Springs great."

The author needed a copy editor. There were local businesses listed on a page called "collaborators." The first five that were listed were the Country Inn; Matthew Omps, the inn's manager; the Bath Christmas Project; Hunter Clark, the man who oversaw the Bath Christmas Project; and Denise Selby. Next, Charlie Curia got a section. So did Sue Evans.

Whoever was behind the site then included a few people who were affiliated with the Knights of Columbus Council No. 12191, including Larry Landon, who also worked with the Berkeley Springs Planning Commission. Those on the list also included Barb Wolfe, the sister of Jeanne Mozier, who had since left town.

A section called "affiliates" listed the Brimelows, Kevin DeAnna, and John Derbyshire, as well as Warren Balogh and Emily Youcis. I found the last two interesting, considering that I was the guy who had identified them and I never wrote anything about it beyond my personal notes.

The section included a photo that Lisa Marie had taken when we were together at the inn that evening. I asked Lisa Marie if she'd played any role in mounting this mysterious website, and she said she knew nothing about it. I decided not to interrogate her about it.

Multiple people asked me privately if Trey or Paul had made the website. In public settings, neighbors insinuated it. Someone did it at a meeting for Travel Berkeley Springs, the tourism board. Trey denied having any connection to the website there.

Then Geoffrey Wendel emailed me from his new home base in Costa Rica to tell me he thought it was Trey and Paul. "Sigh, this is reading like the Johansons needing funds for something," he wrote. "They do donation drives to get funds under various guises."

Someone who knew Trey as a friend, but asked to be discreet, also wanted to know if she'd mounted the website. This person called me to ask just for the sake of curiosity.

"You think it's Trey?"

"A little," the person said.

"Trey hasn't even denied it to me yet, and I won't ask her because it's just obviously not her," I said. "This person who launched the site is seeking donations in Monero, a privacy-focused cryptocurrency. Does that really sound like Trey to you?"

Trey called me at the end of May with some news. She told me that the Brimelows and the "collaborators" listed on the Castle Watchers website had met at the Country Inn. She had seen them there, having a discussion.

"I'm sure they're looking to sue someone," I said.

"I'm sure that's probably it."

"But they still have no way of figuring out who made the site."

"They probably think it's me!" Trey said.

I told Lisa Marie about the meeting right after I spoke with Trey.

"Isn't that interesting?" Lisa Marie said.

"Why?"

"Because it sounds like they're definitely *collaborators*," she said.

"Everyone thinks Trey made the site," I said.

"Maybe she did," Lisa Marie said.

26

The New Materialists

My family celebrated Father's Day early in 2024 and I drove down to Berkeley Springs on that Sunday, June 16. I rented a black Mustang convertible this time, hoping to build on the pleasure I'd gotten from driving that Camaro. The weather was hot and I took the top down on the highways.

A few positive things started to happen to me around this time. My brain started to remember things I had forgotten. Dr. K started to tune down the drug frequency, relying mostly on lithium to keep me level. The SPLC entered into mediation with my legal team. The wait had been brutal, but I had cause to imagine something approximating a victory there.

I parked the Mustang in the lot behind the Lazy Sundae and then hiked up to the castle again. Purple pre-summer evening light blanketed the town. No one could deny Berkeley Springs' beauty in summer. I passed the castle and then I walked farther, to the edge of where I could see Stucco Drive.

Standing on the edge of the property and obscured by heavy shadows, Lydia looked down at me from the long staircase of the middle house. It looked like she held a mug of tea in her hand.

Lydia waved like she was signaling something very important to a person who could not properly hear her. I raised my hand and waved back to her in an awkward, timid motion. Then I walked back down the road, feeling a little embarrassed.

I wrote to the Brimelows that night: "Hey Peter and Lydia, I'll be in town this week until Pride and I wanted to know if you would be amenable to meeting for coffee. Is that something you would consider? I know it sounds weird but I'm serious."

A little later, a friend sent me a link to Lydia's Gab page. She had a different take on our interaction on Stucco: "I called the cops again today on Michael Edison Hayden. He has trespassed three times in the last six months. The first time, he found my youngest unattended at a private social event and asked her personal questions. This time, he seemed to be taking photos of my 12yo while she walked the dog."

I had seen no twelve-year-olds. I had seen no dogs. I had taken no photos. A Gab user, @WytesOwnley, responded to Lydia with, "Does not sound like he's afraid of you."

The next afternoon, I spoke with the sheriff's office about that alleged racist incident at Sleepy Creek Campground that had taken place in 2020. Four uniformed guys met me outside in a parking lot overlooking the McDonald's and the Food Lion. They folded their arms and made faces like they were studying a new species of dog.

"Are you the writer in town?" an officer with a peach fuzz mustache asked. "We got a call about somebody trespassing."

"I was standing on Route 9. There is no sidewalk there, so I stood on the shoulder of the road," I said. "That's perfectly legal."

Officer Peach Fuzz nodded.

"He's right about that," another officer said.

That night, a group of a little over a dozen Berkeley Springs residents met at the Star Theater. An out-of-town community organizer named Ben Fink came to talk about how to unite people. Paul had orchestrated it.

We sat in a circle and went around it introducing ourselves. A woman named Kathleen said her father had died of coal miner's lung. She had liberal friends and she feared that they wouldn't talk to her if she voted for Trump in the coming election. She said she had complicated feelings about immigration, which made her more likely to choose Trump.

A woman named Joanie Dolina, who had this wonderful silver streak at the front of her dark brown hair, said she had been coming to Berkeley Springs since she was sixteen. Joanie had an activist mother, she said. Someone had burned a cross in their yard when she was a kid.

"And it saddens me so much to see the divisions in the town," Joanie told the group. "I plan on leaving Berkeley Springs. Really, I do. I honestly would try harder to stay here if VDARE were gone."

They put us into one-on-one breakouts. Before I could excuse myself, Patti Miller sat down with me. She hadn't heard about what had happened to me around the SPLC and Palestine until recently and wanted to express her sadness. She also told me she heard about someone affiliated with VDARE buying a coffee shop in Martinsburg.

I told Patti that she was likely talking about Tim Pool, a YouTuber who never appeared in public without wearing a knit cap. His shtick was to rant about the news. Pool had bought up a bunch of property in Martinsburg, including a skatepark.[1] Peter's daughter from his first marriage, Hannah Claire Brimelow, worked for Pool.

Patti didn't really care about Pool. She was only ramping up to the real issue.

"Michael, I have Black friends and they tell me they don't want to come here anymore. Black people feel safer in Paw Paw and in areas beyond that than they do here. Something has *got* to change," she said. "What we need is what you talked about. Our town needs to bring our money together and *buy* that castle. And then we can change the tone, change the way we're seen."

I'd forgotten that I'd talked about that with Patti. I thought it was a nice fairy-tale idea, the town buying the castle back from VDARE. I couldn't claim credit for it. I thought Lisa Swanson had articulated it first.

"I hope you guys can do it," I said. "I love it here."

A day later, the SPLC settled. The money was good. Good enough to keep me writing, good enough to hold things down for my kids for a bit. Lisa Swanson and Joanie Dolina met me at Trey's place that night to celebrate with me. Trey gifted me a comically large bottle of pinot grigio and took pictures of me holding the bottle. It was the same make as the bottles Paul had embedded in the space around their door.

Everyone wanted to talk about Bill Carper, the chief of police who had recently quit. People told me he was an honest person in a dishonest local system. Paul said that Carper had investigated things that had affected him and Trey, including an incident at the inn where Trey believed that someone had tried to drug her. Specifically, Trey believed that one of VDARE's guests at the third conference had put something in her drink. Paul told me that Carper told him that the reason he had quit was that the town wouldn't let him do his job.

The next day, Juneteenth, Judy Gubinski and I met in the basement of the Cacapon Lodge and talked for two hours. She was in the process of finishing off a dream home in the woods nearby. I ordered soggy French fries and drank four cups of Sanka to justify our seat there. We discussed Carper too.

"It's the corrupt good ole boys network," she said.

Judy had relocated to Berkeley Springs from Martinsburg to write. She self-published poems, short stories, and sketches through her own website. She distrusted authority figures and loathed bullies and said she had come from a fanatical Catholic background. I said I understood what that might have been like because of the Arab Christians in my family.

"Normies are the people in this town," Judy said, referring to what Peter had said at the Christmas event. "Normies are the people they're *radicalizing*. Lydia doesn't respect the people in this town. She's using them. Peter is using them too. They look at the town and they say we can get these *normies*—to treat *us* as normal."

Judy blamed some of the normalization of the Brimelows on Amy's Facebook group. Amy, the psychologist who had attended my second talk in town, created her group as an "experiment," she told people. She hoped to encourage a civil discourse that could eventually unite Berkeley Springs again.

The group had attracted a wide range of people, combining reactionaries with people like Judy, Paul, and Trey. Amy co-moderated alongside a woman who did people's taxes in town and leaned conservative. The understanding was that Amy was the polar opposite of any conservative, and because of it, people would get fair-minded moderation from both sides.

Initially, no one challenged Amy's progressive bona fides. She could point to her résumé. She had established an antiracism board for the Mid-Atlantic Group Psychotherapy Society. She presented antiracism as being foundational to her work in psychology. She was molded by the language used in progressive spaces.

Like Judith Shumate, Amy made the trek to the castle as part of that effort to humanize the Brimelows. Those trips emerged through collaborative discussion in Amy's Facebook group. Denise Trent Selby, in her role as a frequent castle helper, had brokered the conversations, and Denise was widely considered to be the most radical person in town other than the Brimelows themselves.

Judy Gubinski recoiled at the prospect of sipping herbal tea with accused white nationalists, so for her, Amy's willingness to connect with the Brimelows served as a reason to distrust her. She found the kind of moderation that Amy applied to the Facebook group even more suspect, particularly after Amy locked her out of the account for a month over a contentious exchange that played out in the comment section of someone's post.

In a phone call in late April, Amy told me she had "been treated worse" by what she called "my own people," meaning liberals, than she had by reactionaries. I met a lot of people like Amy throughout the Trump era. She belonged to a subset of intellectuals and pseudo-intellectuals who wanted people to know that they opposed Trump, but also couldn't stay silent when liberals or socialists embarrassed them with hypocrisy and stupidity.

Once Amy got a taste for pointing out the moral failures of people from her own political side, she made it part of her identity. That's how her friends—later, her former friends—perceived it. People described Amy to me as being cursed with a high-pitched superiority complex. And liberals in town had started to believe that Amy used people up. Judy felt that she baited people into her group under the auspices of open discussion, and then used them as part of a psychological experiment.

"I want to show you something," Judy said as we moved on from Facebook talk.

Judy handed me what looked like a Catholic religious pamphlet. It was yellow and featured an image of the Virgin Mary, presented as a bronze statue, weeping. It said, "*The Divine Mother Weeping: A Mystical Legend of the Springs.* Transmitted by Remy Baudelaire Roche."

"What is this?"

"Take a look inside," Judy said.

Judy's eyes gave away her excitement. It looked like one of the pamphlets you could pick up on the way out of Mass. It imitated an authentic Catholic tract, right down to the extravagant, celebratory prose, but Judy's interest in the pages meant that something else was also there. I read enough to pick up that the author had injected heavy symbolism around the Berkeley Springs water into it.

"Is this some subversive thing about the Brimelows?"

"These pamphlets started appearing all over town. Including in places where Catholics congregate," Judy said.

She flashed a geeky, mischievous smile.

"And you know nothing about how that happened?"

"No!" she said.

"Of course not," I said. I read more of the pamphlet's text:

A false Madonna will be seen praying, in the name of the Lord.
She and hers, the new materialists, will do anything to normalize themselves and their dangerous, conquering ideology.
They will do this rather than recognize the Divine within all humankind, as well as in creature, flower and tree.

The idea seemed to be to sow doubts about the Brimelows—among the very people they sought to befriend—by using Catholic tropes.

That night, the Johansons screened *Django Unchained* as a Juneteenth-themed event. I hadn't ever seen a film at the Star Theater before, and the 1940s atmosphere stood out when the screen lit up the space. The out-of-the-way nature of the theater enhanced that feeling of being in a dream. Only six people attended, including me and Paul.

Few moments in my life have felt as surreal as watching the gore that followed the "white cake" scene from directly underneath VDARE's headquarters. In the film, Calvin Candie, a white supremacist plantation owner played by Leonardo DiCaprio, eats a sugary-looking white cake before the antiracist Dr. King Schultz, played by Christoph Waltz, shoots him through the heart, as an alternative to shaking his hand.

The next morning, I walked to Mountain Laurel Artisans to try to connect with Charlie Curia or Sue Evans and hear their side of the biergarten story. Five seconds after Sue realized who I was, she started visibly shaking. She looked like a pressure cooker. I must have seemed like Satan stepping into her store.

Sue pointed a finger.

"There's the door," she said.

"Hey—"

Some light country music played.

"I'm asking you one time and then I'm calling the police," she said.

"What would the charge be? What would the police charge me with?"

"I'm asking you once," she said.

"I just wanted to know if you wanted to comment on a few things," I said.

Sue called the police. I stood there for a minute debating whether I should stay and talk to the police or leave. I was growing tired of people doing this type of thing to me. I decided to leave. Something even more stupid might happen if I stayed.

"If the police want to talk to me, I'll be at the coffee shop," I said.

I had a bagel and coffee while watching the police come and go. Nobody came to talk to me but Trey. She seemed to get a kick out of the whole thing. She sat across from me, wearing her baking apron.

Charlie Curia emerged from his store and looked at me from a distance. He then gave a piece of paper to a young worker. He had been doing construction on the unfinished biergarten space, which was positioned to my left. The young worker then handed the paper to me. It warned me against trespassing in the future.

"Thanks," I said.

I spent the afternoon in Winchester, Virginia, with Claire Goforth, a reporter from the Daily Dot, the internet news site. Claire's family lived there and in Paw Paw, and she had bright red hair and very fair skin, which she attributed to being Appalachian. She had been home for family reasons and started teaching me different expressions people in the area used. One of them was "flatlander." That described both me and Peter—people who came from outside of the hills. Another was "through hell and creation." I felt I had been through hell and creation the whole year.

That night, I drove back to attend a summer solstice party at a house in town with a porch. Joanie Dolina of the silver-streaked hair was there, and Lisa Swanson, and the Johansons. People drank and smoked cigarettes. Some of the women wore flowers in their hair. People asked me about Sue Evans and the cops. After the incident became Facebook fodder, Paul had gotten into a conflict with Amy's husband, Doug, about it. Paul defended my reputation.

At the end of the night, I was starting to leave, when I saw the largest insect I had ever seen in my life resting on the doorframe. A moth bigger than a side plate flapped its wings once and then did nothing. I felt my groin suck up into my stomach. I pulled Trey aside like she was my mother.

"There's an extremely big moth here," I said.

Everyone gathered around the giant moth and roared like it was the most wonderful thing in the world. Someone deftly goaded the beast off the doorframe and it fluttered down onto the wood of the porch. I looked down on it, longing to leave, but unable to raise my foot to walk by it.

"It's not going to hurt you, don't worry," Trey said.

I celebrated my settlement with a stay at Potomac Peak, a cabin overlooking that mystical view of the river and three intersecting states. At night, when I returned from the moth's house, I sat watching the distant lights of the trains draw closer before they filled the green hills with their howls. It was incredible, one of the most transcendent travel experiences I've ever had.

I wrote there and drank coffee. I showered outdoors, which I despised, and then headed down to the Country Inn for Pride. When I stopped at the Prospect Overlook on the way, to take pictures, I became fixated with some of the graffiti written on the guardrails. "Spanky = Big Dick." "Piss Cock."

My number one favorite simply said, "Cursed Town."

When I arrived in the cursed town, I met Scott Collinash, and he gave me the kind of hello you give someone who carries a reputation. I disliked the vibe. I felt like all of a sudden I was caught up in the town's bullshit as a character myself. I tried to cheer him up by buying a few raffle tickets in support of Pride. Scott had a gentle-looking face. He gave me a smile after I made the contribution.

Lisa Swanson and Amy were sitting together inside the inn, and I joined them. It was the first time I had met Amy in person; we'd only talked on the phone once and exchanged some text messages. When she smiled she looked vulnerable, like she was afraid someone might snatch the smile away from her.

Amy came across as a kind person and spoke empathetically in my defense regarding Sue Evans calling the police. But during the conversation, I made a few comments criticizing Lydia. It was just a few days after she'd called the police on me, of course. I was tired of the Brimelows lying about me.

"Well, Lydia has always been nice to *me*," Amy said.

She leaned into her remark with a sprinkling of defiance. Lisa Swanson popped her head back for a beat. Then she raised her eyebrows at Amy.

"Well, I'm sure Eva Braun was a very nice person," Lisa said.

27

Ten Hyenas

Drought consumed Morgan County that July. I sat under a forbidding sun at a convenience shop on Route 9 and read about it in *The Morgan Messenger* over a cheese sandwich I'd bought inside. The drought was causing brush fires. As I read, and ate, Aadya called. She said Joe Biden had dropped out of the race. Then, I lost reception.

The convenience store was halfway to Berkeley Springs from Paw Paw, where I had just camped in a converted school bus. Claire Goforth, the Daily Dot reporter, took me through the backroads in a side-by-side, a little buggy ideal for rattling around the hills. From the rear seat, with branches flying by, Paw Paw looked like a jungle. It reminded me of parts of India. People sat on their porches to watch nature and smoke cigarettes.

We saw nine other side-by-sides, and each time, the riders gave us big waves. By the time we arrived at Claire's stepfather's house, the purple basketball shorts I was wearing were caked in dirt.

The day after Biden dropped out, I did my usual trip to the baths and then had beers with Lisa Marie. The ascendancy of Kamala Harris as Biden's replacement became the only thing anyone could talk about. Lisa Marie had no faith in Harris and she hated the Dems. She viewed them as complicit in building the culture of Trump.

The drought broke as we walked back and sheets of rain fell along Mercer Street. I let Lisa Marie hang out in my room to wait out the rain. The Airbnb had a view of the castle—we could see it through the window—and we felt a cool shift in the air as moisture sucked away the dryness.

On July 23, 2024, my colleague Hannah had been scrolling X when she saw something VDARE had posted. She called me a little after 2 p.m. to tell me about it. I was doing my laundry at Trey's house.

"Mike, open your fucking messages!"

Hannah had just sent a flurry of the same text to people, including sources in the movement. It was a link. Peter Brimelow had announced the disbandment of VDARE.[1]

"Wait, what?"

"Yes."

Hannah and I laughed together.

"They're just fucking *gone*?" I said.

"Just like that."

The whole thing seemed absurd to me. I started texting people from town. No one else could believe it either. They'd fought VDARE for years, and then, abruptly, nothing.

Peter announced his decision to kill VDARE in a video shot from the conference room where Hannah and I had taken pictures of each other seven months prior. He wore a navy blazer and a greenish tie in the video, and he looked pale and weak, like a sick man announcing a bad diagnosis.

"The end of VDARE.com is like the collapse of a small civilization," Peter said. "There's a surprising number of people who have been working with me for a long time, in some cases twenty years, who are dependent on VDARE.com, who are never going to find work in the mainstream media. I feel very bad for them."

Peter said that he had hoped to turn a well-funded organization over to a younger generation of immigration "patriots." He guessed that now this wouldn't happen. Then he said the part that bothered me: "The irony is that the issue of immigration patriotism has never been hotter. Opinion polls are out of control in favor of immigration restriction. In fact, even mass deportation, which the political class absolutely doesn't want to think about, is very popular among ordinary grassroots Americans. I'd like to think that VDARE.com has played a part in that development."

I hated what he said because I wanted it to be false. It was true, though. In an ironic twist of fate, VDARE's crucifixion, to apply Peter's framing, happened as half the country prepared to vote for mass deportation raids. I had watched the Republican National Convention a few days before, after riding in that side-by-side around Paw Paw, and had flinched when I saw scores of people waving signs that said "MASS DEPORTATION NOW." Peter could accurately claim to have influenced that shift in our culture.

When I worked at the SPLC, I could point to something a politician or mainstream pundit said and call it "VDARE shit." Or I could call it "Daily Stormer shit" or something else that was similar, depending on what was happening—but it was always a way to convey that someone mainstream, someone in a position of power, had jumped from Fox News talking points to something more radical. And most of Trump's mass deportations proposal was absolutely "VDARE shit." The conservative movement had started to emulate Peter at the same moment that conservatives abandoned him, leading to the termination of his nonprofit.

"I've worked on VDARE.com essentially every day for twenty-five years," Peter said. "That's a third of my life. I don't know what I'm going to do next. And even if I did, I'm not sure what I could say about it in the current legal environment. But I guess I won't have any excuse not to take my daughters on the 4-H camping trip. So, I want to thank all of you who've been with us for so long. And we hope to see you on the other side."[2]

That afternoon, I met Amy at her home, which was embedded in the woods, closer to the silica plant than the courthouse. It was a beautiful house, perfect in the way it signaled seclusion and quiet meditation. Amy offered me a cold La Croix with a strange flavor and we sat outside.

"I'm scared to talk to you because you're friends with those people," she said.

Amy seemed shaky and defensive. I felt bad for her.

On the day I'd entered Berkeley Springs from Paw Paw, Judy Gubinski, Joanie Dolina, and the Reverend Robert Emerick, a former Methodist clergyman from New York, had met me at Judy's still-developing dream home.

Over Judy's desserts and appetizers, she told us she had been considering launching an ethics complaint against Amy with the West Virginia Psychological Association. Reverend Bob, a gentle, pensive guy, encouraged her to do it. People described Reverend Bob as being a quiet leader who was against the culture that VDARE had brought to town.

Amy had described her discussion page as an "experiment," and both Judy and Reverend Bob insisted this was in violation of a rule prohibiting doctors from conducting experiments without consent. At first, I doubted Judy's instincts. I assumed that Amy meant that she was experimenting with ways to bring the town together, and when I visited her later, I asked her a question hoping that she would correct me.

"So, I think some of the people I've talked to think that you're using the group as an experiment to produce some kind of psychoanalytical paper," I said.

"Why not?" Amy said.

I froze when she said it.

"I did this for *me*," she continued. "So, what if it led to a psychoanalytical paper? A lot of people are encouraging me to do something like that."

"I don't know—how it works."

"You know, a lot of the people who have these opinions about me are people who are jealous because they tried to put together what I put together but didn't succeed."

"Well, I know that Paul and Trey have their group," I said, sheepishly.

I turned the topic to VDARE. I wanted to know how Amy reconciled their alleged normalization with some of their actions and beliefs. Amy had told me on the phone in April that the average Republican today believed in essentially the same things that VDARE did, which was true.

In the conversation at her home, I also stressed that VDARE was influencing our culture to become a place where people believed those things. They had moved the great replacement conspiracy into mainstream discourse. Shouldn't there be some kind of accountability for that? I mentioned the friend-or-enemy dynamic in VDARE's writing and the civil war talk.

"Are liberals not doing that to Trump supporters?" she responded, referring to the practice of otherizing their political opponents.

Amy said it as if she were bringing up something I had never previously considered. Her soft-spoken husband, Doug, joined us, and I got the sense that he felt protective of his wife, because he knew that people were talking about her behind her back. It was understandable. People were definitely talking about Amy behind her back.

"What Trey and Paul have done is sap up all the energy in the town around their issues with Charlie Curia and they've used VDARE as an excuse," he said.

"What do you make of those videos that Sue Evans posted purporting to show the Johansons doing horrible things?" I asked. "Like where it said Paul nearly ran over her? Nothing really happened."

Amy and Doug rocked back like I had said something truly incredible.

"You have to imagine the smell!" Doug said. "The exhaust in that woman's face!"

"What do you think of the biergarten now? Paul and Trey don't think Curia will actually ever finish it," I said. "I heard other people say that too."

"Of course, that's wrong. A lot of people support the Curias and I think their biergarten will absolutely succeed," she said.

After we ended the conversation, Amy showed me what looked like a luxury tree house at the back of their property. It was an elevated cabin with a cozy interior. It was cozy enough to pass for a hotel room. Amy said she sometimes saw patients there.

"Seems like a good place to go if you have an argument with your spouse," I said.

I drove back to Trey's place, where seven of us drank wine to celebrate VDARE folding. Judy. Joanie. Pamee Howard, one of the founders of Trey and Paul's Facebook group. Roger Lyle, who cracked jokes about Trump in a charming drawl. The appearance of momentum behind Kamala Harris's nomination served as a secondary reason for celebration for the guests.

I put ice in my white wine because the heat was too disgusting. Everyone sat around my laptop and watched Peter deliver his statement on VDARE's demise. Everyone drank their wine, eyes flashing with little sparkles of excitement as I held up the screen from my lap.

"Very soon, the VDARE.com website will be suspended. We are currently unsure for how long the archives will remain accessible, or even if they will be accessible at all," he said. "So, my role here has been destroyed. After twenty-five years, I am resigning as editor of VDARE.com and from the VDARE.com foundation board."[3]

Peter's local opponents snickered and laughed at him as his voice sagged with sadness. It was not enough that his site would stop publishing. Peter appeared on screen looking like a shattered man.

"What happens now?" Trey asked me.

I had said in some of my earlier visits that I thought the New York State investigation could make it impossible for VDARE to go forward. But when I'd said it, I wasn't sure I believed it. Now, because of that prediction, I looked like I had answers.

"I think it's over," I said. "The only way I could see them getting out from under this and rebooting would be if Trump won the presidency, and activists within the government like Stephen Miller somehow intervened. I don't know how that would even look, exactly. I think we should be open to interesting things if Trump returns but—"

"Trump's not gonna win," Roger interjected.

"I doubt the Brimelows would be a priority even if a scenario like this played out," I said. "Even if they got their money back from New York State and everything, Peter Brimelow is old. And he's been through a lot. I think he's tired. I think he's mentally preparing to die. We'll see."

"We'll see," Trey said.

Later, Judy and Joanie cornered me to ask about Amy.

I told them that when I'd asked whether she'd write about her experiment, she'd said, "Why not?" "As in, she would be within her rights," I said. "I don't know if that's true or not, but that was how I took it."

Lydia followed Peter's video up the next day with a statement of her own. She analyzed how "cancel culture" had starved VDARE of financial resources and the tools to run a functioning website. She made a convincing case that the tech and finance companies had refused to work with VDARE and that this destroyed them. She named dozens of tech and finance companies big and small that had refused their business.[4]

"We thought that VDARE.com was rolling, slowly at first, but picking up momentum, and would soon be unstoppable," Lydia said, wearing a cream-colored blouse and an elegant cameo pendant necklace with matching earrings. She continued:

> However, it has become clear that we are not unstoppable. My sense is that we are a lion succumbing to hyenas. First one hyena attacks, then another, and the lion throws them off. But the pack is large, and the lion is alone. Two hyenas are now four, now six. No other lions come to his aid. He continues to fight. Now there are ten hyenas. No handful of them could take him down, but there are so many now. The lion is completely weighed down by these scrawny, nasty things. He can't stand up. It's over.

The hyenas thing stayed with me. I found it so vivid and so utterly bizarre. Reactionary posters on Elon Musk's X bestowed pity on VDARE for barely twenty-four hours after Peter's sad monologue went online. After that, it seemed like everyone just forgot about them. The country had plunged into a volatile presidential race with multiple assassination attempts. No one had ink to spare for an expired movement leader and his castle.

The Brimelows kept a low profile around town before resurfacing in a comical way that seemed loaded with cartoonish symbolism. As

September drew closer and a new school year rolled around, a rockslide stripped away some of the foundation of the castle, leaving parts of it exposed along Route 9.

An X account purporting to speak for the Berkeley Springs Castle posted a line saying, "Port-o-let no longer needed, sewer damage from the rock slide is fixed!"[5] Gossip dictated that the Brimelows were stuck in the castle, unable to release their bowels. When Claire Goforth of the Daily Dot spoke with him, Peter Brimelow called the sewage-leak talk "another lie invented by hysterical local communists."[6]

Amy messaged me on July 31 asking why Trey had unfriended her on Facebook. She said that it really hurt. She asked for my advice. I said that Facebook seemed to be a little too important to Berkeley Springs and to let it cool off.

Amy's Facebook group had hosted a picnic in the park earlier in the summer, and Paul and Trey had gone to it, bringing some of their friends along. Curia was there too. Many regular contributors to Amy's Facebook group were participating in the "experiment," if that's indeed what it was. *The Morgan Messenger* covered the in-person Facebook group gathering with a story highlighting Amy and her thoughts about political disagreement.

Then Trey and Paul stopped going to the events Amy hosted, and this undercut the group's promise of building unity in town. The liberals started talking more about Amy and her group in the context of it being an experiment, giving added weight to Trey and Paul's absence. Amy messaged me again at the end of August, as this tension continued to build, telling me that she felt uneasy about having spoken with me.

"I do not want to be part of any more drama in this town," she wrote. "It is actually trying to mend itself: Our community events are getting eighty-plus people and it has been lovely. People are saying that the Facebook page and the community events are doing more to heal this community than anything else in over ten years. It is good here despite ongoing attempts to undermine the progress."

Judy Gubinski and I also emailed one another when I was back in New York. She told me she wanted to pursue science fiction and I recommended that she read *The Left Hand of Darkness* by Ursula K. Le Guin. Judy sent me some of her poems, and she self-published them online so anyone could read them. Everything she wrote had a distinct, ethereal quality to it. Some of her work grappled with death. When Judy posted her poems, she sometimes embedded images from neoclassical or Victorian paintings or a photograph of a cathedral.

On September 11, Judy sent me something else, an email marked "Fwd: [Amy] McGrath Howard official complaint":

> This complaint is against ["Amy"], Psy.D., M.Ed., CGP, for violation of section 8.02 of the Ethics Code of the American Psychological Association. She seems to be conducting what she acknowledges to be an experiment on Berkeley Springs / Morgan County, WV residents, without their informed consent. ["Amy"] has acknowledged to several people she might do a potential research project based on this experiment, which she alleges colleagues have encouraged.

I didn't know whether Amy thought she was experimenting on people to benefit her career or genuinely trying to heal the divide. Maybe it was a mixture of the two things. She had invited me into the Facebook group a few months earlier to see it and then withdrawn the invitation after her husband, Doug, said he thought it was against the spirit of the thing to have me there. The whole situation made me feel terrible for everyone. I felt bad for the entire town.

28

Cursed Town

Whoever put up the Castle Watchers website never took it down, and it continued to infuriate the people listed as VDARE collaborators. Late in July 2024, Castle Watchers added the Country Inn's head chef, Scott Collinash, based largely on his comment to *The Washington Post* calling Lydia "a delightful woman."

Scott felt heartbroken to be called racist. He marshaled Trey and others to speak up in his defense. Trey campaigned hard for Scott. She boosted a letter he wrote and demanded that the person behind Castle Watchers remove him. I wondered if people still believed she ran the site after that.

Scott's letter to the anonymous person behind Castle Watchers, which they published on their site, also demanded that his name be removed. He called the instigator "the keyboard coward." "Everyone who knows me, the Berkeley Springs community included, knows who I am, and how I strive to make the community a better place for everyone," he wrote. "I have spoken with people hoping to mend the division we have within our community. Some of the division [is] being caused by The Castle Watchers, and the keyboard coward."[1]

As summer transitioned into fall, Scott, supported by others in the local queer community, attempted to push an equality ordinance through the town council. There wasn't much to it, just a modest rebuke against discrimination. It contained language similar to what was used in ordinances passed in other West Virginia towns. But it had symbolic firepower, especially in a town mired in accusations of bigotry.

Scott said at a town council meeting that the biggest advantage of passing the ordinance would be to distance the town from VDARE's reputation. "Recent months, the division in this town, caused by whoever it may be, is making us look like a bunch of antisemitic, white supremacist [types]," he said in the meeting.[2]

Proponents of the ordinance figured that no one had anything to lose if they passed it. Potentially the biggest conflict would arise from angering the loudest Christians. But pessimists believed the town would be too reactionary and too cowardly. The town proved those pessimists right.

I spoke to one resident, Darren O'Neill, about it on October 7 on the phone. Darren and I had met before, in person, at Trey's shop. He was broad shouldered, of late middle age, with impressive facial hair and icy blue eyes. When we met, it was soon after the hospital had discharged me. We got along, but he expressed reluctance to tell his story to a writer.

Amid pushback against the ordinance, someone in town insinuated that Jason—Darren's husband, who worked at Berkeley Springs High School as the athletic director—had exploited his position there to "perv" on boys. That changed Darren's perspective on speaking to me.

"Jason didn't really have anything to do with this ordinance fight," he said.

"I had people smear me as a pedophile before. The Brimelows tried to do it. It's horrific," I said.

"Well, it's the worst thing anyone can call you."

I was walking in Queens and the streets were loud. I wanted to hear him better.

"I'm coming down for the election. Let's talk then," I said. "Please tell your husband I said I'm so sorry to hear about this. I'll be thinking about him."

I rented a Hyundai Kona on Saturday, November 2, and drove it that night to Gettysburg. I saw Trump signs from Gettysburg down to Berkeley Springs the next day, after leaving the Civil War site. My favorite of them was a mini-billboard that a guy had erected on his farm. It once had said, "Trump-Pence" and "Make America Great Again," but he'd just spray-painted over Pence in blue.

I drove through the center of town along Route 522, down near the mouth of Cacapon Resort State Park, and turned left into the wooded complex where Judy lived. She had told me about a cabin for rent near her place. She said there was a woman there who had a huge "ULTRA-MAGA" sign across her garage who had called the authorities on multiple people who had stayed at her rented cabin, claiming they had been speeding on the road to the cabin. So Judy had said I should be careful not to speed.

The Trump signs continued into Judy's sparsely populated neighborhood, dotting every single home that I passed there. One of the homes had a Morgan County Sheriff's Department car in the driveway and Trump signs outside. Some of the homes had more obscure signs, like ones with JD Vance's face. I also saw two deer and six foxes dashing in and out of the trees.

When I found the ULTRA-MAGA house, it was just one of dozens done up for Election Day, but the owner had clearly put more enthusiasm into it than her neighbors had. She had seven smaller election signs out front in addition to her year-round ULTRA-MAGA banner. One of them said "FIGHT FIGHT FIGHT," which is what Trump had yelled to the crowd after someone tried to blow his head off in Butler, Pennsylvania, that July.

The cabin was cavernous, big enough for two families, and Judy came over that night with snacks and wine. We talked about the election and the nervous excitement she felt. Harris would win. She had to. People would come to their senses. The miles of Trump signs made me wonder about Judy's day-to-day life in the woods.

"You don't feel isolated here?" I asked.

"Well," she said. "Not really. Well, a little. But take a look at this."

Judy took out a copy of Amy's response to her ethics complaint. Amy had submitted it with the help of a lawyer, and Judy had received a copy from the West Virginia Board of Examiners of Psychologists.

"I have been accused of using the page as an 'experiment,' completely out of context," Amy's statement said. "I used the word colloquially to try to mean something new: To see if we had the capacity to disagree about politics without becoming disagreeable. We have been successful some of the time and not so successful some of the time."

In other words, Amy described the type of experimentation I had originally thought she meant. The statement went on to say, "I have not presented myself on the Facebook page as a clinical psychologist. The information linked about me is on my professional website or on my LinkedIn page. I have never claimed I'm conducting a clinical research protocol to anyone, nor have I acted in a professional capacity as a clinical psychologist on the Berkeley Springs / Morgan County Discussion Group Facebook page."

Amy had already referred to running the group as a "headache" to me in an April conversation before later boasting about how impactful it was. Of course, it could be both things at once, but it was hard to imagine how the headache was worth it.

"She described it as an experiment multiple times," Judy said. "You can't conduct psychological experiments without consent."

Judy relayed what I'd told her about Amy in her next correspondence with the board. When Amy saw that on the day after Thanksgiving, she texted, accusing me of sharing off-the-record quotes. But we'd never agreed to go off the record, and I hadn't even published anything. In a reply text, I told her the truth. I never knew I was participating in an ethics complaint against her. I also explained that I never agreed to go off the record.

"And, lest you take that statement as confirmation that I agree with the accuracy of your statements, I do not. You used my words deceptively and out of context in an effort to harm me," she wrote in response. "I don't want to hear from you again."

Judy's ethics complaint against Amy ultimately went nowhere.

On the eve of Election Day, I ran late to the park to meet Darren O'Neill, because I got lost digging my way out of the woods. When I got there, I also found his husband, Jason, and Alicia, the woman who owned the periwinkle blue store near Trey's coffeehouse. Alicia was the one who had urged Trey to respond after VDARE first bought the castle, back at the beginning.

I hadn't been in Berkeley Springs on a November afternoon since 2022, but I remembered the overcast, ominous tint. The air was just frigid. I had to return to the car for more clothes.

Darren wore one of those South Carolina Gamecocks hats that said "COCKS" on it. His husband, who came across as being a sensitive man, squirmed under a hoodie that looked too thin for the weather. They seemed like a quirky and charming couple.

"The ordinance is a very toothless document," Darren said of the proposed equality ordinance in the town council. "There's no litigation that's gonna occur because of this document. But. Despite being toothless, it lit a fire. It lit the fire that blew this town up. And it wasn't just about *La-bit-ih-quoi*," he added, using slang based on a pronunciation of the LGBTQ acronym. "But the town latched on to that issue. Solely on that aspect. Not people of color, not religious freedoms, not anything. *That* became the flag that everyone was waving."

"You would hear a lot of 'I'm not homophobic, *but*,'" Alicia said of town council meetings. "Each person who spoke said 'I'm okay with XYZ,' but the Pride flag was a no."

"The whole message was that gay people are okay if you don't put them in my face," Darren said. "Be silent and stay out of the way."

I asked if the Brimelows had weighed in on the ordinance.

"Their surrogates in town weigh in for them," Darren said.

Darren and Alicia took turns explaining that on September 3, an older woman named Veta had spoken up at a town council meeting and said the athletic director of the high school was gay and had access to the boys' locker rooms. She was describing Jason but didn't use his name.

"Were you there?" I asked.

Jason picked his head up for the first time.

"I don't even know who this woman is and this is my third year at that high school," he said and dropped his head again.

"Where did she hear about it?"

"At the Total Image hair salon. There were mothers talking, so she thought she should bring it up," he said.

"Where is that? Near the Food Lion?"

"It's down there, yeah."

"Everything is near the Food Lion," I said.

We went quiet, briefly. Jason struggled to brighten his mood long enough to do more than issue a few lines of light chitchat. Alicia said she had been tempted to leave Berkeley Springs for good.

"So many people in the last few months have just had this one-foot-out-the-door, 'can we all really exist here?' moment. Even if the election goes in the direction of goodness. What's it gonna look like here? It's not gonna look as settled as it will in, say, Philly, Baltimore, New York," she said.

Alicia said she knew of people holding off on real estate transactions to find out what would happen in the election and how Berkeley Springs would respond to it.

"People have been asking me if I'm going to watch parties and I'm like, 'No, I'll be sheltering in place this week!' " Alicia said of the election. "I'm not leaving the house until the gunfire subsides."

"My great concern for Berkeley Springs, Morgan County, if Trump does get elected, what does it do to empower the neighbors on the hill?" Darren asked, and raised his hand behind him to the castle. "Do they get resurrected?"

I looked up the hill. The castle looked empty.

"We'll see," I said. "They would certainly be better off with Trump."

As we packed up to leave, I mentioned that I was planning to watch the election results at the Star Theater with Trey.

"Trey Johanson has been wonderful for this town because she—," Darren said, searching for the words, "united all the haters around a common target."

I met Judy at the Country Inn for dinner and then we drove in separate cars to the Prospect Overlook, where Trey, Paul, and Joanie were reconstructing a restaurant. When I pulled my car up to the guardrail, I looked for that "Cursed Town" graffiti I had seen back in June. I found it and patted it with my hand.

Joanie had given up her impulse to split town and decided to invest in the new restaurant project with Trey and Paul instead. Trey and Paul had in turn ditched the Lazy Sundae, adding that ice cream to this menu. The old roadside restaurant and bar, replete with beautiful wood and a fireplace, looked like something unfrozen from 1982. In front of the bar's windows, customers would get access to that spectacular view.

Trey gave me a hug and squeezed my hand.

"You're *home*," she said.

"Thank you," I said.

I couldn't recall ever seeing Trey so obviously happy before. She had told me earlier that she thought Harris would win. James Carville had encouraged that idea in her head. But Trey's happiness came from a deeper place. It was like she was out from under something. The dissolution of VDARE had signaled the end of a struggle.

I watched Paul move from thing to thing, always working. He was setting up a draft area that would have sarsaparilla, a native West Virginia product, in addition to beer. Trey and Joanie took Judy and me around to show us everything. The space had a dreamlike quality. It recalled some forgotten trip I had made with my parents as a boy.

I approached Joanie when I saw that she was alone.

"So, I thought you were leaving town."

"I was. But I'm doing this now."

"That's amazing. Congratulations."

"Thank you."

"It looks awesome."

"I love it."

"VDARE ending probably helps too."

"It helps. But hey—" She leaned forward. "I heard that the Brimelows are trying to sell the castle. That's just what I heard."

"Well, that would be everything you could ask for," I said.

In the weeks that followed, I emailed Lydia to ask whether they'd started the process of selling the castle. To my surprise, she actually responded. She wanted to know where I had heard that particular story. I told her I couldn't say.

That night, I drove back through the dark, winding roads of Route 9, hung a right onto 522 at the 7-Eleven, and, after a string of lonely miles, turned left into the wooded complex near Judy's place. Cutting through the darkness, I heard the sound of horrific screams. It sounded like a madman killing children. I froze, listening to the shrieks of terror. Four deer dashed past. The screaming went on.

I called my friend Stefanie. She was always up late at night and lived in the woods in Montrose, New York. Stefanie told me that foxes sometimes make sounds like they're humans being tortured. I was relieved to hear it.

The next morning, Election Day, I woke up to find that Judy had placed a scone and a napkin in a small Ziploc bag outside the door of my cabin. I brewed some coffee and ate the scone while reading the last-minute election hype.

I saw something Peter had written on X the night before: "VDARE's D.C. consultant friend Patrick McDermott told us on eve of 2020 election that polls were underestimating Trump by 3–4 points. He was right. Now he says the underestimate is 1 1/2–2 points = Trump will win popular vote by that amount—and, he says, all swing states."[3]

I took a screenshot of it.

I headed out in the afternoon for what I thought might be my last trip to the Roman Baths for a long time. I immediately felt afraid to lose these trips as I slipped into the hot water again. I had convinced myself that I possessed some cosmic connection to the baths. I had undoubtedly survived something in them.

I had stopped going down to Berkeley Springs for a few months after the summer, and the five-hour drive had seemed a lot longer this time around. Peter and Lydia still occupied the castle above me, but with

VDARE finished, the pronounced power dynamic they wielded had weakened.

I knew that I would be unlikely to visit as frequently, or do as much while I was here, as I had in the days between the pandemic and the 2024 election. Sometimes, I fantasized about moving to Morgan County and just disappearing into a holler with a couple of guns, like Lisa Marie. It could never happen though.

I heard police talking outside the door of the bath. Someone distinctly said, "He's very agitated," like they were talking about a dangerous chimp. When my time ended I asked what had happened. A worker said a bather had had too much to drink.

On the way out I saw a burly policeman cruising through the path toward the baths. This man was really rumbling.

"What happened?" I asked. "Something happened at the baths?"

"Why don't you have a look at that man's *ass* hanging out of that window and you'll have a pretty good idea of what's going on here," he said, panting.

The policeman resumed his rumbling. I saw the exposed ass. It was skinny and white. The drunk had jarred open the window of his bath, stuck his ass out of it, and refused to leave. I snapped a picture of the scene and kept on moving.

I walked up to the town council meeting to watch Reverend Bob petition for the town to reexamine the biergarten space and whether Trey and Paul losing the property had infringed on their rights. The mayor and council acted like someone was making them sit through bad puppet theater. Sue Evans and Charlie Curia were there. I ducked out, not wanting to deal with them. I thought they might think I was there for them and accuse me of stalking.

I picked up a six-pack at 7-Eleven and noticed white lights at the castle, where the night before there had been none. It looked like something was stirring there on election night. I joined Trey and her friends inside the Star Theater. Some ceiling lights made the spectacular space seem a little more pedestrian that night. The group had an upbeat energy until about ten, when they took the cue from MSNBC that Harris's prospects were flatlining.

Judy looked dazed, like she was witnessing a car accident. Trey wore lipstick and was dressed nicely in black and gray clothing. She had posted a food pic to Facebook in the morning and connected it to a celebration of cultural diversity.

"Election Day breakfast: Paul's homemade kimchi and basmati rice. Yes... Korean cabbage with Indian rice. (Background music 'Ain't That America' by John Cougar Mellencamp)," she wrote.

I went out with her and Joanie to smoke cigarettes as reality sank in. We batted around the different theories as to how Harris could potentially scratch back and make it a race. There were counties in places with lots of college kids. There were places in big cities. In 2020, a bunch of votes came in later to change the dynamic.

"It just doesn't look good," I said, trying to cut through the bullshit.

The Star has some big couches at the back. No one had been sitting that far back at the beginning of the party, but Joanie and I ended up there at the end of the night. We sat there scrolling our phones as that drip of defeat fell all over us. I made a hastier goodbye than I should have and sped back to the cabin.

"Please come and see me before you leave tomorrow," Judy texted me.

The next morning, Berkeley Springs residents woke up to a paid letter to the editor from the Reverend Bob Emerick in *The Morgan Messenger.* He highlighted the Non-Discrimination Ordinance and requested that the town reconsider its decision to reject it. "Please consider this," he wrote. "The reputation of our historic, welcoming and world-famous town is now in doubt. Do we really want to become known as a place that wants to protect discrimination?"[4]

Judy would call me at the start of December to tell me that Reverend Bob had Stage 4 cancer in his lungs. Before the end of the year, he died. No one had known Bob was sick until near the end, and everyone looked back on his final flurry of activism in a new light. Judy called him "the heart and soul of Berkeley Springs" in a phone conversation with me.

That morning after Election Day, I packed everything up and passed through Judy's gate before driving off. She had a lonely-looking Kamala Harris yard sign and a hand-painted yellow decoration that said "Love One Another." Something about it looked childlike in the fresh light of November 6.

Judy was on the verge of tears when I saw her, so I gave her a hug. She right away started sobbing into my chest. We just stood there for a bit like that until we said our goodbyes.

I paid my last visit to Lisa Swanson at her place, with her porch that overlooked the castle. Lisa had knocked on doors in Pennsylvania and sent postcards targeted to voters. She had really tried to move the election any way she could to stop Trump.

"So, do you think we have another election in 2028?" I asked her.

It sounded insane to say it out loud, but we were entering a new time.

"So, you're asking the fundamental question, will America continue to exist?" Lisa asked. "Anyway, I would tip in favor of our institutions being strong enough, or enough of them . . . ? What do you think?"

"It's hard to make a prediction now," I said. "I don't know what Trump's health is going to be, his mental acuity. It could be a JD Vance, or someone else, who inherits whatever they want to do. But I do know they'd rather not have to bother with democracy, even if it worked for them here."

We walked down to Mi Ranchito for lunch, past the house where the sex offender lived, and past Lighthouse Latte, a Christian-owned coffee shop that served as an alternative for those who wanted coffee without the Pride flag.

Lisa wanted to know if it sounded crazy to worry about the new administration targeting activists like her, people who do voter turnout work.

"Look, the stuff that is gonna be about internal enemies, and antifa, could be used for McCarthyist stuff," I said.

"Yeah. Yeah."

"If you think about the war on terror, for example, once someone is deemed a terrorist, you can do anything to them."

"Right."

We dropped the dystopian talk, gossiped, and ate our meal. After we finished, Lisa wanted to show me two new businesses that had opened up in town. New businesses meant new hope. The first one was The Cardinal Bar. The other one was a little tidy-looking shop called Creekside Provisions.

When Lisa and I walked into Creekside Provisions, Darren O'Neill stood there, tall, casting a powerful shadow, and ready to make a purchase of some kind. I skipped up to him as if to say, "Hey, remember me?"

"How's it going?" I asked.

He looked at my smile with a mix of disbelief and anger. I had completely forgotten the election had happened. My mind had blanked it out after lunch.

"What do you think?" he snapped.

EPILOGUE

522 North, Leaving Berkeley Springs

To my knowledge, no one in town ever discovered who created the "Berkeley Springs Castle Watchers" website that purported to identify neighbors with links to Peter and Lydia Brimelow. I figured out who ran it, but I decided not to confront the creator. It really wasn't my business.

Peter and Lydia Brimelow kept a lower profile after VDARE folded. The couple attended the Heritage Foundation's Open House to watch Trump's second inauguration, and then they went to a ball hosted by Passage Publishing, a group that publishes books with illiberal themes. They later tried to raise money for their legal fight against New York State, but it's unclear if they were able to do it.

The Brimelows continued to allow tours of the castle in 2025. They also appeared to host Patriot Front. The neofascist group published pictures to the messaging app Telegram in March 2025 showing their men inside the castle, faces blurred, occupying the same dais where Hannah and I had posed for pictures in December 2023. In September 2025, Letitia James, New York's attorney general, finally sued VDARE for over $1 million, claiming they abused their nonprofit status for personal enrichment.

Charlie Curia opened The Vine Trattoria in the space where the biergarten was supposed to be built. Curia announced that it served Mediterranean food "with a modern twist." My friends in town said Peter and Lydia attended the opening.

Lisa Marie told me that she wanted to leave the country after Trump won reelection. Things became dicey for trans women in a hurry, particularly for the ones living in red states. Lisa Marie explored moving to Denmark but felt that her heart still belonged to "West by god Virginia."

Darren O'Neill and his husband, Jason, did move. They moved to Pittsburgh. Darren called Pittsburgh "a good little city" to me in a text message. The men decided they couldn't deal with the bigotry of Morgan County any longer.

Lisa Swanson continued being Lisa Swanson. Trey and Joanie continued to focus on their new restaurant, the Panorama Public House. Judy Gubinski continued to build her dream house in the woods and sent me pictures of it. She took the Reverend Bob Emerick's death harder than anyone.

West Virginia's Board of Examiners of Psychologists threw out Judy's complaint against Amy. A few months later, Paul alleged that Amy's husband, Doug, had confronted him while he was working on someone's retaining wall, making wild gestures, and blaming him for the situation with his wife.

I gave myself a shoulder injury while writing *Strange People on the Hill*. I would write the book for twelve or more hours at a time, until as late as five in the morning, while I was going through that legal mess with the SPLC. Then I'd lift weights for a bit and crash as the sun came up.

One week after Trump took power, I stuck my hand out to reach for my glasses at the side of the bed and a hot pain fired up the fingers of my left hand into my shoulder. The combination of sitting hunched over like that, with my shoulders bent forward every day, and then switching to heavy weights is what had done it.

My mental health vaguely improved after a few months of taking lithium and attending regular psychoanalysis sessions. Many times, I had to read my own writing to recall how I was in the hospital. It felt like someone else's life. One thing about a hospitalization like that one, you start to see your life strictly in terms of the time before you went in and the time after you left. Everything becomes about not going back to the hospital or not dying.

Berkeley Springs still lives in my home office. As I write this, I have a map of West Virginia to the right of my desk and a late-1980s Matilda Bay Wine Coolers bar mirror I got at the town's Antique Mall to my left. On my desk, I have two packs of Berkeley Springs tarot cards that I don't know how to use.

Lisa Marie gave me a patch that says "Department of Hopeland Security," and that's resting on my bookshelf next to a stack of Wallace Shawn plays. I also have a bumper sticker advertising Fairfax Coffee House, the coffee shop where the book begins, stuck to my door. I still drink coffee from a mug that I bought in Alicia's shop.

I stopped driving down to Berkeley Springs after I filed the first draft of the book. I stayed in touch with Trey, Lisa Marie, Lisa Swanson, and Judy, but over time I spoke to them less. New stories came up. That's how it goes for writers.

I think when you go through something extremely traumatic somewhere, the setting really stays with you in your mind. That's certainly true of me and Morgan County, West Virginia. Even when I'm far away, I can recall the world in exquisite detail.

I can see the starry sky outside of the Old Roman Bath House and my breath going up in the cold. I can feel what it was like to sit down at Trey and Paul's table, waiting to eat, as her cat, Violet, paced behind me. When I show people pictures of Prospect Overlook on my phone and tell them, "This is the most beautiful view I've ever seen," I can hear the roar of the B&O train rushing by.

It's a lucky thing to find a place that you love, even if you bled there.

ACKNOWLEDGMENTS

Thank you to everyone at Bold Type Books and Hachette for taking a chance on me. I'm a first-time author, and I didn't even have an agent when we started this project.

In particular, thank you to Jeffrey Kusama-Hinte for supporting my vision of a book that focuses on the lives of regular people and the psychological impacts of our poisonous culture. So many books about the radical right center on the extremists. I told Jeffrey that I didn't want to do that, and he said I didn't have to.

Thank you to my great editor, Lisa Kaufman, for her incredible support. My proposal for this book didn't include anything about me going to a psych ward—none of that had happened yet. I was nervous about turning it in, because nobody had asked for that story, and it was very raw. Lisa championed the book as it was. She even introduced me to a literary agent after she read it.

Thanks to Ben Kessler, who has been reading my work since we were writing plays together in college. Ben was the only person I trusted to read this book while it was in progress.

I want to thank everyone in the SPLC Union for their support after the SPLC discriminated against me. We always fought together, and I miss you. The same goes for my lawyer, Deborah, for taking on my discrimination claim.

Thank you to Rachel Janik and Hannah Gais for allowing me to write about them here. They were my sisters at work and got me through the worst days of my life. I hope they feel well represented by what I have written.

I want to thank my family. Katie, thank you for the map in this book and for always imagining a successful future for me when we talked on the phone. Thanks to my sons for making me laugh and for giving me a reason to live. Thanks to Aadya for her support over the years. Even as our relationship has changed, our friendship has stayed strong. Thanks, obviously, to my parents for doing everything for me. Hi, Mom and Dad.

And finally, to my fellow writers who now find themselves threatened by a culture that is rapidly and undeniably bending toward fascism—Madeline, Jared, Luke, Bob, Chris, Oliver, Hannah (again), and so many more wonderful people—I promise you: They cannot stop us. Through our passion, we will win.

NOTES

Chapter 1: The Great Replacement

1. Kate Shunney, "Berkeley Castle Has New Owners," *Morgan Messenger*, February 26, 2020.
2. Russell Mokhiber, "VDare Purchases Berkeley Springs Castle," Morgan County USA, February 23, 2020, https://morgancountyusa.org/?p=4373.
3. Matthew Schaeffer, "Virginia Dare (1587–?)," North Carolina History Project, https://northcarolinahistory.org/encyclopedia/virginia-dare-1587.
4. Mokhiber, "VDare Purchases Berkeley Springs Castle."
5. Jean Raspail, *Camp of the Saints*, trans. Norman Shapiro (Éditions Robert Laffont, 1975; originally published in French as *Le Camp des Saints*, 1973), reprinted at JR Books Online, www.jrbooksonline.com/PDFs/Camp_of_the_Saints.pdf, 5, 89.
6. Shannon Bond, "How Tucker Carlson Took Fringe Conspiracies to a Mass Audience," NPR, April 25, 2023, www.npr.org/2023/04/25/1171800317/how-tucker-carlsons-extremist-narratives-shaped-fox-news-and-conservative-politi.
7. Alex Kotch and Michael Edison Hayden, "Donors Pumped Millions into White Nationalist Group," SPLC Hatewatch, June 17, 2021, www.splcenter.org/hatewatch/2021/06/17/donors-pumped-millions-white-nationalist-group.
8. Alex Kaplan, "YouTube Approved VDARE Channel Defended the El Paso Shooter's Manifesto and a Sandy Hook Conspiracy Theory," Media Matters, September 5, 2019, www.mediamatters.org/vdare/youtube-approved-vdare-channel-defended-el-paso-shooters-manifesto-and-sandy-hook-conspiracy.

Chapter 2: A White Man with Money

1. "Dissident Mama, episode 85—VDARE's Lydia Brimelow," posted by Dissident Mama, December 13, 2023, YouTube, www.youtube.com/watch?v=mvqQjISzLQI.
2. "Lydia Brimelow," interviewed by Tucker Carlson, February 21, 2024, https://tuckercarlson.com/uncensored-lydia-brimelow; VDARE (@vdare), "VDARE's experience was that corporate hotels were willing to pay us . . . ," X, June 15, 2024, https://x.com/vdare/status/1802111118401261619.
3. Peter Brimelow, "VDARE.com Editor Peter Brimelow on the Cancellation of Our Colorado Conference," VDARE, August 16, 2017, https://vdare.com/posts/vdare-com-editor-peter-brimelow-on-the-cancellation-of-our-colorado-conference.
4. Peter Brimelow, "The Sin of Sullivan: Why Donald Trump, Tulsi Gabbard and I Are Suing for Libel," VDARE, April 3, 2020, https://vdare.com/articles/the-sin-of-sullivan-why-donald-trump-tulsi-gabbard-and-i-are-suing-for-libel.
5. "Jared Taylor," SPLC, accessed July 2, 2025, www.splcenter.org/fighting-hate/extremist-files/individual/jared-taylor.

6. Jared Taylor, "Unite the Right: Who Got It Right?," American Renaissance, August 13, 2017, www.amren.com/commentary/2017/08/unite-right-got-right (emphasis in original).
7. Alex Kotch and Michael Edison Hayden, "Donors Pumped Millions into White Nationalist Group," SPLC Hatewatch, June 17, 2021, www.splcenter.org/resources/hatewatch/donors-pumped-millions-white-nationalist-group.
8. Hannah Gais, "White Nationalist Who Met with Peter Thiel Admired Terroristic Literature," SPLC Hatewatch, March 18, 2021, www.splcenter.org/hatewatch/2021/03/18/white-nationalist-who-met-peter-thiel-admired-terroristic-literature; "The J. Burden Show Ep. 204: James Kirkpatrick," posted by J. Burden, June 5, 2024, YouTube, www.youtube.com/watch?v=DKjsj8GpNj8.
9. "The J. Burden Show Ep. 204: James Kirkpatrick."
10. Morgan County Clerk's Office, deed between Berkeley Springs Castle LLC and VDARE.
11. Peter Brimelow, "Time to Rethink Martin Luther King Day, the January 2024 Edition," Peter Brimelow.com, January 14, 2024, www.peterbrimelow.com/p/peter-brimelow-time-to-rethink-martin-luther-king-day-the-january-2024-edition.
12. Peter Brimelow, "Time to Rethink Immigration?," *National Review*, June 22, 1992.
13. Heidi Beirich, "Courting Conservatives," SPLC, November 30, 2008, www.splcenter.org/fighting-hate/intelligence-report/2015/courting-conservatives.
14. Peter Brimelow, *Alien Nation: Common Sense About America's Immigration Disaster* (Random House, 1995), 124.
15. "Acclaim for Peter Brimelow's Alien Nation," in front matter of Peter Brimelow, *Alien Nation: Common Sense About America's Immigration Disaster* (Harper Perennial, 1996 [1995]).
16. "Lydia Brimelow," SPLC, accessed July 2, 2025, www.splcenter.org/fighting-hate/extremist-files/individual/lydia-brimelow.
17. Peter Brimelow (@PeterBrimelow), "Lydia and I watched the Inauguration at Heritage Foundation . . . ," X, January 20, 2025, https://x.com/peterbrimelow/status/1881507419270074627.
18. Peter Brimelow, "In Memorium: Maggy Laws Brimelow," VDARE, February 13, 2004, https://vdare.com/articles/in-memoriam-maggy-laws-brimelow.
19. Lydia Brimelow, "We Got the Keys to the Castle," VDARE, February 26, 2020, https://vdare.com/articles/lydia-brimelow-we-got-the-keys-to-the-castle (emphasis in original).

Chapter 3: What Matters to Us

1. "Peter Brimelow," SPLC, accessed July 7, 2025, www.splcenter.org/fighting-hate/extremist-files/individual/peter-brimelow.
2. Josh Moon, "SPLC Fires Founder Morris Dees: Internal Emails Highlight Issues with Harassment, Discrimination," *Alabama Political Reporter*, March 15, 2019, www.alreporter.com/2019/03/15/splc-fires-founder-morris-dees-internal-emails-highlight-issues-with-harassment-discrimination.
3. Geoffrey Wendel, Facebook, February 26, 2020, www.facebook.com/geowend/posts/pfbid02N4VHoCjpwroa2sN3SWK9VVGChAJLP7kU15KExEuAL516waBP5hHuz8nk6pSqW3Qml.
4. "ArtVoiceWV: Jeanne Mozier," posted by 78degreesfilms, July 26, 2014, YouTube, www.youtube.com/watch?v=ZgqrHRKkQFQ.
5. Jeanne Mozier, *The Story of Berkeley Castle: What's True and What's Not* (High Street Press, 2016), back cover.

Chapter 4: Ghosts

1. Berkeley Springs Museum, "A Timeline History of Bath," n.d., Berkeley Springs Museum.
2. Native Land Digital, accessed February 2024, Native-Land.ca.

3. Frederick Thomas Newbraugh, "Bath: That Seat of Sin," Morgan County Public Library, 1958, 1.
4. Berkeley Springs Museum, "A Timeline History of Bath."
5. Newbraugh, "Bath: That Seat of Sin," 5–7.
6. Barbara Jeanne Fields, *Slavery and Freedom on the Middle Ground: Maryland During the Nineteenth Century* (Yale University Press, 1987), 1.
7. "The Civil War in Morgan County," posted by Travel Berkeley Springs, WV, September 3, 2020, YouTube, www.youtube.com/watch?v=_LvhthyQMtw.
8. "Engagement at Great Cacapon: Struggle in the Snow," Historical Marker Database, August 22, 2012, rev. November 7, 2020, www.hmdb.org/m.asp?m=58636.
9. Civil War Trails, accessed January 2024, www.civilwartrails.org.
10. "West Virginia Statehood, June 20, 1863," National Archives, accessed July 7, 2025, www.archives.gov/legislative/features/west-virginia.
11. Vicki Smith, "Ghosts of Parties Past," *Tampa Bay Times*, July 9, 2020, www.tampabay.com/archive/2000/07/09/ghosts-of-parties-past.
12. Jeanne Mozier, *The Story of the Berkeley Castle: What's True and What's Not* (High Street Press, 2016), 13.
13. "Berkeley Springs Castle," Travel Berkeley Springs, accessed February 2024, https://berkeleysprings.com/berkeley-springs-castle.
14. "Berkeley Springs Castle," Travel Berkeley Springs.
15. West Virginia Board of Pharmacy, "Prescription Opioid Problematic Prescribing Indicators County Report," Help & Hope, WV, October 2017, www.helpandhopewv.org/docs/PFS_County_Reports/Hampshire_PfS%20County%20Reports_Final.pdf.
16. Geoff Fox, "The Raging, Spreading Inferno: Firefighters on the Scene of Hotel Washington Recall Tragedy 50 Years Later," *Morgan Messenger*, August 20, 2024, www.morganmessenger.com/2024/08/20/the-raging-spreading-infernofirefighters-on-the-scene-of-hotel-washington-recall-tragedy-50-years-later.

Chapter 5: High Weirdness

1. James Fulford, "Yes, SPLC (And Ayatollah Ahmari), of Course Stephen Miller Reads VDARE.com—Just Not Enough," Unz Review, November 12, 2019, www.unz.com/article/yes-splc-and-ayatollah-ahmari-of-course-stephen-miller-reads-vdare-com-just-not-enough.
2. Stephen Singular, *Talked to Death: The Life and Murder of Alan Berg* (Beech Tree Books, 1987), 226–227.

Chapter 7: America Is Burning

1. "This Week in Morgan County—Oscar Robles," posted by Morgan County Arts Council, November 23, 2015, YouTube, www.youtube.com/watch?v=C3owM8Lgtgo.
2. Michael Edison Hayden, "West Virginia Tourist Hub Rejects VDARE's 'Negative' Message," SPLC Hatewatch, March 19, 2020, www.splcenter.org/hatewatch/2020/03/19/west-virginia-tourist-hub-rejects-vdares-negative-message.
3. James Fulford, "SPLC Thug Michael Hayden Demonizes VDARE.com's Castle Purchase. His Twitter Followers Plot Violence. WHERE IS FBI!?," VDARE, March 26, 2020, https://vdare.com/articles/the-fulford-file-splc-thug-michael-hayden-demonizes-vdare-com-s-castle-purchase-his-twitter-followers-plot-violence-where-is-fbi.
4. Peter Brimelow, "The Sin of SULLIVAN: Why Donald Trump, Tulsi Gabbard and I Are Suing for Libel," Unz Review, April 3, 2020, https://ftp.unz.com/article/the-sin-of-sullivan-why-donald-trump-tulsi-gabbard-and-i-are-suing-for-libel.

5. Will Sommer, "Facebook Bans Anti-Immigrant Group VDARE for 'Inauthentic Behavior,'" Daily Beast, May 5, 2020, www.thedailybeast.com/facebook-bans-anti-immigrant-group-vdare-for-inauthentic-behavior.
6. LeBron James (@KingJames), "We're literally hunted . . . ," Twitter (now X), May 6, 2020, https://x.com/KingJames/status/1258156220969398272.
7. See Nikki McCann Ramirez, "Far-Right Figures Are Attempting to Twist the Facts and Defend the Shooting of Ahmaud Arbery," Media Matters, May 8, 2020, www.mediamatters.org/white-nationalism/far-right-figures-are-attempting-twist-facts-and-defend-shooting-ahmaud-arbery.
8. John Derbyshire, "Establishment Reprising Emmett Till Narrative, Again. But White Lives Don't Matter," VDARE, May 8, 2020, https://vdare.com/articles/john-derbyshire-establishment-reprising-emmett-till-narrative-again-but-white-lives-don-t-matter.
9. John Derbyshire, "Why It's Time to Repeal the 1964 Civil Rights Act After the Brunswick Three Atrocity," VDARE, August 9, 2022, https://vdare.com/articles/john-derbyshire-why-it-s-time-to-repeal-the-1964-civil-rights-act-after-the-brunswick-three-atrocity.
10. Jason Wilson, "White Nationalist Has Long Worked at Conservative Outlets Under Own Name," *The Guardian*, February 3, 2020, www.theguardian.com/world/2020/feb/03/paul-kersey-michael-j-thompson-white-nationalist-report.
11. Paul Kersey, "The Great Replacement in Minneapolis," VDARE, June 23, 2021, https://vdare.com/posts/the-great-replacement-in-minneapolis-from-99-white-in-1910-to-60-white-in-2020.
12. Lois Beckett, "'Boogaloo Boi' Charged in Fire of Minneapolis Police Precinct During George Floyd Protest," *The Guardian*, October 23, 2020, www.theguardian.com/world/2020/oct/23/texas-boogaloo-boi-minneapolis-police-building-george-floyd.
13. James Kirkpatrick, "Where Have You Gone, Donald Trump? A Nation Turns Its Yearning Eyes to You," VDARE, May 31, 2020, https://vdare.com/articles/where-have-you-gone-donald-trump-a-nation-turns-its-yearning-eyes-to-you.

Chapter 8: America's Twenty-First-Century Fort Sumter

1. Russell Mokhiber, "Berkeley Springs Fire Engulfs Fairfax Street Building," Morgan County USA, April 27, 2015, https://morgancountyusa.org/?p=1801.
2. Matthew Umstead, "Three Rescued from Burning Building in Berkeley Springs," Herald Mail Media, April 27, 2015, www.heraldmailmedia.com/story/news/local/2015/04/27/hree-rescued-from-burning-building-in-berkeley-springs/45165727.
3. "'When the Looting Starts, the Shooting Starts': Trump Tweet Flagged by Twitter for 'Glorifying Violence,'" CBS News, May 29, 2020, www.cbsnews.com/news/trump-minneapolis-protesters-thugs-flagged-twitter. The video accompanying this news story includes a screenshot of Trump's May 29 tweet "when the looting starts, the shooting starts."
4. Allan Smith, "Trump Declares Antifa a Terrorist Organization as GOP Points Fingers at Extremists," NBC News, May 31, 2020, www.nbcnews.com/politics/politics-news/trump-says-he-will-designate-antifa-terrorist-organization-gop-points-n1220321.
5. VDARE (@vdare), "One of these pictures . . . ," Twitter (now X), June 1, 2020, https://x.com/vdare/status/1267566529949962240.
6. See JM Rieger, "Trump Team's Effort to Explain Away Lafayette Square Hits Yet Another Snag, One Year Later," *Washington Post*, June 10, 2021, www.washingtonpost.com/politics/2020/06/09/how-trump-administration-has-tried-explain-clearing-protesters-lafayette-square. See also Steve Hull, "For Derwood Woman, a Harrowing Experience at Lafayette Park Protest," *Bethesda Today*, June 3, 2020, https://bethesdamagazine.com/2020/06/03/for-derwood-woman-a-harrowing-experience-at-lafayette-park-protest.

7. Ruth Graham, "The Inconceivable Strangeness of Trump's Bible Photo-Op," Slate, June 2, 2020, https://slate.com/human-interest/2020/06/the-inconceivable-strangeness-of-trumps-bible-photo-op.html.
8. "VDARE.TV's Roving Reporters Attend a Protest (Not a Riot—White Liberals Were Involved)," VDARE, June 1, 2020, https://vdare.com/articles/vdare-tv-s-roving-reporters-attend-a-protest-not-a-riot-white-liberals-were-involved.
9. Michael Edison Hayden and Hannah Gais, "White Nationalist Group Posed as VICE Reporters While Identifying D.C. Protesters," SPLC Hatewatch, June 4, 2020, www.splcenter.org/hatewatch/2020/06/04/white-nationalist-group-posed-vice-reporters-while-identifying-dc-protesters.
10. Maya Shwayder, "YouTube Permanently Bans White Nationalist Channel VDARE," Digital Trends, August 10, 2020, www.digitaltrends.com/news/vdare-youtube-ban-white-nationalist-twitter-peter-brimelow.
11. VDARE (@vdare), "This is amazing . . . ," Twitter (now X), June 10, 2020, https://x.com/vdare/status/1270778032450670594.
12. VDARE (@vdare), "Kneel before Jared Taylor . . . ," Twitter (now X), June 10, 2020, https://x.com/vdare/status/1274873555554107392.

Chapter 9: In a Town with All Whites

1. "Dissident Mama, episode 85—VDARE's Lydia Brimelow," posted by Dissident Mama, December 13, 2023, YouTube, www.youtube.com/watch?v=mvqQjISzLQI.
2. Jason Kessler, "Don't Compare the George Floyd Riots to Charlottesville! (Oh, On Second Thought, Antifa Was Guilty There Too)," VDARE, June 1, 2020, https://vdare.com/articles/don-t-compare-the-george-floyd-riots-to-charlottesville-oh-on-second-thought-antifa-was-guilty-there-too.
3. Michelle Malkin, "Get Up Off Your Knees," Creators Syndicate, June 3, 2020, www.creators.com/read/michelle-malkin/06/20/get-up-off-your-knees.
4. Lydia Brimelow, "Never. Kneel.," VDARE, June 9, 2020, https://vdare.com/posts/never-kneel.
5. Russell Mokhiber, "Protesters Gather at Berkeley Springs State Park to Condemn Killing of George Floyd," Morgan County USA, June 3, 2020, https://morgancountyusa.org/?p=4483.
6. Mokhiber, "Protesters Gather."
7. Kate Shunney, "More Than 100 Gather at Park to Condemn Racism," *Morgan Messenger*, June 10, 2020.
8. Shunney, "More Than 100 Gather."
9. Audra D.S. Burch, Weiyi Cai, Gabriel Gianordoli, Morrigan McCarthy, and Jugal K. Patel, "How Black Lives Matter Reached Every Corner of America," *New York Times*, June 13, 2020, www.nytimes.com/interactive/2020/06/13/us/george-floyd-protests-cities-photos.html.
10. Matthew Richer, "Is It Time for Americans to Start Talking About the Devil?," VDARE, June 26, 2020, https://vdare.com/articles/is-it-time-for-americans-to-start-talking-about-the-devil.
11. VDARE (@vdare), "Where were you at the turning of the tide?," Twitter (now X), June 28, 2020, https://x.com/vdare/status/1277429299730145281.
12. VDARE (@vdare), "Monuments can be replaced . . . ," Twitter (now X), June 28, 2020, https://x.com/vdare/status/1277444439686950917.
13. Juliana Menasce Horowitz, Kiley Hurst, and Dana Braga, "Support for the Black Lives Matter Movement Has Dropped Considerably from Its Peak in 2020," Pew Research Center, June 12, 2023, www.pewresearch.org/social- trends/2023/06/14/support-for-the-black-lives-matter-movement-has-dropped-considerably-from-its-peak-in-2020.

14. James Fulford, "Black Lives Matter Is a Blood Libel Against White America. Here's Why," VDARE, July 11, 2020, https://vdare.com/articles/black-lives-matter-is-a-blood-libel-against-white-america-here-s-why.
15. Mark Graves, "100 Days of Black Lives Matter Protests in Portland," *Oregonian*, September 5, 2020.

Chapter 10: The Land of the Rednecks

1. David A. Graham, "The Mysterious Death of Freddie Gray," *Atlantic*, April 22, 2015, www.theatlantic.com/politics/archive/2015/04/the-mysterious-death-of-freddie-gray/391119.
2. "History of Inequity in Baltimore," Baltimore City Department of Planning, Historical and Architectural Preservation Division, accessed April 2024, https://planning.baltimorecity.gov/sites/default/files/History%20of%20Inequity%20in%20Baltimore%209-12-18.pdf.
3. "Photos from the Riots in Baltimore," Slide 26, ABC News, April 28, 2015, https://abc7ny.com/baltimore-freddie-gray-ferguson-protests/684081.
4. Mark Puente, "Undue Force," *Baltimore Sun*, September 28, 2014, https://data.baltimoresun.com/news/police-settlements.
5. *State of West Virginia v. DeGraw*, David Floyd, Filed 8/11/2021, Morgan County Circuit Clerk.
6. *State of West Virginia v. DeGraw.*
7. Michael Edison Hayden, "Antifa Supersoldiers Are Coming to Kill White People Within Days: Right-Wing Conspiracy," *Newsweek*, November 1, 2017, www.newsweek.com/antifa-supersoldiers-coming-kill-white-people-right-wing-conspiracy-699037.
8. *State of West Virginia v. DeGraw.*
9. *State of West Virginia v. DeGraw.*
10. Portals Metaphysical, "Good morning to all! We live in interesting times . . . ," Facebook, August 20, 2020, www.facebook.com/portalsnewage/posts/pfbid02zFwHsXXeVJyrQx46i3ypuq6wZU3VTAP91X1Qfhj2NyrjcYaWM5cBeUUpwzhkZfuil.
11. See "White Supremacists in Small Town WV Arrested for Terrorist Threat and Does This to a Flag," and "Same White Supremacist Explains His Own Crime . . . and Arrest," archived on YouTube, August 22, 2020, by Yellow Sunshine (@yellowsunshine1117), www.youtube.com/@yellowsunshine1117.

Chapter 11: The Hidden Prejudice That Causes Fear

1. Peter Brimelow (@PeterBrimelow), "Quotes one 'Far-Right' donor, my wife Lydia—'Nobody understands deplatforming issues like Laura' . . . ," Twitter (now X), August 21, 2020, https://x.com/peterbrimelow/status/1296915303411195905; Tess Owens, "The Big-Name Conservatives Bankrolling This Far-Right Troll's Run for Congress," *Vice*, August 21, 2020, www.vice.com/en/article/v7gjq9/who-is-donating-to-laura-loomer-florida-alex-jones.
2. US Census Bureau, "S1701: Poverty Status in the Past 12 Months," US Department of Commerce, Census Bureau, accessed April 2024, https://data.census.gov/table/ACSST5Y2020.S1701?q=S1701:%20POVERTY%20STATUS%20IN%20THE%20PAST%2012%20MONTHS&g=010XX00US$0400000,&tid=ACSST5Y2020.S1701.
3. Kate Shunney, "Competing Protests Bring Hundreds to Downtown Area," *Morgan Messenger*, August 21, 2020, www.morganmessenger.com/2022/08/30/competing-protests-bring-hundreds-to-downtown-area.
4. Shunney, "Competing Protests Bring Hundreds."

5. Barb Wolfe, Facebook, August 21, 2020, www.facebook.com/barb.wolfe.547/videos/10158157359265020.
6. Shunney, "Competing Protests Bring Hundreds."
7. Wolfe, Facebook, August 21, 2020.
8. For the video, see Noah Arnold, "Patriot Strength in Numbers Stopped BLM in Berkeley Springs WV. And, Yes Virginia (Dare), There ARE Black Trump Supporters," VDARE, August 26, 2020, www.vdare.name/articles/patriot-strength-in-numbers-stopped-blm-in-berkeley-springs-wv-and-yes-virginia-dare-there-are-black-trump-supporters; see also Noah Arnold, "Patriots Rout Black Lives Matter in Berkeley Springs WV!," archived in a post by Ann Corcoran, "The Good Folks of Small Town West Virginia Push Back Against BLM," Frauds, Crooks and Criminals, September 1, 2020, https://fraudscrookscriminals.com/tag/vdare.
9. Arnold, "Patriot Strength in Numbers."

Chapter 12: Ruling-Class Angry Apes

1. Barb Wolfe, Facebook, November 26, 2020, www.facebook.com/barb.wolfe.547/posts/pfbid0HzFguwkg1nKmGZuJ3cX84GtCkZawhvhBL6TSFCqmHaNfgwyrHbQZ7pJehssxDBcMl.
2. Kate Shunney, "Mozier Honored," *Morgan Messenger*, December 2, 2020.
3. Jeanne Mozier, "The NYT Did the Research and Called Everyone in Charge in Every State . . . ," Facebook, November 13, 2020, www.facebook.com/jeanne.mozier/posts/pfbid0V5coQD4BuVBscWvz8baxSZ7fwTT5Px8nemsTNeuoNNBxUQhQrN3pDsD3BtyJPDmil.
4. Mimi Dwyer and David Shepardson, "Faced with Defeat, Armed Protesters in Arizona Insist Election Stolen," Reuters, November 8, 2020, www.reuters.com/article/world/faced-with-defeat-armed-protesters-in-arizona-insist-election-stolen-idUSKBN27O02H.
5. Amanda Moore, "'Yeah That Was Too Far': Private Facebook Chats for Gavin Wax's Liberty Conservative Littered with Racial Slurs, Holocaust Jokes," Daily Dot, July 30, 2023, www.dailydot.com/debug/liberty-conservative-leaked-chats-gavin-was.
6. Nick Fagge and Peter Allen, "Exclusive—Revealed: Mysterious French Blogger Who Made $520,000 Bitcoin Donation to Capitol Rioters Booked into Luxury Paris Hotel Room and Killed Himself with Drugs Overdose," *Daily Mail*, January 30, 2021, www.dailymail.co.uk/news/article-9202857/French-blogger-killed-drugs-overdose-day-520-000-Capitol-rioters-donation.html.
7. Brimelow v. New York Times Company, No. 1:2020cv00222, Document 32 (S.D.N.Y. 2020), last modified December 17, 2020, available from Justia at https://law.justia.com/cases/federal/district-courts/new-york/nysdce/1:2020cv00222/529799/32.
8. Charlottesville Survivor, "Why I'm Going to the Jan. 6 Stop the Steal Rally—While We're Still Allowed to Have Them," VDARE, January 4, 2021, https://vdare.com/articles/why-i-m-going-to-the-jan-6-stop-the-steal-rally-while-we-re-still-allowed-to-have-them.
9. Charlottesville Survivor, "Why I'm Going to the Jan. 6 Stop the Steal Rally."
10. Ryan Goodman and Jonathan Hendrix, "Exclusive: New Video of Roger Stone with Proud Boys Leader Who May Have Planned Attack," Just Security, February 6, 2021, www.justsecurity.org/74579/exclusive-new-video-of-roger-stone-with-proud-boys-leaders-who-may-have-planned-for-capitol-attack.
11. Frontline Staff, "What Conspiracy Theorist Alex Jones Said in the Lead Up to the Capitol Riot," PBS Frontline, January 12, 2021, www.pbs.org/wgbh/frontline/article/what-conspiracy-theorist-alex-jones-said-in-the-lead-up-to-the-capitol-riot.
12. Lydia Brimelow (@Lydia Brimelow), "We just said goodbye to some friends . . . ," Gab, January 7, 2021, https://gab.com/LydiaBrimelow/posts/105515580939883616k.

13. Peter Brimelow, "Ruling Class Angry Apes Don't Like It, but They Taught America That Violence Works," PeterBrimelow.com, January 6, 2021, www.peterbrimelow.com/p/ruling-class-angry-apes-don-t-like-it-but-they-taught-america-that-violence-works.
14. Noah Arnold, "VDARE.com Exclusive Video of the Capitol Protests," VDARE, January 8, 2021, https://vdare.com/articles/vdare-com-exclusive-video-of-the-capitol-protests.
15. John Derbyshire, "'Part of Me Was Cheering Them On'—The Case for 'Turbulence,'" VDARE, January 8, 2021, https://vdare.com/articles/john-derbyshire-part-of-me-was-cheering-them-on-the-case-for-turbulence.
16. James Kirkpatrick, "US Capitol Protest: Ruling Class Tantrum Shows Americans We Must All Hang Together," VDARE, January 9, 2021, https://vdare.com/articles/us-capitol-protest-ruling-class-tantrum-shows-americans-we-must-all-hang-together.
17. "First 2020 Presidential Debate Between Donald Trump and Joe Biden," posted by C-SPAN, September 29, 2020, YouTube, www.youtube.com/watch?v=wW1lY5jFNcQ. See also Kathleen Ronayne and Michael Kunzelman, "Trump to Far-Right Extremists: 'Stand Back and Stand By,'" Associated Press, September 30, 2020, https://apnews.com/article/election-2020-joe-biden-race-and-ethnicity-donald-trump-chris-wallace-0b32339da25fbc9e8b7c7c7066a1db0f.

Chapter 13: The Motive, the Means, and the Proximity

1. Jared Taylor, "Ruling Class Weaponizing 'White Supremacist Armed Insurrection' Hoax," VDARE, March 10, 2021, https://vdare.com/articles/ruling-class-weaponizing-white-supremacist-armed-insurrection-hoax.
2. Jacob Silverman, "The CEO Trying to Build a White, Christian, Secessionist Tech Industry," *New Republic*, August 23, 2021, https://newrepublic.com/article/163285/andrew-torba-gab-white-christian-internet.
3. Peter Brimelow, "Gab's Torba Talks to VDARE.com's Brimelow," PeterBrimelow.com, January 23, 2021, www.peterbrimelow.com/p/gab-s-torba-talks-to-vdare-com-s-brimelow.
4. Ann Coulter, "Derek Chauvin, Human Sacrifice," VDARE, March 31, 2021, https://vdare.com/articles/ann-coulter-derek-chauvin-human-sacrifice.

Chapter 14: Let His Way Be Dark and Slippery

1. Andrew R. Flores, Jody L. Herman, Gary J. Gates, and Taylor N.T. Brown, "How Many Adults Identify as Transgender in the United States?," Williams Institute, June 2016, https://williamsinstitute.law.ucla.edu/wp-content/uploads/Trans-Adults-US-Aug-2016.pdf.
2. Lisa Marie (@L_isaMarie), "Yes we have nazis in a castle, it's a long story . . . and yes they suck at life," Twitter (now X), June 26, 2021, https://x.com/L_isaMarie/status/1408767939105345539.
3. Michael Edison Hayden and Alex Kotch, "Donors Pumped Millions into White Nationalist Group," SPLC Hatewatch, June 17, 2021, www.splcenter.org/resources/hatewatch/donors-pumped-millions-white-nationalist-group.
4. Lisa Marie (@L_isaMarie), "Thank you @splcenter for your great work reporting on hate groups like VDARE . . . ," Twitter (now X), July 16, 2021, https://x.com/L_isaMarie/status/1416056439538282498.
5. Peter Brimelow, "SPLC Thug Michael Edison Hayden Fears VDARE.com's Prowess!," VDARE, June 18, 2021, https://vdare.com/articles/splc-thug-michael-edison-hayden-fears-vdare-com-s-prowess.
6. Washington Watcher II, "Ohio's J.D. Vance Shows That Immigration Patriotism Is on the March," VDARE, July 2, 2021, https://vdare.com/articles/ohio-s-j-d-vance-shows-that-immigration-patriotism-is-on-the-march.

7. VDARE (@vdare), "Hayden apparently doesn't have the courage to 'punch a Nazi,' so he hides in his $PLC sinecure and pushes Twitter followers on the one hand and Corporate America on the other to punch for him—literally and figuratively. He's Antifa's propaganda minister," Twitter (now X), August 22, 2021, https://x.com/vdare/status/1429651547445768194.
8. Jason Kessler, "Doxing the Doxers: Half-Egyptian Rich Kid SPLC Enforcer Michael Edison Hayden Is a Weirdo. What Else Is New?," VDARE, August 22, 2021, https://vdare.com/articles/doxing-the-doxers-half-egyptian-rich-kid-splc-enforcer-michael-edison-hayden-is-a-weirdo-what-else-is-new.
9. Edward James (@godsinyou), "Disgusting, demonic slime . . . ," Twitter (now X), https://x.com/GODSINYOU/status/1429662300902920193. The wording of the tweet alludes to Psalm 35 in the Old Testament.
10. Michael Karlik, "Right-Wing Group Fails to Show Colorado Springs Mayor Violated Their Constitutional Rights, 10th Circuit Rules," Colorado Politics, August 23, 2021, www.coloradopolitics.com/courts/right-wing-group-fails-to-show-colorado-springs-mayor-violated-their-constitutional-rights-10th-circuit/article_ddb87c20-042b-11ec-ace5-f79eb58f1eee.html.
11. Lisa Marie (@L_isaMarie), "Fascist activity alert . . . ," Twitter (now X), December 5, 2021, https://x.com/L_isaMarie/status/1467651500390371330.
12. Lisa Marie (@L_isaMarie), "So tied [*sic*] of middle class white activists . . . ," Twitter (now X), December 7, 2021, https://x.com/L_isaMarie/status/1468226820495585286.
13. Peter Brimelow (@peterbrimelow), "This is treason. #IMPEACHBIDENHARRIS," Twitter (now X), December 7, 2021, https://x.com/peterbrimelow/status/1468207418064658441.
14. Lisa Marie (@L_isaMarie), "Everyone I know in West Virginia . . . ," Twitter (now X), December 7, 2021, https://x.com/L_isaMarie/status/1468236625239060502.
15. Lisa Marie (@L_isaMarie), "Update: they may have canceled the event!!! After 2 days of protesting, the shuttles to the castle seem to have been canceled or they had to find a new place to pick people up . . . ," Twitter (now X), December 8, 2021, https://x.com/L_isaMarie/status/1468753915667795971.
16. Lisa Marie (@L_isaMarie), "It is our hope to deny . . . ," Twitter (now X), December 7, 2021, https://x.com/L_isaMarie/status/1468388377959583744.
17. Lisa Marie (@L_isaMarie), "Wanna bet? . . . ," Twitter (now X), December 8, 2021, https://x.com/L_isaMarie/status/1468694325064355847.
18. Lisa Marie (@L_isaMarie), "Nothing is more insidious . . . ," Twitter (now X), December 13, 2021, https://x.com/L_isaMarie/status/1470613399281176580.

Chapter 15: Next Stop, America

1. James Fulford, "Video of James Kirkpatrick's Address to the First VDARE Conference Now Available," VDARE, June 5, 2022, https://vdare.name/posts/video-of-james-kirkpatrick-s-address-to-the-first-vdare-conference-now-available.
2. Cyan Quinn, "VDARE's 2022 UnCancelled Conference," Counter-Currents, April 27, 2022, https://counter-currents.com/2022/04/vdares-2022-uncancelled-conference.
3. Bill Hutchinson, Julia Jacobo, and Emily Shapiro, "Buffalo Shooting: Remembering the 10 Lives Taken a Year Ago in Tops Massacre," ABC News, May 8, 2023, https://abcnews.go.com/US/shoppers-regulars-retired-police-officer-victims-buffalo-shooting/story?id=84731033.
4. Alisha Ebrahimji, Dakin Adone, and Amir Vera, "Buffalo Shooting Victims: 'Hero' Guard and a Teacher Who Was a 'Pillar of the Community' Are Among 10 Killed," CNN, May 18, 2022, www.cnn.com/2022/05/15/us/buffalo-shooting-victims-what-we-know/index.html.

5. Quil Lawrence, "The Victims and Aftermath of the Buffalo Supermarket Shooting," NPR, May 16, 2022, www.npr.org/2022/05/16/1099244614/the-victims-and-aftermath-of-the-buffalo-supermarket-shooting.
6. Peter Brimelow, "Was the Buffalo Massacre (Bad!) Caused by the Great Replacement (Undeniable)?," VDARE, May 16, 2022, https://vdare.com/articles/was-the-buffalo-massacre-bad-caused-by-the-great-replacement-undeniable.
7. Peter Brimelow, "VDARE v. Stein: A Patriot Victory in Berkeley Springs WV," VDARE, June 30, 2022, https://vdare.com/articles/vdare-v-stein-a-patriot-victory-in-berkeley-springs-wv.
8. Peter Brimelow, "VDARE.com Wins a Great Victory over NEW YORK TIMES—For Now," VDARE, November 20, 2022, https://vdare.com/articles/vdare-com-wins-a-great-victory-over-new-york-times-for-now.
9. James Fulford, "Trump Speaks Out Against NYAG Letitia James' Lawfare—Which She's Also Waging Against VDARE.com," VDARE, April 5, 2023, https://vdare.com/posts/trump-speaks-out-against-nyag-letitia-james-lawfare-which-she-s-also-waging-against-vdare-com.

Chapter 18: May You and Yours Get Everything You Deserve

1. Peter Brimelow, "WASHINGTON POST'S Ellie Silverman Is Coming for VDARE.com (and Christmas)," VDARE, December 29, 2022, https://vdare.com/articles/washington-post-s-ellie-silverman-is-coming-for-vdare-com-and-christmas.
2. Steve Cohen, "West Virginia Sheriff Says Bodycam Will Reveal 'the Totality of the Incident' After TikTok Arrest Video Goes Viral," WTRF, December 15, 2022, www.wtrf.com/west-virginia/west-virginia-sheriff-says-bodycam-will-reveal-the-totality-of-the-incident-after-tiktok-arrest-video-goes-viral.
3. Ellie Silverman, "A 'Hate Castle' or Welcome Neighbor? VDare Divides a West Virginia Town," *Washington Post*, January 4, 2023, www.washingtonpost.com/dc-md-va/2023/01/03/vdare-berkeley-springs-castle-brimelows.
4. On Michael Farris, "Coffee and a Mic: Lydia Brimelow #525," podcast, November 23, 2022, https://coffeeandamike.libsyn.com/lydia-brimelow-525.
5. Luke O'Brien, "Alex Jones' Lawyer Violated Legal Ethics by Soliciting Porn Bribes. Just How Dirty Is Marc Randazza?," HuffPost, December 27, 2018, www.huffpost.com/entry/alex-jones-lawyer-marc-randazza_n_5c1c283ae4b08aaf7a86b9e4.
6. Hannah Gais, Michael Edison Hayden, Rachel Janik, and Megan Squire, "Allen, Texas, Killer Posted Neo-Nazi, Incel Content Online," SPLC Hatewatch, May 8, 2023, www.splcenter.org/hatewatch/2023/05/08/allen-texas-killer-posted-neo-nazi-incel-content-online.
7. VDARE (@vdare), "Lydia Brimelow at the 2023 VDARE Conference!," Twitter (now X), July 3, 2023, https://twitter.com/vdare/status/1675888202308091906.
8. "Owner of Fairfax Coffee House and Star Theater Attempts to Run Woman over in Parking Lot," posted by Carmelitta Evans, May 3, 2023, YouTube, www.youtube.com/watch?v=KKgCSZcMfN8.
9. "Owner of Fairfax Coffee House and Star Theater Throwing Glass onto Neighbors [*sic*] Parking Lot," posted by Carmelitta Evans, May 4, 2023, YouTube, www.youtube.com/watch?v=ITpGMod4CMQ.
10. "Owner of Fairfax Coffee House and Star Theater in Berkeley Springs WV Moves Surveyor's Landmark," posted by Carmelitta Evans, May 4, 2023, YouTube, www.youtube.com/watch?v=ITpGMod4CMQ.
11. HLI, LLC, "This made me do a happy dance today. Maybe I should clarify what this is . . . ," Facebook, May 15, 2023, www.facebook.com/33FairfaxSt/videos/674144664522193.

12. HLI, LLC, "Out with the old...new on the way!," Facebook, accessed August 20, 2025, www.facebook.com/reel/1029818424941836.

Chapter 19: Friends and Enemies

1. Alana Goodman, "Southern Poverty Law Center Spokesman Signed Letter Blaming Israel for Hamas Terrorism," Washington Free Beacon, November 4, 2023, https://freebeacon.com/latest-news/southern-poverty-law-center-spokesman-signed-letter-blaming-israel-for-hamas-terrorism.

Chapter 21: The Billion-Year Plan

1. Peter Brimelow (@peterbrimelow), December 8, 2023, "This is the creep who interrogated my 8 year old," X, December 8, 2023, https://x.com/peterbrimelow/status/1733344413449847259, referring to this article by Jason Kessler, "Doxing the Doxers: Half-Egyptian Rich Kid SPLC Enforcer Michael Edison Hayden Is a Weirdo. What Else Is New?," VDARE, August 22, 2021, https://vdare.com/articles/doxing-the-doxers-half-egyptian-rich-kid-splc-enforcer-michael-edison-hayden-is-a-weirdo-what-else-is-new.
2. Michael Edison Hayden and Hannah Gais, "We Went to a Christmas Party at a White Nationalist Castle," Daily Beast, December 12, 2023, www.thedailybeast.com/we-went-to-a-christmas-party-at-a-white-nationalist-castle.

Chapter 23: Tropical Fish

1. William Seabrook, *Asylum* (Dover, 2015 [1935]), 255.
2. "Maimed Men," National Library of Medicine, accessed October 2024, www.nlm.nih.gov/exhibition/lifeandlimb/maimedmen.html.
3. "The Civil War by the Numbers," *American Experience*, PBS, accessed October 2024, www.pbs.org/wgbh/americanexperience/features/death-numbers.
4. Lydia Brimelow, interviewed by Tucker Carlson, February 21, 2024, https://tuckercarlson.com/uncensored-lydia-brimelow.
5. Shannon Pettypiece, "Marjorie Taylor Greene Calls for a National Divorce Between Liberal and Conservative States," NBC News, February 20, 2023, www.nbcnews.com/politics/congress/marjorie-taylor-greene-calls-national-divorce-liberal-conservative-sta-rcna71464.
6. Lydia Brimelow, Tucker Carlson interview.

Chapter 24: A Long Time to Die

1. Peter Brimelow, "IT IS FINISHED—NYAG Letitia James Crucifies VDARE.com," VDARE, March 29, 2024, https://vdare.com/articles/it-is-finished-nyag-letitia-james-crucifies-vdare-com (emphasis in original).
2. Ben Finley, "Liberty Will Pay $14 Million, the Largest Fine Ever Levied Under the Federal Clery Act," Associated Press, March 5, 2024, https://apnews.com/article/liberty-university-clery-act-fine-ac7f365762fb8ac8a4abb86cf4613d33.

Chapter 25: All Kinds of Evil People

1. Michael Edison Hayden, "Far-Right Propagandist Turns Up in Moscow After Jan. 6," SPLC Hatewatch, September 1, 2021, www.splcenter.org/hatewatch/2021/09/01/far-right-propagandist-turns-moscow-after-jan-6.

Notes

Chapter 26: The New Materialists

1. Will Sommer, "The Skate Park Was Thriving. Then a Right-Wing YouTuber Bought It," *Washington Post*, August 12, 2024, www.washingtonpost.com/style/media/2024/08/12/tim-pool-martinsburg-skatepark.

Chapter 27: Ten Hyenas

1. VDARE (@vdare), "Why We've Suspended VDARE and I've Resigned After 25 Years," X, July 23, 2024, https://x.com/vdare/status/1815810301864075542.
2. VDARE, "Why We've Suspended VDARE."
3. VDARE, "Why We've Suspended VDARE."
4. Lydia Brimelow, "VDARE.com vs. Cancel Culture: My Story," VDARE, July 25, 2024, https://vdare.com/articles/vdare-com-vs-cancel-culture-my-story-lydia.
5. Berkeley Springs Castle (@BSpringscastle), "Port-o-let no longer needed, sewer damage from the rock slide is fixed!," X, September 4, 2024, https://x.com/BSpringsCastle/status/1831309992000958899.
6. Claire Goforth, "This West Virginia Castle Is HQ to an Infamous Anti-Immigrant Website That's Influenced Mainstream Republicans. Their Neighbors Are Fighting Back," Daily Dot, September 5, 2024, www.dailydot.com/news/berkeley-springs-vdare-equality-ordinance.

Chapter 28: Cursed Town

1. The letter was still archived at Internet Archive, WayBack Machine, https://web.archive.org/web/20240823082153/https://berkeleyspringscastle.net/uploads/scott.pdf, as of August 20, 2025.
2. Claire Goforth, "This West Virginia Castle Is HQ to an Infamous Anti-Immigrant Website That's Influenced Mainstream Republicans. Their Neighbors Are Fighting Back," Daily Dot, September 5, 2024, www.dailydot.com/news/berkeley-springs-vdare-equality-ordinance.
3. Peter Brimelow (@peterbrimelow), "1/3 VDARE's D.C. Consultant Friend Patrick McDermott . . . ," X, November 4, 2024, https://x.com/peterbrimelow/status/1853623489644675188.
4. "Paid Letter to the Editor," *Morgan Messenger*, November 6, 2024.

INDEX

Index

Index

Index

Credit: Katharine Antoun

Michael Edison Hayden is an investigative reporter and a leading expert on far-right extremism. As a reporter, he broke some of the biggest stories on the radical right over the past decade, and his analyses—featured in outlets like NPR, MSNBC, and CNN—helped shape perspectives on the authoritarian, anti-democracy movement that took over the Republican Party. He resides in New York.